THE CLASSICS OF GOLF

Edition of

THE DOGGED VICTIMS OF INEXORABLE FATE
by
Dan Jenkins

Foreword by Herbert Warren Wind
Afterword by Dave Marr

ISBN 0-940889-03-X

Foreword

He stands out vividly from the majority of the writers in the press tent. At the close of a golf tournament, most of the others scramble for their typewriters (or the modern machines for transmitting their copy) and thrash out their reports at high speed. They have got to get them done as soon as possible. Dan Jenkins is different. A tall, slim, silver-haired man in a double-breasted blue blazer, he sits at his typewriter the picture of ease as his fingers deftly tap out his story on the Crosby Pro-Am or the Masters or the British Open or the Ryder Cup match. He has a deadline to meet all right. Now, as during the many years he was with Sports Illustrated, *his editor at* Playboy *or* Golf Digest *wants his stuff as soon as he can get it to them, which means yesterday if he is describing the play-off of our Open or the British Open. You would never guess this from Jenkins' demeanor. He sits at his typewriter with his back as straight as a cadet's, his eyes practically expressionless as each new line succeeds the line above. When someone comes over to ask him a question, he is never harried and, as often as not, he is light-hearted during the exchange. From time to time he interrupts his*

*magisterial calm to light up a cigarette. In about
two hours his story is finished and on its way to the
magazine. He tightens the knot in his tie, adjusts
his jacket, and glances at his watch to see how
much time he has at his disposal before he meets
some friends for a late dinner.*

*When people across the country read Jenkins'
right-after-the-event articles, they marvel at their
off-beat introductions, the humor which illumin-
ates the reportage, the soundness of his treatment
of the principal figures and the core of the action,
the idiosyncratic asides that he tosses in because he
likes them, and an ending that is sometimes ironic
and at other times echoes a point he has made.
Invariably, the reader has no sense whatsoever that
the man who banged out the report had a deadline
to meet, and, don't forget it, most people who write
would rather meet Primo Carnera than a tight
deadline.*

*At one time it was fashionable to say that Dan
Jenkins seldom went out onto the course to watch
the play in a golf tournament, preferring to mosey
over to the headquarters television trailer where the
director, studying the numerous screens grouped
around him, calls out which camera's coverage he
wants to appear on the telecast. Dan knows the
directors well, and he is happy to accept their invitation to drop in at the headquarters trailer. It is
both a pleasant and sagacious thing to do. Out on*

the course, a reporter can't watch the various contenders and see all the shots that have to do with the winning and losing of the event. Jenkins, however, spends a lot of time on the course. With his sense of where the key action may take place, he sees as many of the crucial shots as nearly anyone. He knows the players well, and during a tournament he spends a good deal of time chatting with them off the course. On the day of the final round, he often chooses to watch the decisive holes in the Hospitality Room, listening to what the players who finished earlier have to say about the climactic action of the tournament. He never scribbles anything down. With his wonderful ear, he takes note of and retains their savvy and incisive comments.

As a natural editor of the immense amount of material he gleans, Dan has the time and the disposition to relax with his friends around a table during the unimportant hours of the long, tedious tournament days. The Jenkins Group, as it has come to be called, is made up of fellows like Bob Drum, Pat Summerall, Blackie Sherrod, Dave Marr, Bud Shrake, Sonny Jurgenson, Ed Sneed, Jack Whitaker, Ben Wright and sundry other writers, telecasters, and retired quarterbacks. At the Masters, they convene at one of the long tables in the upstairs lounge of the clubhouse, but wherever a significant tournament is being held, they stake out a point of assembly and almost instantly make themselves at home. If Dr. Johnson or Robert Benchley were to walk by, they would be asked to pull up a chair. Johnson and Benchley had all the requirements necessary to be eligible for the Jenkins Group: a knowledge of golf and other sports; a sense of humor, preferably droll; a critical wit that knows what is corny and synthetic; a genuine pleasure in listening to their friends' banter; a better than average background in literature, history, and the arts; and, above all, a convivial nature.

Dan Jenkins was born in Fort Worth, and graduated in 1949 from Paschal High, long famous as the high school that Ginger Rogers and Ben Hogan went to. A week before Jenkins graduated, he was hired to cover golf by Blackie Sherrod, the sports editor of the Fort Worth Press. "Blackie knew I'd be entering T.C.U.—Texas Christian University—that fall," Jenkins says. "I went to college with a byline." Jenkins has been around golf all his life. His father, a furniture salesman, was a golf addict. Jenkins Sr. played some golf with another local fellow, Ben Hogan, at a course called Katy Lake, a nine-hole layout with sand greens, which got its name from a nearby spur of the Missouri, Topeka, and Kansas City Railroad. Dan, who had been the medalist in the Fort Worth Junior Championship when he was fourteen and fifteen, went on to become a potent force on the T.C.U. golf team, and in his senior year, 1953, he was its *captain. One thing Dan has in common with Ben Hogan and Byron Nelson is that each of them at one time or another was the runner-up in the Fort Worth City Championship. Another thing he remembers well is a trip he made to Albuquerque to play in an N.C.A.A. Championship. "I thought I was a pretty fair golfer until that tournament," he recalls. "Then I got a look there at a fellow named Ken Venturi fom San Jose State, and I began to understand things better."*

Jenkins got to New York in 1962, when he joined the staff of Sports Illustrated. *He had been a stringer for S. I. when he worked for Fort Worth and Dallas newspapers after graduating from T.C.U. Alfred Wright was then writing the golf for S.I. Jenkins was the back-up golf writer and the head college football writer. In 1967, he became the head golf writer. He was successful from the start, because he was an original. His terse, dry, irreverent style went down so well that it was alleged that young sports writers throughout the country were copying it. One who doesn't is his daughter Sally, who graduated from Stanford about a year ago and is now a sports writer for the San Francisco* Chronicle. *His two sons, Marty (who is Sally's twin) and Danny, have yet to give any decisive indication which profession or business they plan to pursue. Dan lives in Manhattan with his dazzling wife June. She and two other bright girls from*

Texas, who also had an excess of free time on their hands, started and operate two successful New York restaurants, Summerhouse and Juanita's.

A few words about "The Dogged Victims of Inexorable Fate," perhaps Jenkins' best-known book except for his novel "Semi-Tough," an inspired look at professional football that was made into a motion picture. "The Dogged Victims" is a little slow getting off the starting blocks. Don't get concerned if it takes you a while to get into the swing of the first piece, The Game of Golfe, which begins as a sort of James Joycean hallucination that satirizes the all too frequently dispensed adoration of the hallmarks of early Scottish golf by tourists from overseas. By the time that Jenkins has made good his escape from the Cardinal bunker at Prestwick and has moved on to his appointment with the brokerage firm of Heather, Whin, Bracken, and Broom, the tone and the structure of the piece shift into free-wheeling, acute observations on the renowned championship courses, the peculiar mores of Scottish golfers and club secretaries, and other such distillations as seen through the eyes of a percipient Texan who is loving every gulp of the game's astonishing past and present. The subsequent pieces in the book follow vastly different routes. For example, they take the reader back to the 1930s and the first linkages between Demaret and Crosby and the world of Palm Springs and *celebrity golf. They include an exploration of the leaner side of professional golf in the 1930s when Byron Nelson was so overcome by winning six hundred dollars in the General Brock Open in Niagara Falls that he didn't know how any man could cope with such a bonanza; a documented dissertation on how every outstanding putter wants to be known as a great striker of the ball, and how great putters like Jack Burke, Jerry Barber, Gary Player, and Arnold Palmer will heatedly deny that they ever could putt a lick; a close-up of Frank Chirkinian, the maestro of directing tournament golf on television, and how he goes about his work; how the strain of playing the tour week after week is so psychologically destructive that all the seemingly relaxed heroes are obsessed with trying to "keep the dog in them from coming up"; and lots of good inside stuff on Hogan, Snead, the Masters, Palmer, Nicklaus, and Trevino that suddenly takes off and, before you know it, you are reading really purple passages that sometimes turn into authentic poetry and at other times into that rarer commodity, wonderful fountains of humor that gush high in the sky like Old Faithful.*

This autumn, after his long and memorable association with Sports Illustrated, *Dan thought that he would profit from a change of scenery. Henceforth he will be a regular contributor to* Playboy, *with the whole world of sport his oyster, and he will be doing golf articles for* Golf Digest. *He will also from time to time continue to write novels, like "Life Its Ownself," which is due out this year. In the meantime, pull up a chair and join the Jenkins Group table.*

Herbert Warren Wind

The Dogged Victims
of Inexorable Fate

The Dogged Victims
of Inexorable Fate

by DAN JENKINS

A SPORTS ILLUSTRATED BOOK

LITTLE, BROWN AND COMPANY · BOSTON · TORONTO

Sports Illustrated Books
are published by
Little, Brown and Company
in association with
Sports Illustrated Magazine

Published simultaneously in Canada
by Little, Brown & Company (Canada) Limited

PRINTED IN THE UNITED STATES OF AMERICA

*For the gorgeous June Jenkins, of course,
who hates golf but loves Palm Springs;
&
For Bud, Seth, Whit, Mac and all of the
other dogged victims of 5:42 P.M.*

Foreword

To those writers who spend weeks in an agony of composing sentences and making them into paragraphs that fit with other paragraphs to form a page and eventually a story, being in the company of Dan Jenkins at a sporting event can be a humbling experience. At a golf tournament, for example, Dan is usually to be found in good weather on the veranda, probably at a table with an umbrella over it and a waiter nearby. All day Dan may sit there as the other chairs at the table are occupied in turn by golfers, golfers' wives, tournament officials, gamblers, actors, club members, millionaires, pro football players, newspaper columnists, television commentators and various of Dan's friends who have no connection with the tournament beyond a clubhouse badge and an eagerness to tell what they have seen out on the course. Sometimes a table for four will have fourteen people at it, with Dave Marr discussing the town's restaurants, Arnold Palmer mulling over a flight plan, Don Meredith checking his grip on a teaspoon, George Low smiling at the size of the check someone other than he will get stuck with, and the rest rattling on about one thing or

another while Dan, who has never been seen to take
a note in his life, acts as chairman of the recreation
committee.

Someone has said that the trouble with sitting
around is you never know when you're finished. But
Dan has a sense for it. He will rise and wander off and
return in a while, having watched several of the tournament's more consequential shots being played. The
sitting will resume, and the cast at the table continue
to change, and the waiter keep shuttling, and then
Dan is gone again. Two or three hours later he will
turn up at a restaurant where thirty or forty of his
day's companions are having an impromptu banquet,
or at a party in someone's hotel suite, and inevitably
he will be asked where he has been. "Had to write a
story," Dan will say if he feels like explaining.

In the interim Dan has slipped off to the press room
or to his hotel and has written perhaps three thousand
words of prose that is perceptive, funny, evocative,
informative and so well organized that an editor
scarcely ever needs to touch it. Dan does this thirty or
more times a year for *Sports Illustrated*, frequently
working against a Sunday night deadline that he
never fails to make. He writes about golf, football or
skiing for the most part but occasionally turns to the
pop-sociology study of the surfing life in Hawaii, the
high life in Hollywood, or any interesting style of life
anywhere. Meanwhile, Dan manages to produce a
book every year or so, either with his own name on it
or a ghost-writing job, and he can be seen regularly

with his beautiful wife June at Toots Shor's, the "21" Club, P. J. Clarke's or Elaine's in Manhattan or at dozens of other places from Beverly Hills to Kitz-bühel.

One reason Dan is able to live this way is that when he gets at a typewriter he knows what he is talking about. Using golf again as an example — since golf is the subject of the stories in this collection — when he writes of George Low being beaten by a cross-handed Scot in the British Boys championship, Dan understands what such a defeat can do to a person. Dan was beaten in the Texas State Junior by a cross-handed Mexican who wore high-top tennis shoes and a base-ball cap. If Dan ever had any notions of a career in golf, that helped dissuade him. But he used to be an excellent player and still would be except that he rarely plays. Dan was runner-up in the Fort Worth city championship — a distinction he shares with Ben Hogan and Byron Nelson — and was captain of the golf team at Texas Christian University, lofty achievements for one whose idea of practice was to drive a couple of balls into the woods before a match.

In those days we hung around Herb Massey's cafe in Fort Worth eating chicken fried steaks with cream gravy and hot biscuits, drank coffee and beer alternately, and played absurd games on a puck-bowling machine. There was one game in which you put your shirt and pants on backwards, faced away from the pins and slid the puck down the board behind you, as Dan reveals in this book in "The Glory Game," which is his memoir as a municipal course hustler. In another version you stood in the hedge and reached your arm in through the window for a blind shot. Dan was good at all the games we played but best at golf. I recall a match when he arrived at the course wearing a suit and tie just as his opponent was stepping onto the tee. Dan hit one practice putt and it went into the hole. Convinced he was ready, Dan trotted to the tee, shedding coat and tie and rolling up his sleeves. He had already been announced and without a warm-up swing he cracked a mighty duck hook into the forest. "You're in for it today," he told his opponent from the University of Texas. "When I come out of there, we'll have alligators and bears chasing us."

While in college Dan played against Don January, Billy Maxwell, Wesley Ellis, Miller Barber, Ernie Vossler, all of whom have done rather well at the game as professionals. He also played against Earl Stewart, Don Cherry, Joe Conrad and many other names on the Texas amateur circuit, which still offers pretty good schooling for someone trying to learn how to play. The dozen times a year that Dan now plays golf, he still breaks 80. I was playing with him on the great course at Merion a while back when he was researching his book *The Best 18 Golf Holes in America,* and Dan, who had not picked up a club in weeks, shot a 76 in a light drizzle. He has won the National Golf Writers tournament twice, and some other lesser events. But what used to impress us most about Dan Jenkins's connection with the game of golf nearly twenty years ago in Fort Worth was that Dan was the only one of us Ben Hogan would acknowledge. Whenever he saw Dan, Hogan would nod and smile tightly and say, "Hi, fella." We didn't see how you could hope to get any more recognition than that.

Clearly, Dan has done so. After many years as a daily columnist in Fort Worth and Dallas and now as a senior editor for *Sports Illustrated,* Dan is one of the country's most widely known writers. A look at the prose that flows on the following pages will show you why.

EDWIN SHRAKE

Austin, Texas

Golf may be . . . a sophisticated game. At least, it is usually played with the outward appearance of great dignity. It is, nevertheless, a game of considerable passion, either of the explosive type, or that which burns inwardly and sears the soul.

— BOBBY JONES

Tommy Bolt's putter has spent more time in the air than Lindbergh.

— JIMMY DEMARET

Acknowledgment

I N one form or another, and usually in typeface of the
English language, most of the material in this book
appeared originally in *Sports Illustrated*, which sent
the author into a lot of country club bars to gather the
information. It is not true that in order for these stories
to be published in the first place the magazine had to
cancel several thrilling layouts on ice boating, beagling
and orienteering. That would have been the guess of a
subscriber in the 1950's.

I am particularly grateful to the managing editor of
Sports Illustrated, Mr. Andre Laguerre, for holding to
the belief that I know more about the game of golf
than anyone in P. J. Clarke's. I hereby thank the
managing editor as well as the mother company, Time
Inc., for permitting these essays to be expanded and
embellished, and thus to gain the permanence of hard
cover. Also for getting me out of Dallas a few years
ago.

Bud Shrake's Foreword is very flattering and I am
deeply appreciative. Actually, it is something of a
literary masterpiece when you consider that it was
written in longhand on napkins at the Scholz Garden

in Austin during a spontaneous meeting of a group known casually as The Friends of Ellen C. Baggett.

Finally, I must say thank you to Sarah Pileggi, the deputy chief of researchers at *Sports Illustrated*. Aside from the fact that she is a most attractive young woman, she is also intelligent enough to have giggled approvingly at the manuscript while she checked and typed it.

These essays ran in the magazine from 1962 through 1969. I ran in the magazine only a half-dozen times during this period. On each occasion, it was to draw expense money before the window closed. Normally, I can walk and have time to spare.

D.J.

Contents

Foreword	ix
Acknowledgment	xv
The Dogged Victims of Inexorable Fate	3
The Game of Golfe	11
Sam Snead with Hair	49
Lights . . . Camera . . . Double Bogey	79
Lockwrist and Cage Cases	107
America's Guest	131
Down South	153
The Big Window	185
Wide Open	215
Winner and Loser	239
The Glory Game	259
The Dogged Victim	293

The Dogged Victims
of Inexorable Fate

---

*On the golf course, a man may be the dogged
victim of inexorable fate, be struck down by an
appalling stroke of tragedy, become the hero of
unbelievable melodrama, or the clown in a sidesplitting comedy — any of these within a few hours,
and all without having to bury a corpse or repair
a tangled personality.*

— BOBBY JONES

IT first occurred to me that golf was not particularly the grimmest game in the world one afternoon when I was reading *The Brothers Karamazov* on an electric cart. There is nothing in *The Brothers Karamazov* about golf, of course, and very little in the novel about electric carts. But I happened to be reading it, studying for an exam in comparative literature, as I came up the 18th fairway of the Worth Hills municipal course in Fort Worth several years ago. This struck some of my friends as being kind of funny, although not as funny as the fact that I was out of the hole and stood to lose at least fifty big ones.

At any rate, one of the thieves I played golf with in those days said, "I'll tell you one thing, Jankin. You'd be a lot better off if you worked on your golf and paid less attention to them Nazi Roosians."

He was probably right, I said, but it certainly was a bum rap they were trying to pin on Dmitri Fyodorovitch.

My friend laughed, grabbed the crotch of his trousers, and said, "I got your da-mitty damned old dorry-vitch right here. I also got you out, out, out and one down."

Nobody has a soul, I said.

"Naw, they mostly usin' MacGregors and Spaldings now," he said.

A chapter in this book titled "The Glory Game" contains a lot more exciting repartee like this, and it also describes in detail why the author gave up a promising career as a tournament player, a career which might well have led him to the zenith of an assistant pro's job in the lake regions of Wisconsin.

There was another time, later on, when it occurred to me again that golf need not be so grim. This was one day in 1952 when I was covering the Masters tournament for the *Fort Worth Press*, a daily newspaper which folded a long time ago but hasn't realized it yet. A typewriter I was using in the Augusta press room did a quaint and curious thing. On a hasty deadline, it wrote, "Sam Snead won the Masters yesterday on greens that were slicker than the top of his head."

My editor said he thought that was pretty foolish, what I had done, leaving out the where, how and why in the lead, and insulting Sam Snead. Where had I ever heard that this was journalism, or, to use his terms, "good newspapering?" I told him from reading *The Brothers Karamazov*, the new Daphne Du Maurier he most likely had not read yet. So I wrote an example to prove to him that I could do it his way. It went:

"Sam Snead, champion golfer, won the Masters, a big golf tournament, yesterday, which was yesterday, on a golf course. Mr. Snead is losing some of his hair but not all of it."

The final, crushing proof for me that golf should be

taken light-heartedly came in the spring of 1960. I was sitting comfortably in the men's grill of Colonial Country Club in Fort Worth, vividly describing the moment that Harry Vardon invented the grip, when Arnold Palmer and Dow Finsterwald entered the room. They strolled over and invited me to join them in a practice round before the Colonial National Invitation.

No thank you, I said. There will be a large gallery and I don't want to dazzle the crowd with my button-down shirt and my shank. I'm a writer, not a golfer, I said. Palmer said he wasn't sure about that last part, but come along anyhow because it was late in the day and the people had gone home. So I weakened, unfortunately.

There were, of course, at least five thousand people lining the 1st fairway and gathered around the tee, waiting for Palmer and Finsterwald. When I walked timidly onto the 1st tee with my tie off, my sleeves rolled up, and the caddy carrying my white canvas bag, the only thing I overheard in the gallery was a man ask a friend, "Who's this geek?"

Hoping to put myself at ease, I went briskly over to Arnold and Dow, took the driver from Palmer's hands, as if to examine the all-weather grip on it or perhaps the swing weight, and tried to say something snappy.

"Who's away?" I said.

Palmer drove about 290 yards down the middle, and Finsterwald drove about 260 yards down the middle, and then it was time for me to tee off. I had always suspected that trying to play golf in the company of big time pros and a gallery would be something like walking naked into choir practice. And it was. In that moment on the 1st tee, I suddenly felt blinded and flushed, and that I would like to be somewhere else. Bolivia, maybe.

As I bent over to tee up the ball, I could barely see my hand shaking. I remember being able to taste a giant cotton rabbit in my mouth as I addressed the shot. I remember catching a glimpse of my shoes and wishing they had been shined. And I remember that as I took the club back, I overheard another comment in the gallery.

"No livin' way," a man said, quietly.

The drive went somewhere down the fairway, rather remarkably, but the next shot went only fifteen or twenty feet. I topped it. The next one went about ten yards. I topped it again. And the next one went about fifty yards. I hit a foot behind it. Eventually, I managed to pitch onto the putting surface, a feat that was greeted with a ripple of applause, which I took for what it was: a slightly unnecessary sarcasm from a few of my own friends in the crowd.

For a moment or so, I felt all right. I was on the green at last where I could stand around with Arnold and Dow, lean casually on my putter, and smoke. Except when I walked onto the lovely bent grass, I accidentally dragged one foot and my cleats carved a horrible divot out of the turf.

Humiliated, naturally, I quickly got down on my

hands and knees to repair the divot. But when I got back up I noticed that the moisture of the green had implanted a huge damp splotch on each knee of my trousers. I leaned over and stared at the splotches, and began to give each leg a casual ruffle. When I raised up, my head hit something hard. It was my caddy's chin. He had come over to hand me the putter.

I took the putter and went over to my ball. I marked it and tried to hand it to the caddy so he could clean it. I dropped it. We both bent over to pick it up, bumped shoulders, and then got our hands on it at the same time. I dropped my putter. He dropped the towel. I picked up the towel. He picked up the putter. We exchanged them.

At this point, I thought I would light a cigarette to steady the nerves. I removed the pack from my pocket and tapped it against my left hand the way one does to make the cigarettes pop out. About four of them squirted out and onto the green. I picked them up and lit one. But when I went to remove it from my dry lips, it stuck, my fingers slid off the end, knocking the burning head down onto my shirt front. This forced me into a bit of an impromptu dance, which, in turn, resulted in my cleats taking another huge divot out of the green.

When that divot had been repaired, when I had successfully lighted another cigarette, and when I had a firm grip on the putter, I glanced around to see where Palmer and Finsterwald were and realized they had been staring at me, along with the other amused thousands, for God knows how long. It had been my turn to putt.

I won't go on about the rest of that round, or about the blue-red-purple funk that I played in. The point is made. I will say that because of the experience, and many others, I now know most of the pros pretty well. For example, I know Arnold Palmer well enough to call him Arnold. And Ben Hogan, with whom I have also played golf, has become a close enough friend that he never fails to phone me up to chat whenever we happen to wind up in Mratinje, Yugoslavia, at the same time.

This book is about professional golfers for the most part, and about the unique world around them. It is not a book with a continuing story line, except that modern golf itself is something of a story. But Arnold Palmer does not divorce Winnie and run off with Raquel Welch in the end. He marries his three-wood.

There is sometimes a temptation on the part of a writer putting together a collection to try to hang all of the stories on one line, to shape them into something larger and more meaningful than they are. This book doesn't do that any more than it pretends to tell the desperate slicer where his V's ought to point. It is not a history, though there is history in it, and it is not an instructional, though there are theories expounded.

If anything holds the book together other than the binding, it is the fact that a great many fascinating people play this game unconscionably well, and talk about it even better; and most of the more interesting personalities are examined within these covers, playing as I saw them play, and talking as I heard them talk.

The book takes its title from the words of Bobby Jones, who was often capable of writing about the game as well as he played it, which was not exactly with a 12-handicap. Speaking on the topic of golf's pressures, whether in championship competition or in one's normal Sunday foursome, Jones once wrote, "On the golf course, a man may be the dogged victim of inexorable fate, be struck down by an appalling stroke of tragedy, become the hero of unbelievable melodrama, or the clown in a sidesplitting comedy — any of these within a few hours, and all without having to bury a corpse or repair a tangled personality."

We golfers are all of those things at different times, I think. But since I have never known one who did not complain largely and most constantly about bad luck, I believe that we are mostly just the dogged victims of inexorable fate.

Why else, on occasions all too numerous, would we three-putt?

The Game of Golfe

It is statute an ordinit that in na place of the realme be there usit . . . Golfe or uther sik unprofitabill sportis.

— JAMES IV,
*to Parliament in Edinburgh,
May 16, 1491*

I T was a gray, drizzly day like most others in Scotland
and there was I, a lonely shepherd, strolling along a
swollen dune by the North Sea looking for a wee stane
to hit wi' a bit crook. Clumps of heather were up to my
knees and the yellow-tipped whin was up to my chest,
and I was up to here with my sheep because the little
dumplings had wandered away. I had this crooked
stick in my hand which I normally used to keep the
dumplings in line. You know. Firm left side, eye on the
tailbone, slow backswing — and whap. But they were
gone and I was just ambling along when I saw this
chuckie stane, as it was called, this round pebble. I
also saw this rabbit scrape, as it was called, through
an opening in the heather and whin. So I said to myself, "Self, why don't you take your bit crook and try to
knock this here stane into that there scrape? And stay
out of the heather because, boy, it'll make your hand
ring." Well, I guess I took it back a little outside because I cut a low one right into the garbage and almost
never did find it, but anyhow, this is how I came to
invent the game of golf a few hundred years ago.

There are those, of course, who claim that I did not
invent golf in another life, nor did any other Scot.

Some say the Romans did it long before me and called it *Paganica*, which I think, between you and me, sounds like a joint over on East 56th with a big tab. Some say the Dutch invented golf, or a game called *kolven*, which was similar. But no way. *Kolven* has to be a roll of veal stuffed with cheese and chives. Some say that even the French originated golf under the name of *jeu de mail*, but as any European traveler knows, this is a card game for the big players in Monaco. Actually, if the historians want to be picky, you could say that the Chinese a thousand years ago probably played a form of golf by batting a few snow peas around with chopsticks.

The fact of the matter is, golf is a Scottish game. It is naturally Scottish, as natural to our instincts as the seaside links land is natural to the setting. It was the Scots, after all, who took the game and did something with it when everybody else was busy making crossbows. We made the courses and the clubs, the balls and the rules, the trophies and the tournaments. We invented wind and rough, hooks and slices, bunkers and doglegs, and we were just getting ready to invent the overlapping grip when Harry Vardon, an Englishman, beat us to it.

We looked at the seashores, our links land, and said this is where the glory's at. Let the wet wind blow in from Denmark, or wherever it comes from. Let the incursions of the sea make the giant dunes and the tumbling valleys. Let the birds bring in the mixture of seeds that will grow our curious rough — the wiry, purple heather, the bulging whin, the dead fern we'll call bracken, and the green broom that does not have thorns to distinguish itself from whin, or gorse. Let the rabbits and the foxes chew out the first fairways and dig the first cups, perhaps at St. Andrews where The Old Course lies today.

I don't know what the Romans, the Dutch and the French were doing around the 1450's — aside from waiting for the Bible to get printed — but us Scots were playing golfe then, and had been. At least we were when the kings would permit it, there being, from time to time, this nagging problem of national service. Had to go fight the English. Cancel my starting time.

There was this afternoon, I recall, when the game came close to being banished forever. As it happened, I was out on this moor at St. Andrews trying out a new Auchterlonie driving spoon at the 11th — the short hole, of course — when a King's guard raised up out of the whin and handed me a scroll signed by our monarch.

The scroll said, "It is decreetid and ordained that the Fute-ball and the Golfe be utterly cryit doune, and nocht to be usit."

"Guy never could spell," I said.

The guard pointed his crossbow at me and said that the King, Jimmy the Roman Numeral, meant business.

"The golfe is sik unprofitabill sportis," he said.

"Pal, you got that right," I said. "See that shepherd over there with the cross-handed grip on his bit crook? Well, he's got me out, out, out and one down."

"Don't be abusit," the guard said. "It is statute and ordinit that in na place of the realme be there Golfe in tyme cuming."

"Look," I said. "Smell that air. Gaze over this land. Great, huh? Who would want a guy to be hanging around a drafty castle waiting for an Englishman to scale the wall?"

"Aye," he said. "The aire is guid and the field reasonable feir. But can ya na handle the bow for archerie? Can ya na run or swoom or warstle instead?"

"I don't know, man," I said. "Let me put it your way. Here's the deal. I was drivin' the chuckie stanes wi' a bit stick as sune's I could walk."

He nodded his head as if he was beginning to understand.

"Here's something else," I said. "I happen to know that a bow-maker in Perth is fixing up a set of clubs for the King right now. Why? Because the King sneaked out the other day to see what this game was all about and the Earl of Bothwell, who plays to a cool 23, brought him to his knees on the back three at Leith. The King's getting a pretty good price, too. Like only 14 s's for the set, whatever an s is."

The guard put down his crossbow and said, well, go ahead and play if that was the case. And by the way, he added, did I want to buy "a dussen guid golfe ballis?"

"Hold it," I said. "You got featheries?"

"Aye," he said. "Guid featheries that cum from the Laird of Rosyth. Guid featheries stuffed with flock and wuid shavings."

"Four s's," I said. "And not an s more."

"Eight s's," he said.

"They're hot, man. Six s's and we both get out clean," I said.

He went for the six — you can always strike a bargain in Europe — and disappeared back into the whin. And now that I had saved golf, I couldn't wait to try out one of the new high-compression featheries. I heeled up a good lie, and gave the shot a full body turn. Wow. Up, up, it soared — five yards, ten yards, twenty yards, and back to Earth, whatever that was, only a short rake-in from the 11th scrape, a par twelve. There is still a hole in the wind where I hit that shot, and I thought to myself, what a happy and golden time, indeed.

In a few more years, all of royalty would be playing golfe. There were rumors of Mary Queen of Scots shanking all around the fields of Seton when some said she should have been mourning the demise of Lord Darnley. Charles the First got a very bad press for being in a match at Leith when the Irish Rebellion broke out. A lot of Jameses and Dukes of York were seen swinging at Musselburgh, which still claims to be the oldest layout in the world and now sits inside a race course near Edinburgh. There was a Stuart or two spotted in a putting game at Leith, which is where The Honourable Company of Edinburgh Golfers got started before they built Muirfield.

All golfers, I think, should be indebted to a small group of us that got together in 1744 — The Honourable Company. Looking back, I don't know how we managed it without George Plimpton, but what we did was form the first country club. Not only that, we sat down and wrote the first rules of the game, which we called the Articles & Laws in Playing at Golf. At the time, some felt, our days might better have been spent defending Culloden against the English, but it just goes to show how important we thought golf was.

Those first rules have been well preserved along with some terribly clever comments I made at the meeting as I spoke keenly above the roar of our first president, Duncan Forbes. The thirteen rules of our first code are as follows:

1. You Must Tee your Ball within a Club length of the Hole.

(It's going to be uproarious fun, guys, waiting for somebody to drive before you can putt.)

2. Your Tee must be upon the Ground.

(Nothing like teeing up the ball in the air for greater distance.)

3. You are not to Change the Ball which you Strike off the Tee.

(The caddies will take care of this. When I tried to put down a clean one to putt the other day at St. Andrews, my man, Ginger Johnson, tugged at the sleeve of my cashmere and said, "You'll not do that here, laddie.")

4. You are not to Remove Stones, Bones or any Break Club for the Sake of playing your Ball Except upon the fair Green and that only within a Club Length of your Ball.

(Well, we'll get some pretty tricky breaks over the stones and bones.)

5. If your Ball come among Water, or any Watery filth, You are at Liberty to take out Your Ball, and throwing it behind the hazard 6 yards at least, You may play it with any Club, and allow your Adversary a Stroke, for so getting out your Ball.

(Unless your Adversary doesn't see you do it.)

6. If your Balls be found any where touching one another, You are to lift the first Ball, till You play the last.

(I estimate the odds on this happening at, roughly, 9,768 to 1.)

7. At holeing, You are to play your Ball honestly for the Hole, and not to play upon your Adversary's Ball, not lying in your way to the Hole.

(I heard about this across the ocean in a place called East Hampton. They call it croquet.)

8. If you should lose your Ball, by its being taken up, or any other way You are to go back to the Spot where you Struck last, and drop another Ball, and Allow your Adversary a Stroke for the Misfortune.

(And if your Adversary has been seen taking

up your Ball, you may strike your Adversary wi' a bit crook, teeing him upon the Ground.)

9. No Man at Holeing his Ball, is to be Allowed to Mark his way to the Hole with his Club or any thing else.

(And if you do, man, the greens committee will wear your ass out.)

10. If a Ball be Stop'd by any person, Horse, Dog or any thing else, the Ball so Stop'd Must be Played where it lyes.

(Yeah, but with the money up, how do you know if it's a real dog?)

11. If you draw your Club, in Order to Strike, and proceed so far in the Stroke as to be bringing down your Club; if then your Club shall break, in any way, it is to be accounted a Stroke.

(And your forearms will hum a merry tune as well.)

12. He, Whose Ball lyes furthest from the Hole is Obliged to play first.

(This is a good rule, but I'll tell you, the public course players are going to relax it a little.)

13. Neither Trench, Ditch, or Dyke, made for the preservation of the Links, Nor the Scholars Holes or the Soldiers Lines, shall be Accounted a Hazard, But the Ball is to be taken out, Teed and played with any Iron Club.

(Oh, swell, Duncan. So how come you let me make eight passes at it yesterday in the Soldiers Lines with no relief?)

Well, you know what happens. You let one private club get started and down the road another pops up. The noblemen and lairds of Fifeshire couldn't stand it that we had The Honourable Company and some rules, especially, they said, when *everybody* knew St. Andrews was the cradle of golfe. So in hardly any time at all, they formed a group called The Society of St. Andrews Golfers, which later would become known as the Royal & Ancient Golf Club. And you know what happened after that. They had the sport by the old gutta percha and never would turn loose of it.

A lot of arguments have gone on through the years about the history of the game, where it began, who molded the first cleek, and so forth. Over at Muirfield where The Honourable Company still hangs out — merely the world's oldest club — they say that the R&A would still be the Greensboro Jaycees if the Edinburgh code of golf hadn't been written. And at the same time, over at Prestwick on the West Coast, they like to say that the R&A wouldn't have anything to do but run the St. Andrews city championship if Prestwick's members hadn't decided to invent the Open championship and stage it the first twelve years of its existence. The Open championship, of course, is what we call the British Open today.

All I know is, every time somebody at Muirfield or Prestwick or Troon or Carnoustie goes out and finds an old track iron which had to have been made over two hundred years ago, somebody from the R&A will reach down into Hell Bunker or the Swilken Burn and

find a club that is older. One envisions genial Laurie
Auchterlonie, the honorary professional of St. Andrews,
carving and hammering away these days, making an
antique putter dated 1742.

What truly matters, of course, is that the whole
scene is old — the gray clubhouses and the rolling
land, the Minute Books and the scrolls, the wind, and
rain, and heather, the dunes and swales, everything
that makes Scottish golf what it is. It has been said by
many that a golfer hasn't played the game until he has
gone back where it all was, and where it all is.

It is a special feeling, I think, that calls the golfer
back to Scotland as the sailor is called by the sea.
Take me to the grave of Old Tom Morris, a voice says.
Drive me around the Road Hole. Show me where the
Wee Icemon chipped it in at Carnoustie. Lead me
down the long, narrow 11th at Troon where Arnie
made the threes. Let me hear the groan of the Spitfire
ghosts at Turnberry. Carry me over the Sleepers at
Prestwick. Bend me around the archery field at Muirfield. Drown me in all of these treasures of time once
more in this, still another life.

The Scots themselves relish all of this more than
anyone. It is in their faces as deeply as it is in their
poems. They are constantly writing poems about their
bunkers, and burns and braes. "The swallows are high
in an empty sky, so let's to the tee once more." That
kind of thing. Or, "There's none — I'll back the asser-
tion with a wager — can play the heavy iron like the
Major!" It has been estimated that more golf poetry

exists in Scotland than heather. One particular effort keeps haunting me, maybe because I wrote it under the name of Sir Guy Campbell. It is titled "The Old Course Speaks," and I am grateful that J. B. Salmond preserved it in his book *The Story of the R&A*. It is written about St. Andrews, but it could be any links in the old country — guaranteed to hoist the enthusiastic golfer from any land out of his electric cart comfort and set him down on the creeping fescue of a Scottish links. Men have been known to pack as they read it:

I have heard the North Sea
Ceaselessly withdrawing,
Foot by foot receding,
Through the Ages as they spent;
Adding to my Loanings,
My salt and misty loanings,
Gracious ground for Golfers,
Spread far for their content.

Gulls and Terns and Curlews
Left me rich guano;
Sand and silt and sea-wrack —
The Tilth that made my sward.
Cunningies then cropped it,
And foxes followed after,
Fashioning my fairways
And Greens for Golf's reward.

Winter, Spring and Summer,
Autumn, in their seasons;
Snow and haar and sunshine

With wind, and wave, and rain,
Tempered my whole being,
Brought me growth and vigour,
Bent, and whin, and heather
To pattern my campaign.

Countless feet have worn me —
Children, men and women;
Multitudes have scarred me;
Come frost, come wet, come shine.
Service without measure,
Healing for my treasure, —
I renew at leisure.
The secret is mine.

Through long generations
I have watched Golf's pageant;
I have known its Powers,
And Princes in their prime,
Vying with each other
One year to another,
Yet for many changes
The Art is one with Time.

So it was and has been;
So it is and will be.
I abide unchallenged,
And peerless is my Name.
History behind me,
I give all who find me
Welcome and a Blessing,
To the Glory of the Game.

"So let's to the tee once more," I said to the customs official at Prestwick, having de-boarded my Pan Am flight from JFK. "The nature of my visit? Well, to receive a welcome and a blessing from the game. Actually, I have a meeting scheduled with Heather, Whin, Bracken & Broom, Incorporated, one of your very successful brokerage firms."

There was this tour that Keith Mackenzie, the secretary of the R&A, had worked out. Fly to Prestwick, the old World War II air base where everybody played 12 O'clock High, and motor from there down the West Coast to Turnberry, the Pebble Beach of Scotland. Stay at the Turnberry Hotel, which is the only thing there, and covers a whole hillside, overlooking the Turnberry course and the old Spitfire runways. From Turnberry, he said, one could reach two other very famous Scottish links — Troon and Prestwick — simply by driving once a day over the Electric Brae, a road which goes up when it appears to be going down. Cover the West Coast first, said Mackenzie, then move to The Old Course Hotel at St. Andrews where you can play The Old Course, right outside your window, and journey north toward Dundee and Carnoustie, or south toward Edinburgh and Muirfield.

"This is the best possible route for an American," said Mackenzie.

"But I'm Scottish," I said. "I'm just retracing my steps from a few hundred years before."

"Of course, dear chap," Keith said. "We're all Scottish when it comes to golf."

"Aye," I said.

"Simply marvelous tour," he said. "You'll see a bit of it all. Turnberry, for example, pitched right there on the Firth of Clyde. Tees practically hanging on the water like Pebble. And Prestwick with those slender fairways and blind shots, and seven bloody five pars. Too outdated for the Open championship, of course, but, mind you, the Pine Valley of Scotland in a way. And wonderful Old Troon. The 'postage stamp' green. The very first sharp-angled dogleg. I say, Arnie argued a good case there, didn't he?"

"Aye," I said.

"Then to the East Coast. That's your story," Keith said. "You'll quarter in The Old Course Hotel, naturally, right where the railway sheds were on the Road Hole. Walk out on your terrace and spit in the Principal's Nose, by jove. With the new bridge, you can reach Carnoustie in an hour now. Good old somber Carnoustie, the Barry Burn and all that. And then, of course, there's Muirfield. Marvelous place, Muirfield. Not a burn on it, you see. Just one hundred sixty-five bunkers. You'll see a bit of sand there, I'd guess."

"Aye, aye," I said.

"Best of luck," he said. "See you at St. Andrews when you arrive. We'll have a bit of port. It goes well in the Big Room."

For some evil reason, some death wish that perhaps is concealed within us all, the first thing a touring golfer is captivated by in Scotland is the plantlife adjacent to all fairways. The heather, whin, bracken and broom. Turnberry, my first stop, had all of these other landmarks to dwell upon — holes hanging on the Firth of Clyde, as Mackenzie said, the Spitfire runways now bordered by wild flowers, a bird sanctuary on an island off in the distance, the huge hotel on the hill where "God Save the Queen" reverberated from the orchestra pit in the ballroom at night through all of the tea rooms, and an RAF monument at the 12th green commemorating those men from Turnberry's aerial fighting and gunnery school who perished, their name liveth forever with the group captain in the sky. But I was preoccupied with the rough.

You find yourself having this running commentary with your caddy, as if he's a botanist in his checkered James Cagney cap, his coat and tie, and a scruffy face which hasn't been shaved since the last air raid. His name is Jimmy or Peter or Ginger or Tip or Cecil, and chances are he caddied for Hagen at Hoylake in 1924.

"What am I in here?" I asked the one at Turnberry on the very first hole. "Is this gorse?"

"Not likely," he said. "I think that's a bush."

Your caddy is a warm, friendly man who knows his golf. You swing once and he knows your distances. If he says the shot is "a wee seven," you'd better hit it wee-ly, or a dozen of you with machetes won't be able to find the ball behind the green.

Such a hole was the 4th at Turnberry, which bears the name Woe-be-Tide. It is a 170-yard one-shotter. You practically stand on the Firth and hit into a crosswind to a green about as big as your golf bag with more water on the left and hounds of the Baskervilles on your right.

"What am I in now?" I asked, having hit a Firthlock safely to the right. "Is this heather?"

"That," he said, "is gorse. You ca'na swing softly, sir, and be way o' the gorse."

"Gorse is whin, right?"

He said, "Aye, the whins we call it. You can'na plant the whin and neither will the whin die. The whin is just here where it always was."

I took a forceful swing with a sand iron, moving the ball about one foot, and said, "Don't forget to show me the heather when we find some."

"Aye," he said. "That's heather you're in now."

You can't often find the ball in heather. It is a stubby dwarf plant, all matted and wiry, brown at times, purple at others. You can top a shot with a driver and, whereas in America the ball is likely to run for a hundred or so yards, if in Scotland it finds a cluster of heather only a few yards away, it will go flimp — and either disappear forever, or bound straight back at you.

I could see at least half of the ball there in the heather, and I took a full swipe at it with the wedge, so hard that the caddy counted all of the cleats in my shoes and the veins in my legs, and the noise I made sounded like the Stukas had returned to drop another load on the docks at Glasgow.

And the ball didn't move at all.

"When does my hand stop tingling?" I said.

Turnberry has one hole that is more magnificent

than all of the others. It is the 9th, a 425-yard hole
with a tee sitting back on an island of jagged rock,
with rocks and water bordering it on the left where a
lighthouse marks the farthest point of the course from
the hotel. Off to the right, beyond the plantlife, is part
of the old asphalt Spitfire runway. Behind the green is
broom — whin without thorns — and little dabs of
bracken, which the cows won't eat.

One finds in Scotland, however, that if the botany
doesn't confuse you, the scorekeeping will. I drove
well at the 9th, which means safely onto the close-
cropped fescue grass which comprises all Scottish
fairways. I reached the small green with one of my
rare un-shanked four-irons, and I stole a putt of about
twenty feet for a three. Then the trouble began.

"Is this a par-four hole?" I asked the caddy.

"No, sir," he said. "It plays to a bogey five."

"Then I made an eagle," I said.

"It can'na be an eagle, sir," he said.

"Well, what's par for the course?"

He said, "Bogey today is about seventy-six."

"But level fours is seventy-two," I said. "Shouldn't
that be what I would call par?"

He thought a minute and said, "I reckon par to be
about seventy-four today."

"What was it yesterday, for instance?" I asked.

"Oh, in that wind yesterday, par must have been
seventy-seven or so."

I said, "Well, I think I just made an eagle."

"You did'na make an eagle, sir," he said.

"A birdie?"

"Not exactly a birdie with the helpin' wind, sir."

"A par?"

"Oh, much better than a par, it was," he said.

"So what the God damn hell was it, James Cagney?"

He said, "It was a very good score, sir. Your first of the round."

There is much to see in the neighborhood of Turnberry, and along the route to either Prestwick or Troon, like a castle here and there, or a birthplace of Robert Burns, of which there must be a dozen, but never should a visitor miss that hill — that thing — called the Electric Brae. Years ago, bicyclists discovered it, one learns. They found themselves forced to pedal sweatily to get uphill when it obviously looked as if the road were going downward into the woods. It is an optical illusion, and you would lose your wallet betting on it. The proof is this: stop the car at a point where you are certain you are headed uphill. Put a golf ball on the road, a shiny new Dunlop 65. It will roll uphill, that's all.

As mysterious as the Electric Brae is, it is no more mysterious than the course at Prestwick, the course where all of those early British Opens were staged beginning in 1860. Your first impression as you gaze out on a wasteland surrounded by an old stone fence is that this has to be the biggest practical joke in all of golf. I've got it, you say. You pay your green fee, put down a ball and aim at the world, take four or five steps and are never heard from again.

Consider the 1st hole, only 339 yards. On your

right, the stone fence, about ten feet away, separating
you from a train that will come chugging by at inter-
vals. On your left: mounds of heather and whin.
Directly in front: waste. Sheer waste. Small and large
clumps of it, sheltered by thin layers of fog. And the
caddy hands you a driver. The fairway, presuming
one is actually there, can't be more than twenty yards
wide, but the caddy hands you a driver.

"*Where* is it?" I asked.

"Straightaway, sir," said Charles, who was distin-
guished from my caddy at Turnberry by two things.
Charles wore a muffler and had his own cigarettes.
"It's just there," he said. "Just to the left of the
cemetery."

It is asking a lot, I know, to expect anyone to
believe that you can bust a drive about 250 yards on a
339-yard hole, have a good lie in the fairway, and still
not be able to see a green anywhere, but this is
Prestwick.

The green was there, all right, as are all of the
greens at Prestwick, but you never see them until you
are on them, which is usually eight or ten strokes after
leaving the tee. They sit behind little hills, or the ter-
rain simply sinks ten or fifteen feet straight down to a
mowed surface, or they are snuggled over behind tall
wood fences over which you have nothing to aim at
but a distant church steeple.

You would like to gather up several holes from
Prestwick and mail them to your top ten enemies. I
guess my all-time favorite love-hate golf hole must be

the 3rd hole on this course. Like most of the holes at
Prestwick, it is unchanged from the day in 1860 when
Willie Park, Sr., shot 174 to become the first Open
champion. Quite a score, I have since decided.

First of all, without a caddy, it would take you a
week and a half to find the third tee. It is a little patch
of ground roughly three yards wide perched atop a
stream, a burn, rather, with the cemetery to your back
and nothing up ahead except fine mist. Well, dimly in
the distance, you can see a rising dune with a fence
crawling across it — "the Sleepers," the caddy says.
But nothing more. Nothing.

"I'll be frank, Charles," I said. "I have no idea which
way to go, or what with."

"Have a go with the spoon, sir," he said.

"The *spoon?*" I shrieked. "Where the hell am I
going with a spoon?"

"A spoon'll get you across the burn, sir, but it'll na
get you to the Sleepers," he said.

"Hold it," I said. "Just wait a minute." My body was
sort of slumped over, and I was holding the bridge of
my nose with my thumb and forefinger. "These, uh,
Sleepers. They're out there somewhere?"

"Aye, the Sleepers," he said.

"And, uh, they just kind of hang around, right?"

"Aye," he said. "The Sleepers have took many a
golfer."

Somehow, I kept the three-wood in play and when I
reached the shot, Charles casually handed me the four-
wood. I took the club and addressed the ball, hoping

to hit quickly and get on past the Sleepers, wherever they were. But Charles stopped me.

"Not that way, sir," he said.

"This *is* the way I was headed when we left the tee," I said.

"We go a bit right here, sir," he said. "The Sleepers is there just below the old fence. You want to go over the Sleepers and over the fence as well, but na too far right because of the burn. Just a nice stroke, sir, with the four-wood."

Happily, I got the shot up and in the general direction Charles ordered, and walking toward the flight of the ball, I finally came to the Sleepers. They were a series of bunkers about as deep as the Grand Canyon. A driver off the tee would have found them, and so would any kind of second shot that didn't get up high enough to clear the fence on the dune. A worn path led through the Sleepers, and then some ancient wooden steps led up the hill and around the fence to what was supposed to be more fairway on the other side.

It wasn't a fairway at all. It was a group of grass moguls going off into infinity. It looked like a carefully arranged assortment of tiny green Astrodomes. When Charles handed me the pitching wedge, I almost hit him with it because there was no green in sight.

I got the wedge onto the green that was, sure enough, nestled down in one of those dips, and two-putted for a five that I figured wasn't a par just because the hole was 505 yards long. Charles said I had played the hole perfectly, thanks to him, and that I could play it a thousand times and probably never play it as well.

I said, "Charles, do you know what this hole would be called in America?"

"Sir?" he said.

"This is one of those holes where your suitcase flies open and you don't know what's liable to come out," I said.

"Aye, 'tis that," he said.

"One bad shot and you're S.O.L. on this mother," I said.

"Sir?" said Charles.

"Shit out of luck," I said.

"Aye," said Charles. "At Prestwick, we call it the Sleepers."

Prestwick has a number of other charming atrocities. There is a 201-yard 5th hole which the caddies call the "Himalayas" which one plays with anything from a five-iron to a driver, depending on the wind. You flog the shot over a mountainous dune and discover, on the other side, about a hundred feet down, a green. You ring a bell when you've putted out. There is a wonderful 15th hole of only 329 yards, straightaway, but the fairway is total heather except for the width of an umbrella, and there is no green at all that I could find. All in all, I would say that Prestwick is the most unique course in the world. There are eighteen holes but I dare any visitor to find more than, say, twelve fairways and seven or eight greens.

Only a couple of graveyards and trash piles away

from Prestwick lies Troon. In fact, from the 10th tee at Prestwick you can see Troon better than you can see Prestwick. The course is on the Firth, not so much as Turnberry but more so than Prestwick, and the town is filled with small resort hotels and rooming houses which advertise bed-and-breakfast. Troon is the seaside getaway on weekends for the inhabitants of Glasgow. You can fish there, and hike, and go camping in the drizzle. But the best thing you can do if you are privileged enough is play Old Troon, the championship course of the snootiest club on the West Coast. Mr. A. Sweet, sektry, will arrange the round if he approves of the cut of your blazer.

Old Troon is the only Scottish links on the West Coast that the R&A keep on what Keith Mackenzie terms "the championship rota." These are courses fit to host the British Open. In Scotland, they have been narrowed down to St. Andrews, Muirfield, Carnoustie and Troon. And in England they are Birkdale, Lytham and Hoylake. Troon takes immense pride in the fact that it is the jewel of the west, and even more pride in the fact that it was the scene of one of Arnold Palmer's most glorious weeks. Palmer, of course, captured his second British Open at Troon in 1962 by six strokes (276) on a course that Gary Player declared "unfair" before walking off in a rage, and a course that drew such horrid individual holes out of Jack Nicklaus as tens and eights.

For the full haul of eighteen holes, Troon is not all that memorable. The rough, for one thing, is more like

rugged American rough; you *can* escape from it in one
hearty swing if the waist of your trousers is cinched
up. Troon, I found, is what you would call a very
pleasant course and perhaps more modern than most
Scottish courses if any layout without the hint of a
tree can look modern to an American.

This is not to say that Troon is void of character. It
has several holes, as a matter of fact, which are as
good as any to be found, including the single hardest
hole I have ever seen — the 11th — not to forget two
others which have been architectural landmarks since
they were constructed.

The 8th, for example. This is the famed "postage
stamp." It is so named because the green, which clings
to nothing but the lower half of a heather-covered
mound, is not much larger than a stamp. The hole
measures only 125 yards, but it can play up to a four-
iron if the wind is whipping out of the north. Mr. A.
Sweet likes to tell about a member who made a hole in
one at the "postage stamp" in a most unusual way. His
tee shot came to rest atop the mound. He swung at the
ball with a wedge from up there, and missed it. But
the sweep of the clubhead through the grass dislodged
the ball and it trickled down the hill and into the
cup.

"Rightly, of course, the chap made a two," said Mr.
Sweet.

It did not harm the fame of the "postage stamp"
that in 1923 when Troon was first used to stage the
Open championship, none other than Walter Hagen

made a double bogey five there to blow the title by a stroke to a Mr. Arthur Havers.

All over Scotland one continually finds par-four holes where, at one time or another, according to the caddies, Jack Nicklaus was on in one. The hole before the "postage stamp," Troon's 7th, is such a hole. It is renowned for two other reasons; first, it is supposed to be one of the original doglegs, since the fairway curves sharply to the right, and it is also considered one of the most beautiful holes.

With the tee up on a bluff furnishing a wide view of the sea, and with the wind usually helping, you can envision how Nicklaus might have driven it those 385 yards. He caught one just right and strung it out over the sandhills, hit a downslope and burned a path through the whin up to the putting surface.

It might well have been this good fortune back in 1962 that encouraged Jack to take out the driver at Troon's 11th the day he had to sink a fifty-foot putt for a twelve. The 11th hole is 485 yards of railroad track on the right and clusters of whin on the left. The fairway is nothing but moguls all the way with the tiny green hard by another of those old stone fences. This is the hole Palmer won the Open on, for he played it with two threes and two fours — six under — by using a one-iron off the tee and a two-iron to the green.

Nicklaus, however, tried to go with the driver. First, he got acquainted with the whin for a few shots, and once he made it to the fairway, he put a couple over the wall. Here, too, was the point from which Gary Player left for the clubhouse, thence to the airport.

My caddy at Troon, Peter McNeil, who happened to have toted Sam Snead's bag in the 1962 Open, gave me the driver at the 11th, and when we lost sight of it soaring out over the whin, he consoled me the way a good caddy should.

"You're just not with it today, sir," he said.

Troon makes no claim to being among the oldest clubs in Scotland, seeing as how it wasn't built until just the other day — 1878 — but like any other self-respecting private domain for gentlemen golfers, it has a set of relics that are said to be the oldest in Britain. Mr. A. Sweet proudly pointed to the trophy case and said those clubs were found in a cupboard wrapped in a newspaper dated 1741.

"I think Laurie Auchterlonie at St. Andrews is getting ready to discover a set from 1740," I said.

Mr. A. Sweet did not laugh.

The crass American would not think much of a clubhouse at a Scottish links, be it Troon or Prestwick, or most anywhere. There are no tennis courts, of course, and no swimming pool. There is no Mixed Foursome Grill because there is no Mixed. Which means no women or pros allowed inside. The pro stays in his wooden shack nearby, selling rainsuits and mending clubs. The main clubhouse itself is for ex-wing commanders to eat lunch in — no smoking until after two P.M. — to change socks in before or after their daily thirty-six holes, and to slump over their

London *Times* in. If there is a shower stall down some creaking corridor, the water is chilled and hits you with all the force of a leak in the roof. On the walls of the dining room and the reading room, both of which are likely to offer a close-up view of the 18th green, will be portraits of a lot of men who look like George Washington but would rather be dead first. They will be ex-secretaries and ex-captains of the club who not only invented the mashie-niblick but were survivors of the Black Hole of Calcutta.

If you are as poor at geography as I, you have to divide Scotland like this. The West Coast, where Troon and Prestwick and Turnberry are, and where I had been, is the Ireland side. From almost any point on those three courses, in other words, if you could see far enough, you would see Northern Ireland. This is also known to me as the Glasgow side, which, even to the Scots, is not exactly Sutton Place. Where I was headed now was to the East Coast, the Edinburgh side, to the North Sea, to the more posh area of the country where St. Andrews, Muirfield and Carnoustie are. There is a great deal more to Scotland than just this "golf belt," which embraces the land across the mid-section from Troon to Muirfield. There is, for instance, way up north, the links of Dornoch. As good a test as any, according to Keith Mackenzie, but too far away for the R&A to transport its people, chestnut palings, gallery rope, scoreboards and tents for the Open championship. Thanks, Dornoch, but Carnoustie is as far north as the R&A cares to travel.

Actually, if one could grease himself up and swim like Florence Chadwick, he could get to Carnoustie from St. Andrews in about thirty minutes. It is just across a bay. Driving, however, takes a couple of hours because cars have to go through Dundee, which is Yonkers with, as they say, less glamor.

From the viewpoint of providing difficulty for the top professional golfers, Carnoustie is surely the toughest course in Scotland. It is long and windy and wet. It is also smoky, dreary and somber. It is a course with more of a sameness to it throughout than any other. Every hole begins to look like the one you've just played — unreachable. Even the names of the holes are unimaginative. The 2nd: Gulley. The 4th: Hillocks. The 6th: Long. The 11th: Dyke. The 18th: Home.

Carnoustie began to develop a distinction around the 5th hole, I thought. But maybe I felt this because my caddy had me primed. Here was the hole where the Wee Icemon, Ben Hogan, had chipped in for a birdie three in 1953 during the last round. It was where he had made the stroke, from the lower-left bunker, that launched him toward the British Open title the one and only time he ever played in the tournament.

"He stood right here," said Phillip, the caddy. "Aye, it was only a short flick of the wrist."

The 6th, too, had character, most of it provided by an electrical fence down the left-hand side of the fairway. Periodically, a sign in red letters hung on the fence which said: DO NOT TOUCH ANYTHING. IT MAY

EXPLODE AND KILL YOU. On the other side of the wire, as you might guess, was a firing range used by the Ministry of Defense. The hole is 565 yards long, and the Scots named it Hogan's Alley in '53, for Ben birdied it the last two rounds.

Phillip stopped at a point far beyond my tee shot down the fairway. "Here," he said, digging his shoe into the turf. "And here." He moved it a couple of inches. "Then here." He moved it another inch. "And over here." He moved his shoe about a foot.

"That's where the Icemon drove it," he said.

From here until near the finish Carnoustie became something of a blur. The wind wouldn't give my four-wood a rest, and the steady drizzle turned my under and over cashmeres into about seven hundred pounds of inconvenient weight. The most fascinating land-mark near the course, after the firing range, was Anderson Cranes and Stone-Cutting Machinery.

"Phillip," I said. "Did anyone ever suggest to you that Carnoustie is *not* Antibes?"

Somewhere near the end, I vaguely recall, there is a Barry Burn that you have to cross about thirty times on the last three holes, which happen to be a 243-yard three par into the gale that Jack Nicklaus finally reached with a driver in 1968, a 438-yard par four that you are forced to lay up on off the tee, and a 453-yard par four 18th that I judged to be a driver, spoon and full eight-iron. With dry grips, maybe less.

As it turned out, I finished with a flourish. Good driver, good spoon, good eight-iron, four feet from the cup. Of course in my haste to have Phillip show me the spot where Hogan used to go to wring out his sweaters, I blew the putt. And with a number of people staring at me through the clubhouse window, too.

Later on, I was safely indoors trying to dry off and get one of those wonderful hot beers when a tall Britisher in a coat with a crest approached me.

"I say, you're the chap who was out there on the eighteenth a while ago," he said.

"Afraid so," I said.

"Bit dodgey that putt," he said. "Breaks left."

"Sure does," I said.

"Good for me, though," he said. "Took four shillings off a mate at the bar."

Yeah, I thought, well, Hogan won the Open here and he's from my town, and lend lease and — ah, screw it.

Muirfield from St. Andrews is in precisely the opposite direction of Carnoustie, and it is everything Carnoustie isn't. Muirfield is elegance and class, charm and dignity, convenience and pleasure. There is not a true distance on it, nor a fixed par, nor a name for a hole, but it is a course with a championship quality in the purest sense. There is not a tree or a bush or a burn, but there are 165 bunkers and they are trouble enough. It is the only course in Scotland that takes advantage and disadvantage of the full cycle of the wind, for the outgoing nine goes clockwise and back

to the clubhouse, and the back nine runs counter-
clockwise and returns. Par is probably 72, but it is
easy to envision days when the winds would make
it 76.

Muirfield is on the Firth of Forth between Gullane
and North Berwick, not painfully far from Edinburgh.
It is on a fine shore surrounded by estates, and one
gets the idea that this area is to Edinburgh what the
Hamptons are to New York City. Muirfield's clubhouse is noted for its spaciousness in comparison with
other Scottish clubhouses, and its kitchen is noted for
its cuisine. This, after all, is where The Honourable
Company of Edinburgh Golfers hangs out.

Directly next door to the huge stone clubhouse with
its sprawling veranda and putting green is the Greywalls Hotel, where a member of The Honourable
Company would stay. Greywalls fronts on the 9th
green, and the Scots have long felt that part of the
vast charm of Muirfield is that a fellow can stop after
nine holes and grab a tap at Greywalls — the way
Americans do at their courses everywhere.

The real charm of Muirfield is in its amazing fair-
ness and its splendid pacing, both of which are much
on the order of Merion, that gem of a battleground on
Philadelphia's Main Line where every club comes out
of the bag every time you play it. Muirfield has short
fives and long fives, short, bending fours, and long,
narrow fours, short, tricky threes and long but reach-
able threes. Its fairways are skinny but the lies are
perfect, and there are shortcuts to be taken by the

brave or long-hitting who wish to flirt with more bunkers than the eye can count.

Because of the eccentricities of the wind, for example, as well as the roll of the fairway, Jack Nicklaus was able to drive the 407-yard 15th hole when he won the British Open there in 1966. But he had to lean on a three-wood coming back to reach the 198-yard 16th. It would be difficult to imagine a more implausible course on which Nicklaus could win a tournament because the tightness would practically render his big drive useless. But as they say at Muirfield, "He one-ironed her."

The highest compliment anyone could pay Muirfield, I suppose, would be to say that it is a Hogan type of course. Distances are meaningless because of the wind, and Hogan always said they were meaningless, anyhow. Every shot has a look to it, he said, a certain feel. "I might hit a two-iron a hundred fifty yards," he often said.

I played Muirfield that way. My two-irons went exactly 150 yards, and frequently off the shank of the club to the right.

"This is the course," my caddy said, over and over. "This is the best of the lot."

"I'd like to see it sometime," I said.

There are a number of spectacular holes at Muirfield, but the 6th is perhaps its finest. It is a par four — sometimes a par five — of 475 yards or thereabouts, an uphill-downhill dogleg left which curls around a battered rock wall which separates the course from an archery field. The landing area for the tee shot is no more than twenty yards across, and deep bunkers patrol it. With a career drive you can then get close to home with a career three-wood to a rolling green, again framed by bunkers.

"What a hole," I said to the caddy as I stood there considering the three-wood.

"Have a good go with the spoon," he said. "But a word of caution, sir. A ball played into Archerfield Wood is irrecoverable."

The mystique of Muirfield lingers on. So does the memory of Carnoustie's foreboding. So does the scenic wonder of Turnberry, and the haunting incredibility of Prestwick, and the pleasant deception of Troon. But put them all together and St. Andrews can play their low ball for atmosphere.

To begin with, St. Andrews is an old university town. Spires rise up over narrow streets littered with shops and cozy pubs. Students wearing red cloaks are bicycling around. Statues confront the stroller. An inn is here and there, and the North Sea just beyond.

There are four golf courses at St. Andrews: Old, New, Eton and Jubilee, and they are all available to the public. The *new* course is over seventy years old. Try that on for nostalgia. But no one, of course, is ever concerned about anything but The Old. The Old Course *is* St. Andrews, the R&A, all of those famed hazards. It is Jones, Vardon, Hagen, and old and young Tom Morris, and Keith Mackenzie standing on the balcony of his office in the R&A building just above the first tee surveying the entirety of the layout through a pair of mounted German submarine binoculars.

I was fortunate enough to secure lodging in The Old Course Hotel. Thus, I could walk out on my terrace and it was all there directly below me. To my left, the course stretching out to the 11th green — the short hole, of course — and to my right, a matchless view of the 18th fairway leading up through the Valley of Sin with Rusacks Hotel standing there as it is supposed to be, and with the great gray edifice of the Royal & Ancient clubhouse forming a backdrop.

The Old Course has been called a lot of things because, at first glance, it looks like nothing more than a flat green city park. Some Americans have labeled it a "third-rate municipal course," and a "football field," but Bob Jones knew its subtleties better. It was, he said, the one course he would play forever if he could choose just one.

Two things strike the first-timer at St. Andrews immediately. First, the double greens. No fewer than fourteen holes share enormous putting surfaces, the 2nd also being the 16th, and that sort of thing. There are two flags, naturally, and often they will be as far apart as perhaps eighty yards, with many a dip and turn between them. The erring shotmaker is apt to find the longest putts in golf at St. Andrews. Secondly, The Old Course is something of a paradise for one with a chronic hook. The first nine goes straight out, you see, with all of the heather and the sea on your right. And the back nine returns, parallel, giving the hooker all of those outgoing fairways to land on.

The mystery of why no golfer has ever been able to tear apart The Old Course — 278 is the lowest a winner has shot in the British Open there — lies in the wind and the putting, and the fantastically perfect location of such hazards as Hell Bunker, a deep and somewhat inescapable pit at the 14th, the Swilken Burn, a small brook which rushes right up against the green of the 1st hole and catches many a soft nine-iron, and the Valley of Sin, the cavernous lower level of the 18th green from which three-putts and even four-putts are commonplace.

I attacked The Old Course in the company of Ginger Johnson who had merely been caddying there for forty-five years. For a few holes, he thought he had Henry Cotton again. The wind was behind and my shank, my top, my slice and my putting jerk seemed to have disappeared. Through the 10th, I was only one over par, and I said to Ginger:

"I don't know, but I think I'm bringing The Old Course to its knees."

And Ginger said, "Aye, ya made a putt or two, sir. But now we go home into the wind."

In rapid order, I was lost in the Elysian Fields, lost in the Beardies, trapped in Hell Bunker, gouged in the Principal's Nose, over the fence, smothered in heather, and even out of bounds on an overhang of The Old Course Hotel at the Road Hole. Finally, I limped up the 18th fairway en route to the Valley of Sin. Par for 86.

"You had a wee bit of hard luck," Ginger said. "But it can't spoil the fact that as we cum up the eighteenth, we sense a wee bit of tradition, don't we?"

Keith Mackenzie peered down from his balcony as I walked onto the green. I putted out. One final insult: a straight-in four-footer which broke six inches. The secretary motioned me up for lunch in the R&A dining room — no smoking at all. I toured the club and re-read the letter that Isaac Grainger, then the president of the USGA, had written to the R&A on the occasion of its two-hundredth birthday.

He had said, in part, "What golf has of honor, what it has of justice, of fair play, of good fellowship and sportsmanship — in a word, what is best in golf — is almost surely traceable to the inspiration of the Royal and Ancient."

I thought of those words again as I strolled back outside to stand and look at the sea, and at the town, and all across the gentle green sweep of The Old Course — the oldest course.

I had been there forever.

Sam Snead with Hair

Louise, we've got to hide this $600 before we hit the road. Since we're rich, we're bound to get robbed. But if we hide it, maybe they won't get it all.

> — BYRON NELSON
> *to his wife after winning his first big check in the Thirties*

To the hordes of people who feel that Arnold Palmer invented golf on television around, oh, 1960, and who no doubt think the game is played over just four holes, from the 15th — where Jim McKay is — through the 18th — where Chris Schenkel is — the professional tour probably looks colorful today. Sure it does. After all, there goes Arnold again, streaking back to Latrobe for the evening in his twin-booster, partly deductible rocket ship *PGA One*. And there is Billy Casper eating baked buffalo tongue, or sea-lentil casserole, or whatever, for his diet and allergies. And there's Doug Sanders in his latest lemon-lime ensemble, a cluster of bell-bottomed lovelies foraging after him. And here comes Lionel Hebert on his way to the cocktail lounge to work his handicap down from eight to six on the trumpet. Jack Nicklaus isn't around this week, they say. He's off in Addis Ababa filming a TV series with the President of the United States, the Soviet Premier, the Sheik of Kuwait and eight former fraternity brothers from Ohio State. But all he does is stay fat and win anyhow. This tour is splashed with color without him, boy. You look down that list of entries in our $500,000 Lucky Desert Cajun Festival and

you'll see more excitement than the linoleum salesmen caused when the waiter brought the dinner check.

Well, perhaps not to some of us. The Sixties had
their giddy moments, of course, give or take a Julius
Finsteraaron. But there is another period in the history of golf that keeps coming back to haunt those
who remember the cleek with a certain fondness. The
Thirties. Maybe you have to be a little overaged for
the discotheques to appreciate that decade. It would
help if you could remember who Uncle Fletcher was
on *Vic and Sade*, or if you could still set *One Man's
Family* defensively: Paul's in the library, Clifford and
Claudia are down on the seawall and Hank and Pinky
are up at the Sky Ranch, right? If you can handle that
and also identify a Russ Columbo, a Filipino Twirler,
a black cow, a Ken Maynard, a sinking of the *Panay*
and a Ky Laffoon — well, then. You certainly know
that anyone who thinks the pro tour is fun now would
have gone right out of his Spalding Dot in the Thirties.

For it was the Thirties that gave us Sam Snead with
hair, right there on his head, parted on the left, and a
brooding runt in a snapbrim hat and a wild hook: Ben
Hogan. It was the Thirties that gave us Jimmy Demaret's pink shoes and polka-dot slacks — outfits that
would make Doug Sanders look like a Bond's window
today. It was the Thirties that gave us Lloyd Mangrum's mustache, Dutch Harrison's drawl, and Ky
Laffoon anointing the greens with tobacco juice. It
was the Thirties that gave us Byron Nelson throwing
up between his dazzling rounds, Jug McSpaden's sun

goggles, Horton Smith's ominous squint, Jimmy Thomson's booming tee shots, the sand wedge and steel shafts. It was an era in which Ruby Keeler and Dick Powell in their starched sailor suits couldn't do the Big Apple much better than Joan and Paul Runyon, or Emma and Harry Cooper, or Mabel and Frank Walsh. It was a decade with more individuals in professional golf than there were hominy wagons on the streets. And if the pro couldn't make the most of the spirit and hilarity of these struggling times, and if the fan couldn't enjoy them, then the pro could go back to raking cottonseed-hull greens, and the fan could go back to his radio serials.

One of the things that made it special is that golf, looking back on it, still belonged to the amateurs in the early Thirties, to aristocratic young men with hyphenated names, blonde sisters and portraits of whaling skippers over their fireplaces. A pro was anyone who had caddied beyond the age of fourteen, who knew how to run a mowing machine, who could wrap leather grips and who frequently had to take his meals in the kitchen of a country club. If he happened to be personable and didn't look *too* Italian, he might be very fortunate. He could give a few fifty-cent lessons each week to some kindly gentleman who owned a railroad or the state of New Jersey. Or if the pro looked like he could really play, a kindly gentleman might lend him $300 to go out and see what this tour was all about, what those chaps Tommy Hagen and Walter Armour were up to.

The exact date is not recorded when people first realized that a pro could make a niblick back up with more spin than an amateur, but it occurred somewhere in the Thirties. At about the same time Walter Hagen was finally about to convince everyone that you could let a pro in the front door of your club and he wouldn't steal the crystal. Hagen had been working at it for a long time — outdressing, outspending and out-traveling the rich. These two circumstances began to combine in the years of the Depression, and this is what actually led America into today's age of the alligator shoe. This was the beginning of the big-money tour that has put Conni Venturi in Balenciagas, made Dave Marr a bon vivant along 52nd Street, transformed Arnold Palmer into a permanent, floating, corporate crap game and made a worldly, theorizing, hard-cover author out of every ex-caddy who can chip from sand.

One of the more obvious results of this progress is that going on the tour now is as easy as getting into the University of Houston if you can shoot 65. You birdie four holes in a row at Bending Wedge Country Club and some automobile dealer with a coat of arms on his blazer will step up and hand you $12,000, plus an air travel card. A day later, you're standing on a putting green near Bert Yancey. You're on the tour. To say it was somewhat more of an adventure in the Thirties would be like saying Valerie Hogan has seen a clubhouse veranda or two.

You could get to the tour, all right, by hitchhiking

or riding a freight if necessary. But to *stay* there, that
was the challenge. To put enough chuckburgers down
your neck to fend off the hunger from Flagstaff to
West Palm. If you shot a 74 in the first round somewhere, forget it. Fifteenth place was the last pay spot
in any tournament, and of the thirty to forty regulars
who were out there trying to beat you Ben Hogan was
the least known. "We used to figure $160 a week was
the break-even figure," Byron Nelson remembers. So if
you shot 74 you loaded it and yourself into somebody's Graham-Paige or Essex and drove until the
connecting rod made a double bogey. Air travel? That
was fantasy, something you saw in the movies for a
dime. Air travel was for Noah Beery, Jr., up there
flying the mail in the sleet without any de-icers, while
Jean Rogers wept softly in the control tower.

The tour began in Los Angeles, just as it does today,
but little else is similar. There was none of this three
hundred guys teeing off on both nines of a public
course, everybody trying to finish a nervy twenty-
ninth. The L.A. Open was held at the class clubs,
Riviera, L.A., Lakeside. Nor were the players
scattered everywhere from the Polo Lounge at the
Beverly Hills to the cheapest motel in Santa Monica.
Everyone piled into the Hollywood Plaza for a dollar
a day, single, or five dollars a day for a suite, the hotel
providing a whole private floor for the competitors.
And at night the established stars congregated at
Musso Franks, or the Brown Derby, or Clara Bow's It
Cafe, to drink with Richard Arlen, Clark Gable, Ran-
dolph Scott, the serious golfers of Hollywood who also

entered the tournament. There, they contemplated the happy fact that L.A. offered the biggest purse on the tour. First place was worth $3500, and that, for example, was five pay windows higher than the U.S. Open.

L.A. also lured the largest galleries of the year, crowds sparkling with movie celebrities and rising starlets. There were so many one year, in fact, that Dick Metz had to park two miles from the course before the second round and buy a ticket to get in. This would not have been so embarrassing for the sponsors if Metz hadn't been leading the tournament at the time.

"We knew everybody in Hollywood," says Jimmy Demaret. "It was pretty impressive to be hanging around Bing Crosby and folks like that all the time. And there were an awful lot of dandy little old gals around. We didn't know who they were. They had different names then. But we realized later that they were Susan Hayward and that kind of thing."

The tour might stay on the Coast for a month. It would go from L.A. to a Riverside Open, where the players would stuff their golf bags with fruit from the citrus trees in the rough, or it might go to a Pasadena Open, where they scooped niblicks around the Rose Bowl. It might go to an Agua Caliente Open. And one they certainly didn't miss was the Bing Crosby Pro-Am at Rancho Santa Fe, which was only thirty-six holes. It would also head north to a weird thing called the San Francisco Match Play championship. The pros would get into the Sir Francis Drake Hotel, dine at Vanessi's and Nujoe's with a wealthy host and work up the pairings in the locker room. "You figured out who you thought you could beat and challenged him," Demaret says. "And you hoped you didn't get Leonard Dodson because he'd pay a guy to follow you around with a camera and click it on your backswing."

After the flamboyant times on the Coast, fan belts permitting, the tour moved lazily through the Southwest, the South, the East and the Midwest, until, quite sensibly, it came to a dawdling end as football season began. It embraced a variety of tournaments, many of which sounded as if they ought to be on a billiard circuit, namely, the Miami-Biltmore Four-Ball, the Goodall Round Robin, the Westchester 108-Hole Open, the Dapper Dan and the Vancouver Jubilee.

It was not always easy getting from one place to another. Hogan and Nelson would be more intent on reaching a destination than some of the others because they wanted to practice. They would form a mini-motorcade, Byron and Louise following Ben and Valerie, and dart for shortcuts like Bonnie and Clyde. "Ben wanted to get there and start hittin' golf balls," Demaret says, with a slight trace of bewilderment. "Nobody ever practiced. First guy I ever saw do it was Bobby Cruickshank, about 1932. I didn't know what he was up to. But Ben *really* practiced. I'm sure he invented this business of spending two and three hours hitting balls."

Demaret, of course, would be late because he would

still be throwing a party from the previous week. And
Lloyd Mangrum, with Buck White or Leonard Dod-
son, would have found a card game — seven-card low,
pitch, auction bridge, casino — while Sam Snead
would have to sit around and wait for them in the car.
Johnny Bulla's car. "For a while, we traveled in Bulla's
Ford sedan. Can you imagine anyone loaning Lloyd
Mangrum, Sam Snead and Buck White his car?" Mangrum says. Some cars made the next stop easily, like
Walter Hagen's front-wheel drive Cord, or Denny
Shute's Graham-Paige. But others didn't. Johnny Revolta has vivid memories of a fan belt going out
somewhere in the infinity of a Texas horizon. His
companion at the time, Henry Picard, sat in the car
and held his head while Revolta hiked twelve miles,
got rescued by a Mexican family, finally found a belt
to fit and, six hours later, returned.

This would have been on the way to San Antonio
for the Texas Open, the oldest of the winter events
(1922). The tournament was distinctive for a number
of reasons, not the least of which was that it was usually played among the willows and pecans of Brackenridge Park, a short, tight little public course featuring
rubber mats for teeing areas. It was on this course that
the most headlined practice round of the era was
played one year. In a group with Hogan, Nelson and
Paul Runyan, the easy-going Jug McSpaden, wearing
sun goggles as always and putting with a mallethead,
shot a stunning 59. The round was accented by the
fact that Nelson had a 63, Hogan a 66 and Runyan a

71. And it was also at Brackenridge Park one year that Wild Bill Melhorn, who made most of his expenses at the bridge tables, finished with a seventy-two-hole score that looked as if it might win, provided Bobby Cruickshank didn't par the last hole. Melhorn climbed a live oak and tried to heckle Cruickshank into a three-putt on the 18th, but when Bobby survived, Melhorn toppled off the branch and into the crowd, without backspin.

From San Antonio, the tour normally frolicked onward to New Orleans, which was both a good and bad town for a riverboat gambler like Lloyd Mangrum. He once arrived on Mardi Gras Eve with the town so crowded — and himself so busted — that he joyfully bunked in the city jail for two days. "The only hard part was going without cigarettes," says Mangrum. "Try that course sometime."

Mangrum went on the tour with a $250 stake he got from John Boles, the singer. Cards kept him on it when his golf didn't. "I never won as much as everybody thought at the card tables," he says. "But the first time I ever got enough money to afford it, I bought me a big LaSalle with a couple of four-foot chrome horns on the front fenders, and folks thought I was rich." Stories would spread on him. And grow. When he won $4000 at gin rummy in Arizona it would be $25,000 by the time it reached Toots Shor's in New York. "The public thought you got thousands from the club companies," he says. "But all I know is I thought it was a big lick to get $300 and some clubs and balls out of MacGregor."

There was usually a way to get something out of somebody. If Mangrum couldn't do it with cards, Leonard Dodson would think of something else. "We're in Niagara Falls, I think it was," says Lloyd, "and I've got about $1.35 and Dodson's got $1.25. Together we can't buy enough gas to get half-way where we're going. So Dodson scares up this Canadian millionaire and bets him $500 he can outrun his automobile at 100 yards. Now we can't get $500 up if we rob everybody on the tour, and I don't think Dodson can outrun me if I got a heart attack. But Leonard takes the guy out in the country to an old dusty farm road where the tires can't get any traction in the deep, soft sand, and damned if Leonard doesn't win the race on his start."

The tour had its elegant stopovers where the foolishness gave way to a more formal atmosphere. Pinehurst was one, where the North and South Open was held. You had to have a tux and your wife needed a gown for dinner or it was off to a roadhouse for pork and beans. The same was true at the Masters when everyone stayed at the old Bon Air Hotel and went to millionaire Bill Wallace's ante-bellum mansion for ham cooked in wine, biscuits, barbecue and corn whiskey in a pitcher. There was also the fanciness of Palm Beach — golf amid the lockjaw accents — a place where Paul Runyan had a fascinating partner in the Seminole Pro-Am one winter.

"He drove three hundred and ten yards off the first tee and hit his approach about eighteen inches of the flag," says Runyan. "Now, I'm thinking to myself, we've got this thing all wrapped up. Nobody told me this guy could play like that." But then Runyan's partner took out the putter and tapped his gimme roughly eighteen feet past the hole with all of the gifted feel of a coal miner. His name: Gene Tunney.

It was in Florida that the pros first began to suspicion that they might be semi-celebrities — and all because of the Miami-Biltmore Four-Ball. This was a partnership tournament sponsored by a hotel, which guessed correctly that a lot of sports-page stories with the word Biltmore in them could give ideas to tourists. The Four-Ball tournament also invented "appearance money," for it paid the current U.S. Open and National PGA champions $1000 each to show up, as if they had somewhere else to go. Promoters were everywhere. Each birdie scored won a bottle of White Horse Scotch for a player plus a tin of Lucky Strikes. Daily, for those willing, players and wives were hoisted by autogyros over to Miami Beach for a swim. Occasionally, when the sponsors grew lax at providing entertainment, some of the players would take over. Such as the evening that Walter Hagen and Joe Kirkwood came back from fishing in the Everglades and dumped their entire catch in the hotel lobby, including an alligator.

Early in the Thirties not much was made of the identity between a pro and the club where he spent at least part of his summer or winter teaching. Ben Hogan would later make this a profitable thing through his connection with the Hershey Country

Club in Pennsylvania. But before that only a few of the stars were closely associated with certain clubs — Vic Ghezzi with Deal, New Jersey, Craig Wood at Winged Foot, Tommy Armour at Medinah and Sam Snead at Greenbrier, to list a few. Being dragged to his first promotional breakfast by the tour manager, Fred Corcoran, back in '37, Snead told Corcoran, who became Sam's manager as well, "Would you mention that I'm from Greenbrier? Those folks pay me a nice $45 a month to say so."

The Miami Four-Ball, being publicity-conscious, helped promote the clubs to which many of the pros were attached, and it also helped to convey the idea, through its partnership format, that there were certain cliques and friendships on the tour. Hogan and Demaret were nearly always partners, for instance, as were Nelson and McSpaden, Snead and Ralph Guldahl, Horton Smith and Paul Runyan, Johnny Revolta and Henry Picard. The teams, few realized at the time, were mostly formed by the club manufacturers.

As the tour moved through the South the players would note from time to time the emergence of a strange, squealing species that came to be known — Denny Shute is credited with the name — as "Sammy's Lambies." These were the crowds that traipsed after Snead, a pre-war Arnie's Army, so to speak. The South was quail and wild turkey country as well, and part of the fun of the Thomasville, Georgia, Open was being permitted to shoot as much game in the fields and thickets as you could between rounds, no limit.

Trying to cook quail and turkey gave the wives something to do besides compare verandas. Hettie and Denny Shute liked to think that the wives broke up into three categories, and they named them: ramblers, setters and shadows. The ramblers walked about the course, chose vantage points, and viewed the tournament distantly, sunning, gossiping and getting exercise. The setters were generally older and clung to the porches or lawns with their embroidery or played cards or pondered the possibility of getting a permanent wave like Carole Lombard's. The shadows never left their husbands. They tied bandannas on their heads and did the full eighteen holes, shot for shot.

Potential sponsors for all of these tournaments were mostly where Fred Corcoran could find them, and they came in all shapes and sizes and bankrolls. A sponsor was usually the first to leap in front of a camera, putting his arm around a Snead, a Hogan or a Nelson, buddy-buddy. But not all of them were like that in Corcoran's day. There was this one gentleman, quite amiable, who put up a good portion of cash for the 108-hole Westchester Classic in 1938. Except no photographs, please. Corcoran himself had to present Snead with the victory check so the sponsor could hide from the press. Four years later everyone discovered why. The gentleman was convicted of printing bogus whiskey labels. And no one has yet, to anyone's knowledge, tracked down one of the sponsors of the Indianapolis Open of 1935. It took Al Espinosa, the winner, three years to get his thousand dollars prize money from the PGA because the Indianapolis fellow skipped town with the purse.

In all there were no more than twenty-five tournaments a year, compared to forty-five today. If the total prize money added up to $150,000, that was sensational. It looked as good as the $5.5 million of 1968. And a player in the Thirties knew that if he could reach most of those tournaments, if he could attach the clubheads, which were made in Scotland, to the shafts, that were made in Tennessee, if he could assemble a set he liked, and if he could survive the card games and the parties and the fan belts, he could bank as much as $6000 for the year and rate as high as fifth on the money list.

Of course if he *practiced* — that odd ritual Ben Hogan originated — hitting old balls into a vacant lot for Stepin Fetchit to pick up, there was no saying how affluent he could become. It could lead to victories, which could lead to exhibitions, which could lead to club affiliations and on and on, conceivably into movie contracts. A man might become good enough to make some of those marvelously plotted instructional shorts, like Bobby Jones did with W. C. Fields or Buddy Rogers. ("Say, Bobby, since my car seems to have broken down right here by the golf course, how about a tip on playing the mashie-niblick?") It might even help a man get one of those incredible deals that Johnny Farrell had: smiling and holding a pack of cigarettes on the back cover of a magazine. Farrell got $1000 for that, somebody said.

Sam Snead saw the ad one day and took it to Fred Corcoran, his agent.

"What they call that there?" Sam asked.

"That's an endorsement," said Fred.

"How come you don't git me some of those?" Sam said.

"You don't smoke," Corcoran explained.

Snead thought for a moment and said, "Reckon them folks know that?"

Winning had been outrageously simple for Snead. His big, graceful, natural swing and his hillbilly personality made him an instant star, and Corcoran sold him well. Almost oversold him, in fact. Snead had no sooner begun to earn money on the tour when reporters were phoning Corcoran long distance to ask if this West Virginia guy was real. "He has the finest swing since Jones," Fred would reply. And a few days later Corcoran would see a headline proclaiming: SNEAD PICKED TO WIN US OPEN. That, of course, was something Snead never did, although he gained a negative fame for coming close.

While it was never a problem for Snead, winning that first pro tournament is still, even today, one of the most difficult things for a young player, regardless of how talented he may be. Byron Nelson's baptism in the hazards of near victory makes one of golf's better horror stories. Unknown and unsure, thin, young, broke, nervous, married, armed only with a good, quick, upright swing, Nelson learned the hard way. He was playing along in the General Brock Open at

Niagara Falls when, suddenly, at the end of the third round he was the leader.

On Sunday morning it took Nelson a while to adjust to the headlines in the papers. That was Byron Nelson they were talking about. Guy from Fort Worth. Then he looked closer at the stories, at the pairings for the last round. Good God. He was paired with Walter Hagen. He turned to his wife, Louise, and in something akin to a death rattle, he broke the news.

"I, uh, I have to play with, uh, Hagen today," he said, as if to apologize for the 88 he was bound to shoot and the no-money they would leave with.

Now in a situation like that a pro got to the course early, and Nelson did. He chipped awhile, putted awhile and worried awhile. He blushed a lot and hung his head and hid and kept checking to see if his trousers were buttoned. Finally it was time to tee off, but Walter Hagen, naturally, had not arrived yet. "Looks like Mr. Hagen is late again," sighed the starter, unconcerned.

"Late?" Nelson said. Of course. Late was part of it then, what a real pro did to a rookie without penalty or disqualification; in fact, what Hagen usually did to everybody. Didn't he once send to the clubhouse for a folding chair so that Gene Sarazen, the man who introduced the sand iron and steel shafts, could sit down and rest while he, that cunning Hagen, studied a simple chip shot? Wasn't it Hagen who liked to psych guys out by strolling over to their bags, peeking in at their clubs, shaking his head mournfully and walking away? Others, like Horton Smith, just squinted peculiarly at the rookies until the sad young men worked themselves into incurable hooks. And still others, like Dutch Harrison, would sweet-talk a rookie out of his game. "Man, can you massage that ball," Dutch would say. "I ain't seen a swing that good since Mac Smith." But prince of the Slow Plays, that was Hagen.

And so it went for Nelson, the starter telling him, "Go ahead and tee off with Willie Goggin, Byron, or with Ed Dudley. We'll pair Mr. Hagen with someone else when he arrives."

"But Walter Hagen's my idol. I've wanted to play golf with him all my life," Byron said, torn between high privilege and dire necessity.

"Well, we're very sorry."

"But I'm leading the tournament," Nelson said.

"Yes, we know."

Nelson practiced some more and paced and sat and paced and putted, his slacks ballooning in the Niagara breeze like the Graf Zeppelin, his wide-bottomed tie whipping past the curled-up collar tips of his dollar-nineteen shirt and on around his neck.

Fidget, pace, putt, stroll, throw up went Nelson until, thanks a million, two hours later along came Hagen in his white-on-white silk shirt, his gold cuff links and more oil on his hair than they were pumping out of the East Texas fields.

"Hi, boy," he said.

"It's — it's a real big honor," said Nelson in a trance,

a trance he did not recover from until forty-two strokes later on the front nine holes.

The disaster was not total. Nelson somehow rallied himself, shot a 35 on the back for a 77 and salvaged second place in the tournament. He won $600, which was almost as much money as Andrew Mellon had, he thought.

"Louise, we've got to hide this $600 before we hit the road. Since we're rich, we're bound to get robbed. And if we hide it, maybe they won't get it all," Byron told his wife. She agreed. So $50 went in the glove compartment, $100 in the suitcases, some more in the purse, some in the pockets, a little more under the seats, until it was neatly put away where the Dillinger mob would never find it. As a matter of fact, it took the Nelson mob a couple of hours to find it all when they reached a motel down the road.

If Jimmy Demaret had won the money he would have been 8 to 5 to leave it in a bar or blow it on a handmade pair of orange and purple saddle oxfords. The man who singlehandedly led golfers out of neckties and into knit shirts had little trouble getting rid of money. On the contrary, Demaret's problem was that he destroyed it with the same ease of the wealthy people he loafed with.

When Demaret left his native Houston to become a tour rookie in 1935 he had a set of clubs, a car and $600 loaned to him by Sam Maceo, a Galveston nightclub operator, D. B. McDaniel, an oilman, and Ben Bernie, the bandleader. He also had the fervent hope that he could drive through Juarez without stopping. But no such luck. All it took to nearly ruin him during what he hoped would be a brief stopover was for a man to ask him a question.

"Hey, señor, you want to shoot a leetle pool?" the man asked.

Demaret lost the car the first day, the clubs the second and the $600 the third. The only reason he didn't lose the River Oaks Country Club of Houston was because nobody in Juarez would take an IOU for it. The only thing he did right was save the pawn slip for the clubs so his brother, Milton, could retrieve them and ship them to the West Coast where Demaret hoped to wind up on the freight train he boarded.

Jimmy got there, and he did squirm through the first couple of weeks on a diet of sandwiches and muscatel. But as destiny often ordains for free spirits, especially if they can fade a high two-iron, he cashed in for a few hundred the third week, and Demaret has been throwing a party ever since.

From almost the instant he arrived Demaret's quipping nature, his friendliness and his passion for clothes that screamed made him golf's unofficial publicity agent. If the sports pages ever nurtured a grander cliché than "Navy won the toss and elected to receive," it was "colorful Jimmy Demaret, golf's goodwill ambassador."

Demaret wore lavender, gold, pink, orange, red and aqua slacks; yellow, emerald, maroon, plaid, checked, striped and polka-dot coats; and more than five hundred hats — berets, Tyroleans, straws — importing all of it from Europe. He paid $250 for the coats as soon as he could and $125 for the slacks in an era when that kind of money could avert a bonus march. He ordered ladies' pastel fabrics from abroad and had them tailored in the U.S. His idea about shoes was to give a factory swatches from his slacks and have matching saddle oxfords made.

Not only did Demaret have a color for every occasion, he also had a quip. Some of the more classic were these:

To an L.A. radio announcer who asked him which player on the tour had the most even disposition: "Clayton Heafner. He's mad *all* the time."

To a sportswriter who asked him if Ben Hogan had said much to him while they were winning the Inverness Four-Ball: "Once I think he said, 'You're away.'"

To Robert Trent Jones, the golf architect with a reputation for building monster courses: "Saw a course you'd really like, Trent. On the first tee you drop the ball over your left shoulder."

To Roberto De Vicenzo at the Masters: "Play good, Roberto. I'm betting on you to be low Mexican."

When the Thirties didn't have Demaret for comic relief, they had Ky Laffoon. He was a portly, balding part-Indian who got his start by caddying for Titanic Thompson, the famed hustler who liked to bet on this and that and usually won. Titanic liked to say to an opponent, "Hell, my caddy could beat you," and Ky Laffoon could.

Except on the tour. Laffoon never won as much as he probably should have, and his temper was largely responsible. It wasn't a legendary temper, the kind which caused earth tremors or broke up a party. It was more of a lovable temper, they say. Almost. Kind of.

Laffoon would wander off into the rough and discreetly, or not so discreetly, flog all of the leaves off of a small tree. He would miss a short putt and spurt tobacco juice into the cup, enough so that a man putting next would reach for his ball rather gingerly. And he would sometimes curse so audibly around a gallery that his wife, embarrassed, would stalk to the clubhouse and call a lawyer.

Once Laffoon had three putts from five feet to win the Cleveland Open. He missed the first, missed the second and thereupon became so violent that he slammed the putter down on top of the ball, not caring whether he finished first or eighth. But the ball ricocheted up in the air and — truly, truly — plopped right into the cup. Seeing it in the newsreel later, Laffoon is said to have let out a screech that cleared three rows.

Lloyd Mangrum remembers being paired with Ky when the Indian threw away one club per hole, finishing with Mangrum's clubs from the 15th in. Paul Runyan was with him one day when he broke the head off of his putter out of anger, but stepped up to putt again with the jagged shaft. When he realized what he was doing Laffoon, who had a tendency to stutter when he grew mad, said, "W-what the h-hell h-happened here?"

To appease his wife during a rare period of resolution, Laffoon decided he would play through a whole tournament without cursing. Surprisingly enough he scored fairly well in the first round and succeeded in doing it. He then started decently the second day, but he soon played himself into the lead and things got touchy. He held back for a while. But when an approach shot soared over a green on the back nine and landed in a bed of honeysuckle, that did it.

A jungle guerrilla with a machete could not have attacked the ball more furiously. One swing. Two. Three. And out came a torrent of get-even words that had spectators blushing as far away as the parking lot, which was precisely where his wife headed. Ky chased after her, caught up and began a panting, futile plea.

"I-I w-wasn't cussing," he said. "N-no k-kidding, d-darlin'. It w-wasn't a-anything to d-do w-with the g-golf. I just don't like honeysuckle."

The group to which Ky Laffoon felt the most philosophical kinship was a self-confessed pack of wolves acutely aware that prize money was not the only means of supporting oneself on the golf course.

Dutch Harrison, the Arkansas Traveler, eventually became a consistent money-winner, but he spent his first six years without earning a single penny of official cash. He lived off the fat of other men's golfing egos. In this respect he was much like Leonard Dodson, or better still, the brilliant trickshot artist, Joe Ezar, from Waco, Texas, who could make a golf ball sit up and speak. Ezar would stow away on freighters to Europe and hustle his way back on the *Queen Mary* balancing golf balls on top of each other on a bet. He could balance one ball on top of another — Lord knows how — hit the bottom ball onto a green and catch the other in his hand before it reached the ground. For money. Ezar would turn up at a tournament armed only with a derby hat, an overcoat and a pair of street shoes. "Loan me the equipment, and I'll pay you back double," he would say, and do it.

Dutch was never greedy. All he and his pal, Bob Hamilton, wanted was a couple of "nine-dollar pigeons" a day, enough to make expenses. Harrison had that splendid talent of being able to name his score. If his opponent shot 71, Dutch shot 70. If his opponent shot 80, Dutch squeezed out a 79 and convinced the guy how unlucky he was.

One afternoon on the Coast in 1937, as Dutch and Hamilton negotiated on the first tee for a game, a stranger asked if he could play along. He had a raw swing and a country voice, like Dutch, which meant he couldn't be all bad.

Hamilton, ever eager with loot in sight, said something subtle like, "How much you want to play for?"

"Well, I don't know much about betting," the man said.

"You come along with us," said Hamilton.

No more than a few holes had been played before

Dutch and Hamilton were distracted from their game with the nine-dollar pigeons. For every good shot they hit, the stranger hit one better.

"My, my, son, you sure got yourself a pretty swing there," Dutch said. "That old hook grip don't bother you none at all, does it?"

Birdie, birdie went the innocent fellow.

Presently, Harrison lashed a spoon shot into a green — a career shot — and he thought to himself, "Now we see who the men are."

To which the stranger put a two-iron inside of him.

"Bob," Harrison said to Hamilton. "We done got ourselves a-hold of something here."

Later on, after Dutch and Hamilton had paid off, the young stranger said, "Sure do thank you fellers. Say, what time you gonna be here tomorrow?"

"Son," Harrison said, "you work your side of the road, and we'll work ours."

"That," Dutch says today, "is how I met Sam Snead."

The tour had no sooner become acquainted with Sam than along came another newcomer who would help fill the glamorous void that had been created by Bobby Jones's retirement. Fellow named Hogan. He was a loner and a brooder, weighing in at one hundred thirty pounds with an uncontrollable hook off the tees. No one thought he would ever make it. And he warmed up to only a few of his contemporaries — Demaret, whose humor he admired, and Henry Picard, a gracious and helpful veteran who loaned money and advice, and Harrison, whose ability to survive he found intriguing.

Harrison discovered one evening when he was rooming with Hogan just how determined the Texan was. As Dutch tried to sleep, Ben gently beat his fists against the bedposts in their hotel quarters.

"You done gone crazy?" Dutch said.

"I'm strengthening my wrists," said Hogan.

The thumping continued until the manager arrived, having been summoned by an annoyed guest next door.

"I'm through," Hogan explained, contentedly. "I just figured out what's wrong with my grip."

He almost had. Hogan struggled through the Thirties by settling for such stunning successes as third place in the North American Long Driving Contest behind Jimmy Thomson and Porky Oliver at Niagara Falls. He would get a check here and a check there. It wasn't until 1940 at Pinehurst that he finally won a tournament, the North and South. He found it so much to his liking that he quickly won two more, at Greensboro and Asheville — three in a row. And for the next twenty years there never lived a better golfer.

Throughout the Thirties only one player came on the tour in absolute comfort, unfettered by financial worries. That was Lawson Little, golf's first bonus baby. He was a handsome, husky, carefree Californian with a square face, curly hair and white duck trousers. He had been the greatest amateur since Jones, winning both the U.S. and British Amateur championships in 1934 and again in 1935 — a feat that sports-writers called, rather clumsily, the Double Little Slam.

Little's decision to become a touring pro was final proof that amateur golf was minor league. And when he signed up with Spalding for $10,000 and all expenses to play golf and be a public relations man, it was the most amazing thing the pros had heard of since beltless slacks. Not until twenty-five years later, when Jack Nicklaus made a deal twenty times as big, did amateur golf produce so dazzling a celebrity.

Once Little was in the Spalding stable a group was formed that became known as the "trained seals." They were Little, Horton Smith, Thomson and Harry Cooper, and they were a popular exhibition team. They traveled together, mostly by luxurious train, and staged their own pre-tournament matches and clinics. "Can you fellows really balance golf balls on your nose?" Demaret would ask them.

Horton Smith was the boss and the bookkeeper. At the clinics he demonstrated the short game, Thomson hit the woods, Cooper, a nervous man who had a habit of jingling coins in his pocket, especially when someone stood over a putt, displayed the mid-irons and Lawson Little hit the long irons, the strength of his game.

Gallery ropes were nonexistent in the Thirties. Spectators literally formed a barricade around their favorite players; a golfer hardly had room to take a backswing. Self-appointed officials would stand in the middle of the fairways, puff on their pipes and say, "You're away, Byron." During one match Harry Cooper, who carried up to twenty-six clubs in his bag before the fourteen-club limit was set in 1936, kept finding a spectator's shadow over his ball when he addressed it. "Very unethical," Cooper would mumble and hit a fine shot. It happened all the way around the course until about the 16th hole when the shadow disappeared. Cooper then hit a ball roughly ten feet. "You bum," he called out. "Why'd you step on those leaves just as I was swinging?"

There were occasions when the fans were permitted to be so indelicately close to the players that a championship could be settled by them. Very nearly. A spectator almost cost Little the U.S. Open. The Californian never became the big winner that everyone expected, possibly because he was so well-fixed, but he did achieve a week of glory at Canterbury during the Open of 1940. He tied with Gene Sarazen for the championship, and they played off over eighteen holes the next day. It was a duel of different personalities. Little was friendly, outgoing, a fine socializer, particularly when he had Jimmy Thomson to drink with. Sarazen was grim, independent. When the pros switched to knickers, Gene introduced slacks. When they switched to slacks, he went back to knickers.

Little took an early lead in the play-off, but even as he led Sarazen he public-related. At the 5th hole a fan came up to him and wanted to ask a question. Sure, said Little.

"What I want to know is whether you inhale or exhale on your backswing?"

"Are you serious?" Little said.

"Quite," said the fan. "As for myself, I think I inhale, but I'm not sure."

Little duck-hooked his next series of shots, trying to figure out if he inhaled or exhaled. He managed to recover, however, and shoot a 70 to defeat Sarazen by three strokes. He was the U.S. Open champion, regardless of how he breathed, and the Spalding Dot was once again guaranteed to give you extra distance.

But that was 1940. The Thirties were gone — sunk slowly in the background like the wooden shaft. A wonderfully unpredictable and rather remarkable era of golf had passed, but the legacies it left were many. Among others it left us the fond memory that somewhere around every dogleg there lurked an individual — a Snead, a Hogan, a Nelson, a Demaret. A Laffoon, a Harrison, a Little, a Mangrum. And all of the others. Individuals is what they had to be, really, to last it out.

And what none of them would ever have guessed at the time is that out there on the tour in the Sixties a pro could hardly scrape by at all without an agent, a manager, a copilot, a secretary, a valet, a tax consultant and a corporate jet.

Lights...Camera... Double Bogey

The thing I've noticed most is that celebrities aren't celebrities on the golf course. They're more relaxed. They don't have to play a role.

— MAC HUNTER,
*head professional at
Riviera Country Club*

I GUESS you missed the item, although it was in all of the trades — right there with the news about George Plimpton's scheme to impersonate an airline captain for his next book, *Paper Mountain*, which has been pre-sold to Epic Pictures. The item explained how I decided to take a plunge into self-involvement journalism myself by challenging some show business personalities like James Garner and Glen Campbell and Vic Damone to a game of golf, a sport to which Hollywood has always been devoted. The item further told how I brought them to their knees one day at Riviera — or rather how my bronchial asthma did — and how Epic is interested in making an epic out of the experience. The tentative title is *The Ugly, the Bad and the Unplayable*, but I think it will be changed to something a bit more commercial, like, for instance, *Midnight Caddy*. At any rate, the studio hopes to get Raquel Welch to star as two hills above Mandeville Canyon and four bearded dropouts from a Berkeley die-in to portray my wood covers. The item told how Epic is eager to begin production as soon as it finishes shooting *Paper Russia*, a film based on the week George Plimpton spent as President of the United States.

The story went on to say that the studio is still considering the possibility of turning the film into a big musical if it can decide that enough spunky tunes could be written about standardizing handicaps, the care and management of hybrid Bermuda and post-flood silt removal. Personally, I am not all that ecstatic about this idea, knowing Hollywood's track record on musicals. I can envision Joe Dey having to learn the banjo just to portray himself, Arnold Palmer in the role of Charlie Coody, Charlie Coody in the role of Orville Moody, and Tom and Jeanne Weiskopf tap-dancing down a globe-lighted stairwell of broken putters in the big production number while the blue-and-white-clad ladies of the Colonial National Invitation motor pool sing a chorus of "My kind of town, Fort Worth is." In any case, Epic Studio, I understand, is going to conduct a nationwide search of municipal courses to find an unknown to play me; someone, the story went on to say, who coughed incessantly from smoking and possessed the wraithlike ability to shank a two-inch putt.

I suppose that, like me, you are a little distrustful of what you read in the trades. I know I didn't for a second buy the rumor that Jim Murray, the columnist, had the title role in the remake of *Arthur Daley Discovers Horton Smith*. And I don't believe the gossip that Billy Casper has the lead in *Jesus Played a Onesome*, which they say will be filmed on actual location at La Scala. I do, however, think you can trust the item about me. Epic is very excited. Only a moment or so ago the head of the studio, Zeth Dorian-

Baker, phoned from the Daisy during a see-through contest to say that everything looked plenty all right from where he sat.

By now, I expect, you are anxious to hear the full story behind the film and something about a lot of the Hollywood celebrities who play golf these days when they aren't digging their homes out of mud slides. Why else would your Guccis be tapping so restlessly on the pegged floor of our Mixed Foursome Room? Well, I will tell you. But first, I think you ought to know something about the history of golf in Hollywood as it has been recorded on napkins at the Polo Lounge.

This background is vitally important, not just because it will give you a deeper insight into my film, but because it relates to something bigger than all of us — the pro golf tour. Surely you realize that the PGA tour, Arnold Palmer and all that, might never have become what it is today without Hollywood's support or perhaps even its consent. The fact is, pro golf sort of grew up with Hollywood the way the bosom grew up with acting. "To know more about Hollywood is to know more about the backswing," said an old philosopher. Forget the name. Bruce Cabot, maybe.

At any rate, it could be argued that the tour might have staggered through its early days of the 1930's on its own. I mean, Jimmy Demaret might have pulled it through by the laces of his pink-and-gold saddle oxfords. But I can look back and see that it certainly did not hurt anything that the tour chose to begin each new season (and still does) out in that strange, almost mystical boomland of southern California. It did not hurt anything in the beginning for the pros to be able to socialize with the Clark Gables, Richard Arlens and Randolph Scotts. It did not hurt anything that the Los Angeles Open often had such stalwarts as those playing in it, with swarms of other celebrities in the galleries. And what a glorious thing, the world took note. Going to a golf tournament on the Coast could be a giddier thrill than attending some world premiere and seeing a million dollars worth of feet, hands, legs and noses being pressed gently into Chinese cement.

What has since made Hollywood's role in professional golf even more meaningful, of course, is the fact that many of these old friendships have endured, and just as many fresh ones have blossomed. I have learned that a celebrity today who is not chummy with at least one touring pro is either a lousy softball player on Sundays or a motorcycle freak who drops acid. After all, the giants of the industry have lent their names to tournaments. Bing Crosby. Bob Hope. Andy Williams. Frank Sinatra for a while. And as one looked at the tour in the year 1969 it was noticeable that no fewer than seven championships were played up and down the coast, from L.A. to Carmel, from San Francisco to La Costa, with more Clint Eastwoods around than you could shake a Raymond Floyd at.

What it has all come down to, I decided, is a happier, gaudier, more glamorous scene than any pro or entertainer could ever have guessed at long ago. There they all are in their insular bedazzlement, speedy swings matched against speedier quips, a snappy time for the sport. Bronzed pros in violet knit and hair-sprayed stars in tight little trousers, all thrust against the glittering backdrop of palms and mountains and sea, not to forget the arrangements of raven-haired, orange-haired, golden-haired, moon-haired starlets in their sideless, backless, frontless fashions.

For a few weeks out of every year, at least, pro golf was a happening. And who among us was strong enough that he could resist being near it, or a part of it, if the opportunity presented itself. Not me, boy.

But first I had to learn more about the fascinating history of golf in Hollywood, which I shall finally unveil. It all begins with a popular misconception: that the game was actually invented by Bing Crosby and Bob Hope. That, of course, is wrong. Golf, as a matter of fact, was invented by Maurie Luxford, a friend of theirs, about 1925 at the Lakeside Country Club. Lakeside is located in the valley area near Warner Brothers, roughly two or three wife-swapping bars from Beverly Hills. Luxford dreamed up the game at Lakeside to provide a healthy, recreational activity for men like Howard Hughes, Guy Kibbee, Adolph Menjou, Richard Arlen and Oliver Hardy. Some people have argued that over in Palm Beach about the same time Chris Dunphy invented golf for Wall Street vacationers and cosmetic executives. Chances are they both invented the game; Maurie Luxford simply got more publicity, Hollywood being second only to Washington, D.C., in the number of press releases that are mimeographed daily.

Recently I asked Maurie Luxford if it were true that he invented golf.

"No two people have done more for the game than Bing and Bob," he said.

Luxford, a pleasant, friendly, gray-thatched gentleman about sixty years out of his teens, has remained very much involved in golf through the years. He has organized and officiated at hundreds of pro-celebrity tournaments up and down the West Coast, and he has held up well under the immense pressure of having to turn down requests of heavy industry presidents to play in the Bing Crosby National Pro-Am.

Now, then, shortly after Maurie Luxford originated golf the sport became very popular with scads of Hollywood celebrities. Among other things it gave them something to devote themselves to other than swinging from balcony to balcony rescuing Myrna Loy, and Lakeside gave them a place to hide from the public. All the public ever saw, the public being mainly back in Des Moines then, were photos in movie magazines of these tanned handsome figures in white shirts and slacks with polka-dot scarves addressing two-foot putts, sometimes a bit too awkwardly to convince anyone they played to a strong six.

There were some good players and, according to Maurie Luxford, fascinating characters during the early days, however. Well, heck, there was George Von Elm, who won the 1926 U.S. Amateur and lost a play-off (over seventy-two holes, the longest on record) to Billie Burke for the 1931 U.S. Open. There were a couple of other strong amateurs, Johnny Dawson and Bruce McCormick, who made the Walker Cup team. And there was the mysterious John Montague, the trick-shot king, who beat Oliver Hardy one day using only a baseball bat, a shovel and a rake. All of these, together with low-handicap celebrities like Bing Crosby, Randolph Scott, Richard Arlen, Buddy Rogers, Douglas Fairbanks and Howard Hughes, inspired Grantland Rice once to write that no golf club in the country could defeat a team from Lakeside.

Gossip columnists of the era also wrote about the huge gambling games at Lakeside, but Maurie Luxford rarely saw more than $5000 lost in a foursome, that foursome usually consisting of Howard Hughes, George Von Elm, Scotty Armstrong and Duke Hinnau. Another group that would bet it up, Luxford remembers, was comprised of Adolph Menjou, Guy Kibbee, Frank Craven and Oliver Hardy. And still another, in later years, was Bing Crosby, using shafts three inches longer than normal and addressing the ball two inches below the spot where it was teed, and Randolph Scott, Dennis O'Keefe and a newcomer, Dean Martin.

"The world knew that Bing liked golf," said Maurie Luxford. "But only the members around Lakeside knew how well he could play in his younger days. He was very accurate and a fierce competitor. After all, he won the club championship five times against some pretty fine golfers."

For a time Howard Hughes, an impoverished lad from Texas who played golf in sneakers because he couldn't afford saddle oxfords, was a 1-handicapper at Lakeside, as strong a player as any in the film colony. But Hughes wanted to be better than that. And one day he asked his close friend, George Von Elm, what would happen if he really worked at golf. Could he, Hughes, get to be good enough to capture, say, the National Amateur? Von Elm said probably not. So Hughes quit the game altogether. He did return on a later occasion, it should be noted, to crash-land a private plane on the course at Bel-Air one day, and the legend is that Howard Hughes, having given up the game, refused to replace his divot.

This about covers the early history of golf in Hollywood, at Lakeside, the "home of the stars." If anything other than the intriguing gossip filtering out of Lakeside served to focus more attention on the fact that the celluloid heroes had adopted golf as their very own game, it was the tournament Bing Crosby started with his brother Larry in 1937 — the now famous Pro-Am. It was first staged in Rancho Santa Fe, where it rained, and subsequently was moved to the Monterey Peninsula, where it snowed. It was first played over thirty-six holes, then was stretched to fifty-four and finally to seventy-two, and Bing's tournament has ultimately become a total must for corporation executives around the land as well as for celebrities and touring professionals.

For a week in February every winter, the only place

for a self-respecting golfer to be is either in the Del Monte Lodge or the Pine Inn of Carmel or in a palatial rented home along the 17-Mile Drive. There one should be having cocktails with Bing or Arnie or Jack or perhaps Clint Eastwood, Jack Lemmon or Jim Garner or the board chairman of Pacific Mobile Homes or Eastern Chemical or some such thing. It has become so much of a status symbol to be invited to the Crosby — only three hundred or so amateurs out of nine thousand applicants are admitted, after all — that businessmen who do *not* make it suddenly find their lives growing dreary if not desperate. They may arrive at their offices to discover their doors locked and their secretaries thumbing through the classifieds. Or they may go to their country clubs and find the locker attendants sullen and unfriendly. Until he has played in the Crosby a business tycoon simply cannot say that he knows anything about life, love, Palmer's hip trouble, Doug Sanders's clothes or whatever happened to Rhonda Fleming.

Conversations between certain happy Crosby invitees often tell you more about the tournament — indeed more about Hollywood golf — than anything else. I happened to have overheard one a winter or so ago in the Del Monte Lodge between two gentlemen I shall call Sims of Nuclear Plumbing and Thurman of Southern Mail Fraud. It went like this:

SIMS: Hi, Thurmo. How'd you play?

THURMAN: We were paired with Jack Lemmon. How about you?

SIMS: We had Phil Harris.

THURMAN: How'd you do Thursday?

SIMS: Jim Garner. Yourself?

THURMAN: Not bad. Dick Shawn.

SIMS: Last year I got Dean Martin.

THURMAN: I've had Bob Hope.

SIMS: I've had Andy Williams.

THURMAN: So have I.

SIMS: How'd it go Friday?

THURMAN: Terrific. Danny Thomas.

SIMS: Yes, I've had Danny at the Springs. Ever been around Indian Wells with Desi?

THURMAN: Well, no. Down there I usually play Eldorado.

SIMS: Not a bad layout, but Frank talked me into joining Tamarisk.

THURMAN: Frank Buck?

SIMS: Sinatra.

THURMAN: Oh, sure. Say, next time you see Frank, ask him about the time I took him to Merion.

SIMS: Fine course, Merion. Gave up the membership though when I joined Pine Valley. Say, ask old Garner about the day I took him to Pine Valley.

THURMAN: I will. Ask Hope about the day I took him to the Augusta National.

SIMS: Was that before or after we built the cottage for Ike?

THURMAN: Well, I'm certain it was before because I remember telling Bobby and Cliff where they ought to put it.

SIMS: Get back there much?

THURMAN: Not really. Somehow I can't get away from Seminole when I go South.

SIMS: Know what you mean. Ever since Joe got me in the R&A I've found it difficult even to play in this country.

THURMAN: Joe *Day*, you mean.

SIMS: Yes.

THURMAN: Quite a fellow. He offered to do the same for me one day at Locust Valley, but I had to tell him that the Brigadier had already handled my case.

SIMS: Nothing like St. Andrews, of course. Ask Dino about the time we ripped up The Old Course.

THURMAN: Sure will. Ask Andy about the day we tore up Muirfield.

SIMS: Glad to. Well, gotta run. Coming over to Bing's for a drink after a while?

THURMAN: I suppose so — if Arnie wants to.

SIMS: Good. The Duke and I will see you there.

THURMAN: Duke Wayne? Is Duke here?

SIMS: Of Windsor.

THURMAN: Oh, naturally. Say, ask him about the day I talked him into abdicating so we could take a pop at Sunningdale.

It would be impossible to assess the impact that Bing Crosby and his friend Bob Hope have had on golf. Hope, of course, also sponsors a tournament for corporate executives, celebrities and pros — the Bob Hope Desert Classic in Palm Springs, or rather near Palm Springs, most of the five courses that are used being located in towns like Indio and Cathedral City and Palm Desert. The sun beams down on Hope's tournament — whereas Bing's has been called The Four Seasons; the players crawl along on electric carts and a lot of orange-haired ladies loiter in the galleries. At night everyone goes to Ruby's Dunes for dinner in the hope that Frank Sinatra will come in. The food is good if, as somebody once said, you like steak and Jade East.

For all of this, however, it may be established one day that the greatest contribution Hope and Crosby made to the game was the creation of the Golf Joke. They have been telling them since they used to take putters along to their radio broadcasts. Crosby would talk about Hope's game for Kraft Foods, and Hope would talk about Crosby's game for Pepsodent. And the world would laugh whether it played golf or not.

"Bob Hope's swing?" Crosby would say. "I've seen better swings on a condemned playground."

"They're making a movie of Crosby's round yesterday," Hope would say. "It stars Bela Lugosi."

According to Crosby, Hope invented the nonbody turn, the interlocking grip on a money clip, the fast backswing and a good short game — off the tee. According to Hope, Crosby invented the pipe, the shirt worn outside the pants, the cocked hat, the impression he was so rich even his caddies subscribed to *Fortune*.

And all of those lines.

But so much for the background of golf in Hollywood. So much for what history there is. So much for all of the noble pioneers. What of today? Where must an autograph seeker go now that no one is left at

Lakeside except an occasional Frankie Avalon, a Gordon MacRae, a Guy Madison and a Don Knotts? I put the question to my main contact man with the stars, a public relations consultant from Chicago named Bill Martin. As far as I could tell, Bill Martin, over the years, had been in Las Vegas, Palm Springs, the Polo Lounge and the men's grill at Bel-Air a lot more than he had ever been in Chicago, although I had never been at Binyon's without running into him.

This time, I had found him at Binyon's with Vic Damone discussing a way for Vic to sing through cigarette machines and entice the buyer into a certain brand.

"You know I've always had the big lights — the baby juniors — in my eyes," I said. "I want to play golf with the stars."

"That's a good story," said Vic. "I'd rather have someone write about my golf game than my voice any day."

"Who you want?" asked Martin. "You want Vic? You got him. You want Crosby . . . Hope . . . Dean? What do you have in mind?"

"I want the really serious players today, like Jack Ging, whom I know. Pretty good athletes. I don't want to listen to a pile of Buddy Hackett jokes," I said. "Where does anybody play?"

Bill Martin explained how it was. There was the Bel-Air crowd: Dean Martin with his group of toy manufacturers and auto dealers, and Dick Martin, Bob Sterling, Richard Crenna, Howard Keel, Bob Wagner and loads of others. There was the Hillcrest crowd:

Jack Benny, Danny Kaye, Milton Berle, Danny Thomas, a gaggle of top bananas throughout the dining room. There was the Brentwood crowd: Jack Lemmon, Gary Morton, Buddy Hackett, Joey Bishop, Jerry Lewis, Jan Murray — a panel show. There was the Los Angeles Country Club: nobody. Nobody? Yep. Bing Crosby lived near the 14th green of the great North Course for years but could only play at L.A. as a guest. No show biz types allowed. Sooner the Viet Cong should be members. Somebody said Randolph Scott finally got in after he swore that he would never have anything to do with Hollywood again, or maybe it was because the membership decided that, after all, he was never an actor. Anyhow, finally, there was the Riviera crowd: Jim Garner, Jack Ging, Vic Damone, Donald O'Connor, Lindsay Crosby, Bob Wilke, the badman, Jim Backus — the good, serious golfers with a few Robert Stacks and Gregory Pecks thrown in.

"Riviera's quite a course," I said.

"And they go to the back tees there, my man," said Bill Martin.

"A team of show business personalities from Riviera could beat a team from any other club in the area," Damone said. "Call when you're on the Coast and I'll arrange a game."

"Just tell me who you want," said Martin. "Andy? Frank? Duke?"

I told Martin I wanted Jill St. John, Jacqueline Bisset and Raquel Welch and thought no more about it.

A short time later I happened to be at the Crosby

tournament listening to my good friends Sims and Thurman in the Del Monte Lodge when I ran into Jack Ging, who had come to win the Pro-Am with Pro Bob Dickson. And did.

"Come on over to Clint's and we'll talk about a game at Riviera," he said.

"Has Murchison got a house here?" I said.

"Eastwood," he said.

"Oh," I said.

Ging is a curly-haired, enthusiastic, grinning, in-gratiating little man whom I had known better as a halfback for the University of Oklahoma than as the quiet psychiatrist, Dr. Phillip Graham, of the TV series *The Eleventh Hour.*

Jack Ging had apparently become the best golfer in the Hollywood community since his days at Norman. One heard he was a strong 3-handicapper from the back tees at Riviera, which is a mere 7022 yards of bunkers and eucalyptus trees, the course where Ben Hogan won the 1948 U.S. Open. He had been winning a number of member–guest and pro–celebrity tourna-ments regularly, the kind that Bob Sterling and Bob Wilke used to win. And if there had been any question about Ging's claim to being Hollywood's best in 1969, it was surely erased after the Crosby. He not only played extremely well as Dickson's partner through rain and mud, he actually hit the stroke that won the Pro-Am for them — an eight-foot birdie on the final green at Pebble Beach — before a big gallery and a national TV audience.

"Isn't this great," said Ging then. "This is greater than winning an Academy Award."

A little later on he said, "You know how I made that putt? Bob Goalby made it. He walked over to me on the green and said, 'I know you're nervous. We all get nervous. But you deserve to win this, and you're a good putter. It breaks a little left. Just give it a smooth stroke and it'll drop.' Boy, Bob Goalby's great. Isn't he a great guy?"

Ging said he would get with Vic Damone the following week and they would round up a lot of great guys and we would have a Sports Illustrated Open Invitation for celebrities at Riviera so I could see how the stars play golf. He said he would get Jim and Glen and Don and Lindsay and Bob and maybe his Malibu neighbor Jack Warden from *Twelve Angry Men* and *The Bachelor Party* and all my favorite movies for a forecaddy, and I said I would get a photographer, Marty Mills, who was married to Edye Adams, and he said Marty was really a great guy and we would have a great time.

I barely managed to get out of the Daisy, The Factory, The Candy Store and Ging's own night spot, Cisco's, in Manhattan Beach in time to transport my headache to Riviera when the day came. The clubhouse at Riviera, which is in Pacific Palisades, can best be described as early Morro Castle, and I rattled around in it for a while before I found anyone. Mac Hunter, the pro, came along and said I had better warm up my three-wood for the back tees, and he asked what was first prize worth in this tournament Ging and Damone were having.

"The winner gets a tour of the sumptuous Hollywood homes," I said.

Mac and I had a cup of coffee, and the pro talked about some of the stars and their golf games.

"Ging's a hell of a competitor," he said. "It stems from his football days. He has a real winning attitude that I suppose Bud Wilkinson instilled in him. His swing is a neat package — short and compact. He's very consistent and straight."

Mac said, "Bob Wilke used to be head and shoulders better than any of the actors and personalities. And he's still very good. A solid four-handicap, but his putting is deteriorating. Wilke must have won more celebrity tournaments than you can count.

"Bob Sterling is a fine player, of course, a graceful swinger. And Randolph Scott they tell me was terrific several years ago. But I think Wilke must have been better, day in, day out, and now I think Ging is better than Wilke."

I asked, "What about Garner and Damone and some others?"

"Well, nobody loves golf more than Vic. He'll play from dawn till dark," said Mac. "Garner could be one of the best but he doesn't work at it. He's got his racing cars, and of course he's frequently working on a movie."

Mac said, "The thing I've noticed most is that celebrities aren't celebrities on the golf course.

They're more relaxed. They don't have to play a role. Around here they're cheerful, easy-going. They'll play golf with anyone at all who enjoys the game as much as they do. I think this is truer at Riviera than at the other clubs. You've got to like golf a lot to get on this monster. So this is another reason why you'll see the Bob Stacks and the Robert Mitchums out there with just plain folks, playing golf. They don't have to *be* anybody around here."

Until he walked in I wasn't sure I would know Bob Wilke, one of the durable Western villains, a man who had been gunned down by everyone from Wild Bill Elliott to Grace Kelly. But I remembered. Cold, steely eyes, drawling, solemn expression, a slow, cocky, gun-slinger's grin. Tall and evil.

"Didn't Grace Kelly get you in *High Noon?*" I asked.

"Right in the back," Wilke smiled.

"Who else?" I said. "I may want to refresh my readers who aren't that familiar with your name."

Well, said Wilke, Jimmy Stewart had shot him in the belly in *Night Passage,* and Gary Cooper had shot him in the chest in *Man of the West,* and Jim Coburn had stabbed him in *The Magnificent Seven,* and he'd been blown up in James Mason's submarine in *20,000 Leagues Under the Sea,* and he probably had died four hundred other times in films since the mid 1930's.

"Jack Ging killed me yesterday at Riviera," he said.

Presently all of the other players showed up, Glen Campbell, Damone, Ging, Donald O'Connor, Lindsay

Crosby and James Garner. So did Jack Warden, who said he had just come out to watch and see what Hollywood types were really like.

"This is all pretty dazzling for me," he said, looking around at the table of coffee drinkers.

Warden shook hands with Damone and squinted at him and pointed his finger at him and said, "Aren't you that, uh, that fellow that, uh, sings a lot — that, uh, Jack Jones?"

Everyone teased Glen Campbell about being the hottest thing in town and suddenly rich. And didn't it beat backing up Perry Como records on the guitar or playing one-night dates with the rhythm pickers at truck stops?

"You know what they say," said Campbell. "It takes about ten years to become an overnight success. I thought Johnny Hartford never *would* write 'Gentle On My Mind.' "

James Garner addressed me and said, "You're Time, Inc., right?"

"Sort of," I said.

"Did you *read* what they said about my car at Daytona? They referred to it as 'the *implausible* Lotus of Jim Garner.' I know what implausible means. I looked it up."

"Wait till you read what I say about your golf game," I said.

"Oh, wonderful," said Garner. "Ging. Hey, Ging. Where'd you get this one, Sweets?"

Garner had grown a black mass of a beard for a role he was about to play. There were a lot of cracks about it. Marty Mills, the photographer, asked him where he had left the two boards he was nailed to.

And Ging said: "Hey, did you hear what Dino said to Jim at the Crosby when he saw his beard? He said, 'Say, man, when you bite into one of those, you're supposed to turn loose.'"

Everyone traded Dean Martin stories for a while. Funny man, everyone said. Fun-nee. There was this time he was on the 1st tee at Bel-Air with two of his golfing pals, Fletcher Jones and Art Anderson or somebody, and Buddy Hackett came jogging up, hoping to join them. "Sorry, Buddy," said Dean. "We've already got three." And there was this time that Bob Newhart or somebody almost fell down hitting a shot and Dean said, "If you step on my suedes one more time I'll . . ." And there was this time Sinatra hired a guy to dress up in a grizzly bear costume and dash out of the woods to scare Dean, but when the man did he tripped and fell, and all Dean said was, "Look fellows, I think the poor thing's hurt."

After a while we were all out on the 1st tee at Riviera, taking warm-up swings, preparing for the first, only and last Sports Illustrated Open Invitation Hollywood Celebrity-Celebrity Minus One.

A couple of mildly curious members stood by. One of them wore a pair of red, white and blue golf shoes. I made some comment to Marty Mills about the shoes, quietly I thought. Something about how much Ronald Reagan would like them, but Vic Damone heard me.

"Don't joke," said Damone. "I've got a pair like that."

Marty Mills said, "I've got a flag like that."

A few bets were made. Ging announced that it was "Get Wilke Day," and Wilke announced that it was "Get Ging Day." Garner asked for a couple of ups, and Ging offered one or two.

"Oh, please button your shirt before your heart falls out," said Jim.

"Aren't we gonna play seriously?" Damone asked.

"You bet your sweet bippy," Garner said.

"How *is* your bippy?" said Vic.

"Him dust so thweet," Garner said, gripping the driver.

I guess I would put Garner up against most anybody at imitating, let us say, an interior decorator on a golf tee. He wiggled his hips, touched at his hair, as if it had just been rinsed and set, put a finger to his lips and glanced down at the ground.

"Let's thee," he said. "Thith is a club and thith is a ball and that muth be the green down there. Oooo, it's tho far."

Garner has the swing of a good, natural athlete, which he was when he was Jim Bumgardner back in Oklahoma, like Ging, a guy who had played football, been in the service and was laying carpet when somebody made him an actor by accident. And a good one.

Garner hit a fine drive off the 1st tee and swaggered over to the side with his left hand on his hip. With the right he took the driver by the clubhead and slid the shaft down through the left hand, like a cavalry officer placing his saber back in the casing on his leg.

Glen Campbell stepped up next in tight-fitting, stitched, tailored blue denims, pink shirt and a somewhat incongruous yellow hat with a brim, a reminder, it seemed to me, that he had come from Delight, Arkansas. He took a wide stance and I knew he would unleash a big, fast, powerful swing and that the shot would soar away for a mile in one direction or another.

Standing over the ball Campbell said, grinning, "Kill . . . destroy . . . ravage . . . plunder . . ."

Campbell's drive was a big one, and as he retrieved his tee he sang a note or two in his country-style voice.

"Oh, the lace time I seen Paris," he sang. Then he said, "Hear about the hippie who took LSD but didn't take a trip — he went home?"

Donald O'Connor and Lindsay Crosby teed off quietly and nicely. They were to remain quiet, pleasant and concentrating for most of the day. There would be no missing Lindsay for a Crosby either in looks or voice. Had he broken into a chorus of *The Old Ox Road*, ba-ba-ba-boo, it would not have astonished me.

Ging, Wilke and Damone got off the first tee very businesslike. They were intense, it seemed, eager to get at it, and I struck some sort of drive into the rough, and we were away, an eightsome, ten counting Jack Warden and Marty Mills. As we bounded down the hill of the 1st hole, a 508-yard par five, Warden came over to me and nodded toward all of the celebrities up ahead.

"I, uh, I just can't describe to you what a thrill this is for me," he said. "When I go home and tell my wife that I was with Jack Jones and Andy Griffith, well — "

It didn't take long for me to discover that Hollywood has some pretty good golfers. Ging and Campbell birdied the first hole, and Damone, Garner, O'Connor and Crosby parred it. Ging also birdied the 2nd hole, a 526-yard par five, and so did Damone and Crosby, while everyone else made par — except me. Granted, these are probably the two easiest holes at Riviera, but I skillfully managed to play them in 6–7.

By the time you reach the 5th hole at Riviera, the course has started, the real golf course, which is nothing but drives and spoons, particularly on a heavy day as this one was. But Jack Ging was still one under, and the others were only one or two over, and Jack Warden, my favorite actor, was still strolling along beside me, throwing out lines.

"This fellow with the beard," he said. "He looks familiar. Don't he work in the movin' pitchers?"

"Yes," I said. "That's Cary Grant."

Warden said, "That's it. I knew I had something in common with one of them stars."

"Oh?" I said.

"Yeah," he said. "That, uh, Cary Grant over there. The thing is, I used to ball his maid."

The 5th hole is one of the great holes at Riviera, a long par four with out of bounds on the right, a row of trees on the left and a slightly sunken green which hides to the left of a mound.

When Garner sliced his tee shot out of bounds he instantly blamed it on Marty Mills's camera. I remembered that I had heard Garner had a temper at times. I guess I expected him to explode, but he didn't. "Thank you, James Wong Howe," he said.

"Sorry," said Marty.

"Forget it," said Jim. "It's just a double bogey."

"I'm really sorry," Marty said.

"No problem," said Garner. "I'm not picky. I'll take a six, seven, anything. It doesn't matter."

Whereupon Garner walked over and beat his driver against a tee marker.

As the round progressed Ging, Campbell and Garner, all of them being native country boys, developed a rapport that seemed to amuse everyone. When Campbell hit a bad shot he would holler, "Glen Travis Campbell, you come in this house!"

When Ging had a shot go astray, he would shout, "Jackie Lee Ging, get down off that roof!"

And, in turn, Garner, roaming in the rough, would call out, "Jimmy Jack Garner, you're gonna get your ass wore out."

Glen Campbell, a very natural and likable sort, hardly the hairspray king of his television show, eventually fell into the throes of an incurable darting hook, but he kept singing and dropping gems of rural humor.

Once he said, "That sumbitch right there dropped like a bell from a tall cow's neck."

Hitting a good shot he would say, "Oh, Glen Travis, son, you daince so purty."

Before the day was over Riviera nearly wrecked everybody's game, of course. It was not a very clever or energetic eightsome that limped up the 18th, a 443-yard par four known as "cardiac hill." Donald O'Connor was headed for an atrocious 96, his worst score in years, and I was struggling in with 91, my worst since the day before. Vic Damone's loose swing and sort of pale fade had worked him around to 88, far from his best, and Jim Garner, his back aching, was gaining on an 85, hardly worthy of him. Lindsay Crosby was rounding out an 81, which surprised me, since I felt he stood up to the ball better than anyone except Bob Wilke. As for the villain, he'd played a 79 that looked lower and would have been had some putts curled in. Wilke and Ging had both gone out in 39, but Jack had nailed him on the back side with a dazzling even par 36 and a fine three-over 75. Jack Ging, thus, was our winner.

There had been one more intriguing moment on the last green. I stroked a fifty-footer that never came close to the cup, but along the way as the ball curved over two or three breaks it hit a tee that someone had used to mark his ball with and then it skipped again

over an unrepaired divot, and as it bounced and wiggled over its path Jim Garner started to laugh. Then
he said: "This putt will self-destruct within ten
seconds."

Later on we gathered around a huge table in the
bar to trade golf stories and show biz stories and
figure out that Ging had won about $150 and to try
and settle on where we'd go to dinner.

Everyone decided that he was a better golfer than
he had shown out on the course and that if you
eliminated a couple of triple and double bogeys his
score wasn't so bad. I quite agreed.

Donald O'Connor told a story about hitting a golf
ball into somebody's kitchen, I think, and settled back
for a long evening of storytelling with Wilke and
Lindsay Crosby. They weren't going anywhere, they
said. Vic Damone invited everyone up to his office on
top of the Playboy Building on The Strip. Plenty of
booze, he said, a great view and a sound system. Ging
wanted the group to drive out to his joint, Cisco's,
where he had a rock band and nine million stewardi.
"I need that like I need a hole in my git-ar," said
Campbell, adding that he was going home to watch
Wilke get killed on television. Garner also excused
himself, saying he was going home to put his feet up.
"Him tired?" asked Campbell. "Him's little bippy is
three down and two to go," said Garner.

All good guys, I thought. Really regular. Gee. And
what a movie it will make. No sham. No phony pre-
tentions. No tinsel. Who says this town has a popcorn

machine for a heart? Script by Neil Simon. Songs by Jimmy Webb. Direction by Mike Nichols. Realism. Integrity. Only one minor change, I shoot 74 and beat Ging. Jenke Birdie Flick Boffo.

My thoughts were interrupted by Jack Warden who put it all back in perspective. He stared across the table at Jack Ging, put down his drink, snapped his fingers and said:

"Excuse me, sir, but I've been looking at you all day. Aren't you that, uh, that funny guy I seen so much in the flicks . . . that, uh, yeah! Ain't you Peggy Ann Garner?"

Lockwrist and Cage Cases

Hitting a golf ball and putting have nothing in common. They're two different games. You work all your life to perfect a repeating swing that will get you to the greens, and then you have to try to do something that is totally unrelated. There shouldn't be any cups, just flag sticks. And then the man who hit the most fairways and greens and got closest to the pins would be the tournament winner.
— BEN HOGAN,
late in his career, after three-putting several greens

THE devoted golfer is an anguished soul who has learned a lot about putting just as an avalanche victim has learned a lot about snow. He knows he has used putters with straight shafts, curved shafts, shiny shafts, dull shafts, glass shafts, oak shafts and Great-uncle Clyde's World War I saber, which he found in the attic. Attached to these shafts have been putter heads made of large lumps of lead ("weight makes the ball roll true," salesmen explain) and slivers of aluminum ("lightness makes the ball roll true," salesmen explain) as well as every other substance harder than a marshmallow. He knows he has tried forty-one different stances, inspired by everyone from the club pro to Fred Astaire in *Flying Down to Rio*, and just as many different strokes. Still, he knows he is hopelessly trapped. He can't putt, and he never will, and the only thing left for him to do is bury his head in the dirt and live the rest of his life like a radish.

If only, he thinks to himself, I had the confidence, the savoir faire, and the ability of those touring pros. They win those big checks every week — I see it on TV — and they wear those beltless slacks and those

dinosaur-skin shoes. They stand up there before thousands of people, their bronzed faces expressionless,
their mock turtle shirts unsweaty from not traipsing
through the rough, their alpacas hanging just right,
and they ram the ball straight into the cup, or near it.
They must know how to putt, right?

Wrong. When it comes to putting, nobody — nobody — equals the pros for feelings of insecurity, in-
feriority, ineptitude and plain old fear. Despite anything you may pretend to have seen at tournaments,
or on television, the pros are absolutely certain they
can't putt any better than the Shaker Heights Ki-
wanians. Maybe worse, they claim, maybe worse. And
if you heaped up all their theories on the subject of
putting, you would have yourself a mountain big
enough to ski the Arlberg-Kandahar on.

In an attempt to prove this, and to place the whole
tormenting art of putting in some kind of perspective,
a very famous golf writer who knew the pros reason-
ably well and was, himself, suffering a terminal case of
the yips — ahem, me — decided to devote a few days
in 1962 on the PGA tour to observing the styles and
listening to the agonies of the pros. Who could really
putt, and who couldn't? Would Jack Burke, Jr., trade
putting strokes with Arnold Palmer, for example?
Would Gary Player simply allow God to line up the
four-footers for him? Do you overlap, interlock, un-
derlap, reverse overlap or just grip the putter like a
snake and turn your head? Was there really an art to

squatting down behind the ball? And what then did you look at, besides the protuberances on the redhead in the sweater across the green?

One should begin with Jackie Burke, it seemed, because at the time he was generally regarded as the very best putter in the game. He used an old wooden-shafted blade putter from a bygone era, but his touch with it was mystical. It was judged to be so delicate that tiny strands of bent grass had been seen to quiver with delight at his mere approach. He could glance at a putt and, rather uncannily, see a definite line to the hole, as if it were marked with chalk for only him to see. And he had this minor deity in the sky who would always whisper the speed to him. In fact, he sank so many putts during one stretch in 1952 that he won four tournaments in a row — a feat that had not been accomplished since Byron Nelson in 1945, and has not been equaled since. Burke would know all about putting.

"Who told you I was a good putter?" Jack asked. "Listen, I'm just an average putter. I've had streaks. We all have. But I'm no superputter, or I would have won more tournaments."

"But everybody says you're the best."

"Go tell everybody they're lighter than popcorn," said Burke.

Burke, obviously, could not hide the conviction that almost all of the big-time players had about their putting. It was average. It was streaky. And don't go placing him in the same category with whoever won a

tournament the previous week. Whoever that was —
Palmer, Julius Boros, Bill Casper — *he* was a great
putter without question or doubt, and you could just
ask anybody, anybody who lost.

All of which, right away, brought up one of the
fascinating vagaries of golf. No pro ever wants to acknowledge that he is excellent on the putting surfaces,
but he will refuse to admit mediocrity at playing from
tee to green. After all, one calls for skill, but the other
for luck. Slashing at a ball is manly, but tapping it is,
well, womanly. Hitting a shot is muscle coordination,
strength, timing, technique, balance, guts, *athletic*
ability. Stroking a putt is something else. It is an unnatural leaning, bending or stooping. It is giving the
ball a dainty caress and hearing it make a funny noise.
Plink, kind of. Or foomp. In any case, it isn't stepping
up to a drive and going crash, smack, splat and then
hearing the crowd swoon as the ball soars away.

There is a pretty good reason the pros feel this way.
They think of themselves, with some justification, as
highly skilled athletes who have conquered the sophisticated timing of golf through hard labor and
experiment. Their swings have become almost instinc-
tive, so much so, in fact, that these swings never leave
them, even under the most savage conditions, be it
weather or intense pressure. A pro can shoot a 77, horrible for him, but it will be a good-looking 77 to the
average golfer behind the gallery ropes. But the pro,
because he has mastered the game, holds another conviction, not altogether logical. He believes that when

a shot happens to veer off line and float into the
rough — the trash, the garbage, Marlboro Country
(he has a lot of terms for trouble) — he steadfastly
believes that it can only be the result of cruel inter-
ference from that mysteriously evil force that goes
around affecting the flight of golf balls.

"Everyone wants to be known as a great striker of
the ball, for some reason," Gary Player said as he
dropped five-footers by the dozen on the practice
green. "Nobody wants to be called a lucky, one-putting s.o.b., and nobody thinks he is."

Indeed not. Some may remember Player walking off
the 18th green after a televised match with Palmer in
1961 and complaining dismally. "From tee to green, I
was never better. But I couldn't make a putt. And
Arnold was knocking them in from everywhere." And
I remember that Palmer came along five minutes later
and said, "I don't understand it. Every time Gary
reached for his putter the ball was in the hole."

The great strikers of the ball, it's true, are superb at
describing shots they hit but never at describing putts
that drop, or, better still, at admitting they drop. "I
feathered a wedge in there and let it sit," one will say.
Or: "I had a squirty lie, so I hammered a seven-iron."
Or: "I really let that two-iron go at the thirteenth. I
put the hands to it. Sometimes, when you've got to
carry the water, you have a tendency to try to dog-
hump it, but I let that one fly, boy." Gary Player has
always been marvelous at this. Once he told the press,
"It may have been the greatest four-wood anyone ever

hit. It was so much on the flag that I had to lean sideways to follow the flight of the ball."

Terrific. But when did the press ever hear a pro ease into the interview chair, light a cigarette, settle back and say, "Now, you take that putt on the seventeenth. I had to have it, of course. Looking at the way the green sloped, I knew that a gentle rap would bring the ball down over the hill, about eight inches above the cup, and that the grain would catch it there and that it would have to pull slowly into the hole. I stroked it perfectly, as I always do. When you know how to read greens, of course, it shrinks those twenty-footers down to about three feet."

Not hardly. Rather, the man on the PGA tour who happens to be winning the most money in any given season usually carries along the unflattering distinction mentioned by Player: A one-putting s.o.b.

"Just go down the money list," Bob Goalby was saying in the 19th Hole. Goalby was a temperamental fellow who had tried out twenty-five different putters over the past two years. He'd give you a thought or two. "The guys who can putt are the guys who win money," Bob said. "There's nobody winning money who can't putt a little bit."

Gene Littler was with him, and the 1961 U.S. Open champion said he had to disagree with Goalby.

"Bob isn't a real good putter, and he wins his share," said Gene, a calm, pleasant gentleman with a fine, slow-motion swing. "I believe most of us divide up into two basic groups. There are the ones who are better players than they are putters, and those who are worse players than they are putters."

"And what is Gene Littler?"

"Oh, naturally, I'm a better player than I am a putter," Littler smiled.

To which Goalby said, "Gene's a great player, but, for Christ's sake, he's one of the all-time superputters."

Littler said, "You gotta be kidding."

Goalby said, "You can't putt, huh?"

"Not like we're talking about," said Gene.

And Goalby said, "Man, if you can't putt, then we all better pack it up."

Littler argued on. "There are only four superputters out here. Arnold Palmer, Bill Casper, Jerry Barber and Dow Finsterwald. Now, those guys can really putt."

"And Littler," said Goalby.

They were still threshing it out over their steak sandwiches when Jerry Barber came through the room. Barber could putt, all right. At Chicago's Olympia Fields during the 1961 PGA championship he holed putts of twenty, forty, and sixty feet, and practically in the dark at that, on the last three greens to tie Don January for the title. And he won the play-off with more of the same.

"Anyone who puts me on a list of great putters is drunk," said Barber, a studious little man, something of a health faddist. "There are three types of putters on the tour if you want the truth. Good, very good, and super. Nobody is awful, or he wouldn't be out here. I am very good, in the second division so to speak. I have to be. I've worked harder at it. Why?

Because I can't drive the ball very far, and I can't play fairway woods. But I'll tell you. I'm no superputter like Arnold Palmer."

When Palmer was told what the verdict was about his putting he looked startled and hurt, as if Winnie had just asked him for a divorce. "Me?" he squeaked. "They must be crazy. Now I will have some good putting rounds, but I'll also have some bad ones — really bad. In 1960 I had some fantastic rounds, but I haven't putted that good since. When you talk about Barber, well, you can just put him way out there by himself. The rest of us are back here."

Arnold did confide, "Finsty's a good putter, day in and day out. And Doug Ford. Follow Doug around for eighteen holes, and he'll show you something. Now I *will* say this. I don't think my good or bad streaks last as long as they do for most of the others. Casper is like that, too."

Billy Casper said he would modestly yield to Palmer as the game's greatest putter. Yes, yes, he knew he had been winning all of the awards as golf's best putter, the Putter of the Year, stuff like that, but that was wrong. That was a cliché. He was a fair putter, he said, but not brilliant. Palmer was brilliant. "I have my favorite distances and my favorite types of greens," Billy said, "but I go through periods lacking confidence. The reason Arnold is the best putter is because he makes more big ones that he *needs* than the rest of us. How else are you going to decide who's the best?"

By now one had to wonder about something. If the

good putters weren't good putters, what and who were the truly bad putters? Several nominations came up among the pros for the worst putter: Tommy Bolt, Johnny Pott, Gardner Dickinson, Jay Hebert, Paul Harney and big George Bayer. Everyone agreed, pretty much, on this list. Right break, left break, no matter. These guys were just terrible on the greens. Pott would occasionally switch to a cross-handed style. Dickinson was in a state of spreading his legs far apart. Hebert and Harney were simply whip-dog, give up, no confidence. And poor Bayer, he knew he wasn't supposed to be able to putt because he was so big and so long off the tees — the Wilt Chamberlain of the tour. And then there was Bolt, that splendid shot-maker, the first and last angry man of golf.

With everyone Tommy ranked up there near Ben Hogan as a shotmaker, a guy who could "van Gogh it," as the pros say, off the fairways, but never, in any mangling of the imagination, was Bolt a decent putter. Worse than that, he continually blamed fate.

He would hit wonderful shots in wonderful streaks — as he surely did in 1958 at Tulsa's Southern Hills where he won the U.S. Open — but the outrage was always in him, ready to boil and explode. Tempestuous Tommy. Terrible-tempered Bolt. And nothing could make him explode like blowing a short putt. Once, the Bolt legend goes, he missed a short one that cost him a couple of thousand dollars and paused to talk it over with the Lord.

As the putt curled out of the hole Tommy wearily let the putter slide from his hands, grimaced severely and stared up at the sky. "Me again, huh?" he said. He stood there, squinting upward and boiling. And he spoke again. "Why don't you come down here and play *me!*" he said. "Come on, come on," Tom sighed. "You and your kid too. I'll give you two a side and play your low ball!"

Tommy, who often dressed as loudly as he swore, was pleased when told he had unofficially been voted one of the worst putters of the ages. "I'm glad they know *something*," said Bolt. "Why do you think I'm using this kind of machine?" He displayed his putter, which was a lump of odd-shaped lead fastened to a shaft bending outward and down in a giant curve, like the stem of a maraschino cherry.

"That's so I can bend it when I get mad," Tommy winked. "They fine you a hundred, don't you see, if you break a club. This way I can just bend it a little."

"You're *not* a very good putter."

"If I could putt they could all go to the cabin," Bolt said. "All these little dudes out here runnin' around wearin' their Ben Hogan blues and grays, they could hang it right up if old Tom could putt a lick."

"That's right."

"You'd better believe *that*, pal," Tommy said.

"Of course, of course."

Bolt sauntered off a few paces, turned around and called back.

"Tell 'em how it is," he said. "And, hey. That list you got there of bad putters. You can take 'em all off there except me, old buddy."

I was standing around thinking about what great

copy Bolt always was when Gardner Dickinson came along. Poor Gardner. Wasn't he the one who had begun to putt with a wide, stiff-legged stance, looking something like a flamingo with arthritis? And wasn't that embarrassing for him?

Gardner said, "Hell, I'd putt sitting up in a coffin if I thought I could hole something."

Some players say you aren't that bad a putter, he was informed.

"Anybody who says I can putt is more of a cage case than I am," he said. "You better lock them straight up."

"It was Goalby, or somebody, who said you get stoop-shouldered sometimes taking the ball out of the cup."

Dickinson said, "Goalby? *Goalby?*"

"Uh, I think, yeah."

"Man, that's really something, that is," Dickinson said. "Well, you can put this down. There's *no way* I can putt as good as him, or a lot of others. My trouble is, I found out when I was fourteen years old that every putt doesn't have to go in the hole. Palmer and Goalby and some others haven't figured that out yet."

As for his weird stance, he went into theory. "You want to hit the ball square," Gardner said. "Get it rolling good toward the hole — and then pray. This wide stance looks like it might keep me honest. Keep me from moving on the putt. I'm looking for that immovable position that Palmer's got."

Hitting the ball square sounded good, but it only

took a few moments to find a pro who said it was impossible and that Gardner Dickinson might as well go searching for the Dead Sea Scrolls.

"It's not humanly possible to hit the ball squarely every time," said Earl Stewart, Jr., who was more of a teaching pro now than a touring pro. "I think everybody takes it back a little differently every time — a little inside or a little outside. The thing you got to avoid is the old freeze. Lockwrist, we call it."

Lockwrist?

"You betcha," said Earl. "You don't want to take it back because you're afraid you'll miss it. That's lockwrist."

Golf is played by a bunch of *cage cases* trying to avoid *lockwrist*. Beautiful.

"It's mental," Stewart was saying. "But sometimes it's fatal. Why, it finally forced Byron Nelson off the tour when he was only thirty-four, when he probably had several good years left. He'll tell you that."

He did. "Putting affects the nerves more than anything," Byron said. "I would actually get nauseated over three-footers during my prime. And there were tournaments when I couldn't keep a meal down for four days. Missing a short putt is about the most humiliating thing in the world because you're supposed to make it."

Nelson remembered that Clayton Heafner, a big, burly man from North Carolina who was a tour name in the 1930's and 40's, so detested putting as part of golf that he used to tell his fellow pros of a great

ambition. It was to come down to the final hole of the
U.S. Open championship and have a one-foot putt —
a gimme — to capture the biggest, most important
prize in the sport. Heafner then wanted to take several
moments, lining up the putt while the gallery stood
frozen and hushed. Finally, he wanted to walk up to
the ball, gaze down at it, then haul off and backhand
it as hard as he could, knocking it off the green and
into the stunned crowd, saying, "To hell with this
crummy, rotten game."

Byron said that this golfing disease, lockwrist, could
get to anyone, that it had finally got to Hogan, apparently, and that it would eventually get to Arnold
Palmer, but it might take longer for him. Palmer's
technique of staying motionless over a putt, solid as a
statue, was envied by all. "You notice when he ad-
dresses the putt, pigeon-toed and knees pinched together, nothing moves but the hands and forearms,"
said Nelson. "That's the secret."

All good putters have something in common, Byron
added. They have a slow backstroke and they get a
definite rap on the ball.

Jerry Barber said as much. "What you're doing
when you putt is calling on all the years of experience
and practice. You're concentrating and you're confident. When you hole a long one it's because you
have a putter heavy enough to get the ball to the cup,
you've stroked it nicely enough to give it a good roll,
you know the line — and you believe in the first place
that you can make it," he said.

From any distance?

"Somewhere in there skill stops and luck takes over," Barber said. "The scoring range is probably from fifteen feet in. Anything outside that is plenty of luck."

Barber said, "We tend to get embarrassed, you know, if we hole very many putts of any length. There's so much talk about tee-to-green play, it's gotten to where you have to apologize for making a putt. I think that's silly." Barber noted that Arnold Palmer never apologized for making anything, the reason being that Arnold thinks he *deserves* everything that goes in. "He's *stared* the ball into the hole when he needed it a couple of times at the Masters," Jerry said.

For all of his confidence, it was well-known that Palmer spent hours every week in a golf shop, fooling with his putter — changing the grip, bending the shaft, weighting the head, unweighting the head, filing, chiseling, nailing — and doctoring the rest of his clubs as well. A lot of people wondered why. It did seem that Palmer changing his golf clubs was a little bit like Liz Taylor getting plastic surgery regularly, just for laughs. What are you doing in the pro shop with that club sticking in a vise, Arnold?

"When you putt poorly you think you ought to change putters," Arnold said. "But I can't find another one I like. So I do some work on the one I've got. I could possibly leave it alone and the stroke would come back, but all I'd do in the meantime is worry. At least working on the clubs keeps me busy and helps me think I'm doing something to correct the situation."

The Palmer putter, which up to this point in his career had won him three Masters championships, the U.S. Open, two British Opens, the U.S. Amateur and a caddy shed full of lesser tournaments, was an old Tommy Armour model, the one with the rear shaft and slight gooseneck. "The shaft is so weak I can actually bend it with my hands. I've got a nail driven through the head of it. It's been weighted and reweighted a hundred times, I guess. I've tried a lot of others, but I always come back to this one," Arnold said.

Palmer isn't the first great player to stay with one putter. Bobby Jones used Calamity Jane, so named by O. B. Keeler, the writer, a thin blade putter, throughout his career. It was a good weapon for the fast, slick greens Jones always found in the major championships. Ben Hogan also used the same putter to win all of his big titles. His was a handmade invention, a brass-headed, center-shafted relic, actually carved from a doorknob. Hogan got it from a fellow pro, Ky Laffoon, in his youthful days on the tour. I once asked Ben if he intended presenting the club to Golf House, the USGA museum, when he seriously retired, and he said, without sentiment, "I don't know where it is. It was stolen, I think."

Something else was stolen from Hogan by the years: his nerves. But only on the greens was it evident. As late as 1960, when he was forty-eight years old, Hogan still reached more greens in regulation than any competitor in the U.S. Open championship. He could still hit the shots, and still can, for that matter, but as fewer and fewer putts found the hole, Ben's attitude toward the game changed.

It was before the 1961 Open at Oakland Hills near Detroit — the Open Gene Littler won — that Hogan originated an interesting game for those who companioned him in practice rounds. Littler was among them. "You didn't count putts, or the score on a hole," said Gene. "You got a point for hitting a fairway, a point for hitting a green, and a point for getting closest to the pin. He won, of course."

The practice game was not the result of Hogan never being able to sink a putt. He had made some in his day; indeed, anyone who could win five U.S. Opens (counting an unofficial one during the war in 1942), two Masters, two PGA championships and the British Open — ten major championships in all — could, of course, putt. But now in these later years he couldn't, so he made up games and enjoyed holding court in the locker rooms with other players and with writers, discussing that abominable aspect of golf.

"Hitting a golf ball and putting have nothing in common," said Ben, after a round at Oakland Hills in '61. "They are two different games. You work all of your life to perfect a repeating swing that will get you to the greens, and then you have to try to do something that is totally unrelated. There shouldn't be any cups, just flag sticks. And then the man who hit the most fairways and greens and got closest to the pins would be the tournament winner."

Him.

Well, Hogan could have his intriguing games and theories. There were other cage cases on the tour who were far more desperate because of putting ills, it seemed to me.

Bob Shave, Jr., was one to consider. He was on and off the circuit, using a putter with a shaft adjoining the clubhead at the nose rather than in the center or at the heel. The grand design: force himself to strike the putt harder. Shave also liked to keep a portable radio playing near him when he practiced on the putting green. Soft music, smooth stroke. Bob Duden was another. Duden, in his never-ending quest for hitting the putt squarely, went to a croquet style, putting between his legs with a club that vaguely resembled an apple pie on a pogo stick. Freddie Haas was still gripping the club cross-handed and Johnny Pott was trying it. And Sam Snead, of all people, would occasionally separate his hands on the grip by as much as six or eight inches, or, at times, slip his right hand down the shaft to within about a foot of the clubhead, then bend way over and attempt to sort of sweep the short ones into the hole. And Doug Sanders, without resorting to any wild methods, was simply mumbling incessantly about the fact that if he could have sunk one more putt per week — of any distance — the previous year, it would have increased his bankroll by $20,000. Hogan was far from alone.

Men have always had trouble putting on the tour, of course. It was Joe Turnesa of the golfing Turnesas who once won a tournament on Long Island by throwing away his standard-size putter and using one with only a foot and a half shaft and stroking the ball from a low crouch. It was Leo Diegel who originated the style of pointing both elbows out in opposite directions and putting as if he were doing the Suzy-Q. Diegel, a fine putter, eventually wound up putting left-handed because he suffered slow-creeping lockwrist. And it was Ky Laffoon, an early-day Tommy Bolt in terms of temper, who used to open a moving car door and drag his putter along the road to punish it. Laffoon, in fact, who would begin to stutter in his anger, once grabbed his putter by the neck, raced to a water hazard, held it under and raved, "D-drown, y-you, d-dirty, b-bastard."

It is difficult to say whether Cary Middlecoff ever was afflicted by lockwrist or not — whether that was the reason he went into semi-retirement at so early an age. Cary, a splendid champion, was forever a slow player, refusing to strike the ball or a putt until he was absolutely ready. A joke on the tour used to be that Cary gave up dentistry because no patient could hold his mouth open that long.

"I never had any idea I was taking a long time," Middlecoff confessed. "You just don't realize it, especially when you're out there romancing with the high seventies. That's a struggle, believe me. I'm more and more convinced that putting is plain luck. You could take a machine that would stroke the ball exactly the same way every time, feed it ten balls to putt over the same line from about six feet away, and I'll guarantee you the machine would be lucky to make six of them. Too many things can happen to the ball after it leaves the clubhead. The tiniest thing, sun, wind, grass, anything, can move it off line. I've putted poorly and holed everything. And I've stroked it good and missed everything."

A few players share the opinion that putting is entirely mental and that, therefore, one should always think positively on the greens. Don January said it best. "A lot of guys are afraid to make a putt. By that I mean they're afraid to win a tournament, especially a big one. I try to tell myself all the time that I'm a good putter. I try to psych myself into believing I can make anything. But most of us, we like to bleed about putting badly and hope that a good streak will sneak up on us. It's all superstition, I suppose."

January went on, "Some fellows are afraid that if they talk about their putting the touch will go away. So they think the best thing is to moan about it even when they're putting good. One thing is very true. The better you putt, the bolder you play."

But doesn't that work in reverse as well?

"Of course," January said. "You putt bad, you get afraid to take chances. And you start worrying about your quota. You're apt to think: I've made two long ones already today. I know they won't give me another one, so I'd better lay up this time or I'll three-putt. This leads to other distractions. You start lining up putts and you find yourself staring at people across the green. Your concentration is gone."

When a pro starts watching fans in red shirts or ladies in short skirts or a passing jet overhead or the swallows going home to Capistrano his putter may be near the "crystallizing" point. Here is another tour expression. When a putter crystallizes it breaks in half. Hammering it against a tree trunk can speed up the process, needless to say.

Some players have almost crystallized their heads in anger over their putting. Such a man was Ivan Gantz, a man who never quite made it on the tour.

"The first time I ever saw Ivan," January said, "he was walking down a fairway parallel to mine. I hadn't been on the tour long, and when I saw Ivan I thought, 'Hold it, man, this is back in the cat games in Dallas.' Blood was streaming down his forehead over his nose. The man had hit himself in the head with his putter because he'd blown a short one."

January said he'd heard tales of Ivan Gantz leaping face first into a bunker because of a missed putt, of Ivan diving into creeks, of Ivan banging his head with a stone and of Ivan rolling and tossing in the grass. The pros laugh about Ivan Gantz, but they understand the fury that consumed him.

Nor is anger the only reaction to a case of lockwrist. Any pro can recite with warm relish the story of the man who had so much trouble putting he often visualized animals running across a green just as he got ready to tap the ball. One day he came down to the last hole with a chance to win a tournament. But as he prepared to putt a dog ran onto the green, the way a dog somehow always manages to run onto a football field at half time. The golfer just stood there, agonizing in fear, and presently he turned to his playing companion and asked, "Was that a real dog?"

For all of the pain that the pros seem to suffer on the putting surfaces, the good ones can still tell you how it's done, technically.

"Just get comfortable," said Billy Casper. "Then stroke the putt the best way you know how. Don't try to copy anyone else, unless of course you're doing something drastically wrong, like aiming a foot off line or something."

"Get a club that feels right to *you*," said Jack Burke. "Keep your head down, take the putter back slowly, and don't worry about where it's going after you stroke it."

"Stay down and don't move," Arnold Palmer said. "Get a positive stance, a firm position, and be sure you're getting a good, solid rap on the ball."

"Just concentrate on the line and the speed and have confidence that it'll go in," said Jerry Barber.

And do all of these things work, all of them together, with a blade, a mallet, a centershaft, a gooseneck, with any putter you pick up? The club doesn't matter?

"I'll tell you what," said Bob Rosburg, a fast player and a good putter whose theory, mainly, is to hit the putt before it hits you. "You change clubs all you want, but you'll wind up like a guy I knew in Miami. There was a grab barrel in the pro shop. You threw your putter in if you didn't like it and took out another one, giving the pro five dollars. This guy kept doing it through eighteen putters and ninety dollars. He finally got his old one back."

Rosburg, a fairly cynical man, said, "I'll tell you why putts go in. Because the old National Open champion in the sky puts 'em in. How about this? Bud Holscher is paired with Bolt one day in Vegas, and he's been holing out from everywhere all day. Finally he comes to the last green, and he's got a two-footer. He stands there with his putter under his arm, tryin' to get in his pocket for a coin to mark his ball. He gets all tangled up, the club falls, hits the ball and knocks it right in."

"So if you're destined to make a putt, you're destined to make it, is that it?" I said.

"Pretty much," said Rosburg.

"And then from tee to green, does the old National Open champion in the sky ever hit any shots for you?"

Rosburg grinned, "Last I heard he was shanking."

America's Guest

---

*Give me a millionaire with a bad backswing and I
can have a very pleasant afternoon.*
  — GEORGE LOW,
    on the subject of survival in golf

IN professional tournament golf the clubhouse veranda can often be a noteworthy blend of rumble seat, wax museum, promenade deck, theater wings and courthouse steps. As the tour moves from one Crystal Rancho Happy Avocado Creek Country Club to another, the verandas undergo some severe botanical changes — a palm will beget a pine, or a eucalyptus will beget an oak — but the human plantlife will remain practically changeless. Except for the occasional intrusion of a spectator fully equipped with binoculars, periscope, chair seat, transistor, program, pairing sheet, camera and hot dog, and the almost invariable presence of at least one young female in form-fitting slacks, huge dark glasses and a straw bonnet, the regular veranda standers comprise a remarkably homogeneous and identifiable part of golf. They are the hanging-in, cooling-it businessmen of the game. And as they spread across the lawn, gazing toward the nearest leader board while a tournament progresses, they are not unlike a cluster of military commanders observing the glow of shell-fire from a distant valley.

To almost anyone in the 1960's who knew the difference between a Ben Hogan driver and a shooting stick

the faces of these fringe personalities looked as familiar as casual water, but only the true insider was
able to identify them by name. There was the stocky,
pink-faced man in the dark blazer, his hands usually
folded behind him, the one ready with a Sam Snead
anecdote or a story about the 1937 Ryder Cup team.
That was Fred Corcoran, Snead's lifelong agent and
the tournament director of the International Golf Association. There was the tall, blond fellow in the white
shoes, a briefcase in one hand and Winnie Palmer's
arm in the other. That was Mark McCormack, a
Cleveland lawyer and manager of Palmer, Jack Nicklaus, Gary Player and most of the ships at sea. And
there were several others, forming a sort of corporate
blur, spaced equidistantly among the umbrellas: J. Edwin Carter of the World Series of Golf, Jack Tuthill, the PGA tournament supervisor, Bob Rickey, a
Brunswick-MacGregor vice-president, Ernie Sabay-
rac, an equipment distributor, Bob Drum, a hulking
writer, Joe Wolfe, the Wilson clubmaker, Darrell
Brown, Palmer's pilot, Doc Giffin, Palmer's personal
secretary, Malcolm Hemion, a TV director for ABC,
and, finally, the most familiar figure of all, that of a
man called Bubble Head, a man who was always
there, never doing anything.

On or off the verandas, Bubble Head, or George
Low, was (and still is) the stand-around champion of
three decades. He is, all at once, America's guest,
underground comedian, consultant, inventor of the
overlapping grip for a beer can, and, more impor-

tantly, a man who has conquered the two hardest things in life — how to putt better than anyone ever, and how to live lavishly without an income.

For thirty years George Low has been the vaguest, most mysterious man in all of golf. Outwardly solemn and immobile, he stands like an urban renewal project on the verandas in a plaid jacket and an open-collared shirt, deeply tanned, granting interviews only to book-makers and forcing grins only toward those who might seem inclined to buy him lunch or a cocktail. It has been said that if George Low is not on your veranda the tournament simply hasn't started yet. When the Western Open was held at the Field Club in Pittsburgh in 1959, for example, George did not reveal his two hundred forty pounds until the final round, whereupon a friend on the committee scolded him for being tardy and nearly giving the event a bad name.

"Well, you got to understand that a man who don't have to be back to his office for thirty years is some-times gonna be lax," said George.

The only office that George Low has ever had is the trunk of someone's automobile, preferably a Cadillac, which, if he borrowed it for long began to look like a rummage sale of golf clubs, clothes and photo albums. George has no age. His lungs are one hundred, his stomach is one fifty, and his soul is two thousand, says he. The body has been fifty-four or so for a while. For most of these years, at any rate, George's home has been a car seat, a convertible couch in someone's living room, a roll-away bed in a friend's hotel room, or, when he's going good, the vacant wing of a friend's mansion. But always these places have been where the sunshine is — either on or near the PGA tour. He is also very comfortable in Palm Springs, Scottsdale or Miami Beach, whether the tour is in the vicinity or not, or at Saratoga, Santa Anita or Gulfstream.

"I go where some rich guy's got a bed and a kind heart," George says. "Most guys are if-come in this world, but there's a few that ain't phony, and they like having me around. They understand that I got to be where it's warm 'cause I can't afford no overcoat."

To the person who is "strung out," as George puts it, which means he has a steady, respectable job, it may seem that Low's existence is mostly a matter of survival. But George has never thought of it quite that way. On the contrary, George Low has usually lived comfortably, and often far better than the strung-out fellow who rides a commuter train or drives the freeways to work, who is paying off a divan and a Frigidaire and who has to purchase a daily ticket to a golf tournament, not admissible to the clubhouse.

The main reason why George Low has been able to survive in reasonable splendor is that he has one of those personalities that appeal to gentlemen of means. He has a rare sense of humor that makes him one of the superb put-down artists of his time, an unobtrusive manner for being around and not bothering anyone and a crashing honesty, all of which can add up to good company. Aside from these things George knows as much about golf as anyone, and a lot of gentlemen of means like to play golf, apparently while being put down unobtrusively, honestly and without being unduly bothered.

If he *does* have to work he does that on a putting green in Palm Springs or Miami Beach, mainly, where he is apt to putt with a wedge or with his shoe against a wagerer using a putter, and come out all right.

"Put me on a putting green in Miami for a week," says George, "and I'll kill more tourists than the Fontainebleau."

Among the celebrities who have demonstrated that they enjoy George's company and have, therefore, been his happy hosts, are, just to touch on four different sports, Jimmy Demaret, Willie Shoemaker, Horace Stoneham and Del Miller — a golfer, a jockey, a baseball owner and a harness racing mogul, respectively. George has visited with Stoneham in Phoenix during November, he has spent Christmas with Demaret in Houston and he has devoted a lot of weekday drop-ins to Shoemaker in Los Angeles and Miller in Pennsylvania. It was Paul Grossinger of the resort by that name in the Catskills who once labeled George "America's guest."

"After which he come up with a freebie," says George.

Another associate, Bob Johnson, once the president of Roosevelt Raceway outside New York City, may have summed up George perfectly — at least it delights George — for all of his hosts one evening as Low kept badgering Johnson for another hundred dollars to buy drinks for everyone at a Palm Springs party.

"Just loafing with George is better than having a Dun & Bradstreet rating," said Johnson.

All of this helps make absolutely clear George's uncomplicated philosophy of life, or rather his blueprint for leading a life of ease.

"There ain't no use hanging around a broke 'cause nothing falls off," he says. "The only time I pick up a check is to hand it to somebody."

This, for George, sharply divides the world into two distinct categories of people — those who "come up," or pay, and those who "plead the fifth," or don't pay, when a tab appears.

Since most everyone who knows George knows him well enough to keep his pocketbook either handy or hidden, there are never any surprises or embarrassing situations. If George strolls by you prepare to pay or you prepare to leave. "It's an honor to pick up my check," he says. "How many true celebrities do you know? Anyhow, if you plead the fifth I'll go find a live one somewheres."

Low has a carefully thought out term for the man with a reputation for being something less than a wild spender. A very cautious student of the dollar, George calls him. Like Sam Snead.

"When I dine with Mr. Snead he always suggests

that I order as if I was expecting to pay for it myself," says George. "I have known many great destroyers of money, but Mr. Snead is not among them."

Anyone who might happen to stand near George on a veranda at a tournament is likely to be treated to a comic routine. It oozes out naturally from his husky voice and always with a cynical tone. Most of the competitors have learned to feed George straight lines just for the pleasure of picking up a new expression.

Al Besselink came by one day at Pensacola and said, "Loan me fifty, Bubble."

Staring straight ahead at a sheltering palm Low said, "Loaning you money is like sending lettuce by rabbit."

Another time, as George rested himself against the trunk of an elm at Colonial, Billy Maxwell good-naturedly said, "Wish I had your energy, George."

"I wish I had a rock in each hand," said Low.

When Mark McCormack began packaging and selling Arnold Palmer, a close friend of Low's, in ways that no one had ever thought of before and practically printing money in the process, it gave George a lot of ammunition for his veranda standing. If someone were to ask Low if he had seen McCormack lately George would reply, "Yeah, he was sticking up a supermarket about an hour ago."

Mark learned to approach Low delicately, but it would never do any good. George would only tell McCormack, "Driving your getaway car is the best job in golf."

Bing Crosby once told George, who had insinuated he needed a room during Bing's tournament, that he could probably fix him up at the Del Monte Lodge and probably for a good rate.

"Thanks a lot," said George. "Can I loan you a dime to mark your ball?"

The Crosby has never been famed for drawing large crowds to the Monterey Peninsula for two reasons: it is inconveniently located on a 17-mile drive from Earth, and the weather is nearly always deplorable. When Crosby seemed rather excited one year by what appeared to him to be a better than average turnout Low remarked, "I seen more people on the back of a motorcycle."

Though George might frequently have a hangover gaze about him, his mind remains quick. Roasting in the Las Vegas sun one afternoon during the Tournament of Champions, when it was still being held at the Desert Inn course and when Wilbur Clarke was still alive, George noticed something unusual going up on the scoreboard. Arnold Palmer had just posted a nine, a seven and a five, in that order. Turning quietly to Clarke, Low said, "That's twenty-one. Pay him."

One of the better verandas to stand around on is that of the Augusta National Golf Club during the Masters. It has two big shade trees, some crawling wisteria, a scattering of umbrellas and tables and, always, George Low. He will move from a table to a bench to a tree trunk to a slope in the sun and back again, covering his steps, mumbling comments about the wretched state of the world and how many brokes there are in it. One year George arrived fresh from having spent a weekend sharing a hotel room with a friend, Bob Drum, who was then a writer for the *Pittsburgh Press.*

"How do you like rooming with Drum?" George was asked.

"It's okay," he said. "If you don't mind taking a shower with your money in your hand."

And there was the time at Augusta that George was hearing about Oscar Fraley, a former columnist for UPI, getting into a minor argument in a bar and causing some mild excitement. As the tale was being related by someone who had witnessed it, Fraley happened to stroll by. George interrupted the story and called to Oscar. "I hear you didn't start no fight last night for a change," he said. "Where'd you stay? In a room full of nuns?"

George Low may not have been born bourbon-faced or angry, but he was certainly born "energetically lazy," to use his words. "He was born retired," is the way Jimmy Demaret has put it. The event of George's birth occurred before World War I, that much is known, and not three hundred yards, a stout Nicklaus tee shot, from the pro shop at Baltusrol Golf Club in Springfield, New Jersey.

"I like to say I was born in the 19th Hole — the only one I ever parred," Low says.

He was the son of a rather famed Scot, George Low, Sr., who was runner-up for the U.S. Open championship in 1899 and who became the resident professional at Baltusrol. As one of those Scots who came to America to teach the game to an intrigued continent, George, Senior, numbered among his pupils a couple of renowned White House slicers, William Howard Taft and Warren G. Harding.

"There were poor guys like that all around Baltusrol," George remembers. "The Toppings and them kind of charity cases."

Despite the fact that George grew up near the 1st tee of a golf course, he did not try to learn the game until he was fifteen. And this after his father had retired and taken his son back to Scotland. George *had* to play golf in Scotland, he felt.

"What else is there to do over there? Wear a skirt?"

Try as he did to avoid playing golf, two things came naturally to George. A good swing and a deep, nagging feeling about the game. These attributes combined — conspired, more probably — to bring him back to the U.S. in the early 1930's. But in those days George returned as more than just an assistant pro at a variety of clubs in the upstate area of New York. For instance, there was one summer when he was working at a club in the Catskills when he was struck with a get-rich scheme. He found a friend who owned a Ford Tri-Motor airplane and together they dreamed up the idea of shuttling newspapers from the cities to resort areas.

Soon, they decided they could make their business even more profitable by shuttling more than papers.

Like booze, this being during Prohibition. And at the same time, on weekends, they staged what could only be described as the world's worst air show featuring George Low parachuting out of the Tri-Motor.

"I didn't exactly jump," he says. "I'd open the door of the plane, and then I'd open the chute and let it pull me out. Who the hell wants to jump if he don't know the chute's gonna open?"

All of this came to an end one cold evening during a shuttle flight when the plane somehow drifted into a small mountain.

"Me and the pilot got out safe, but the booze died," George says.

It was also during these early, formative years that George developed a special fondness for Saratoga and thoroughbred racing itself. In August during the Saratoga meeting, he got acquainted with the sport by becoming a runner, one of those guys who found out what the swells in the box seats wanted to wager on a race and then ran to the betting tables to get it down for them.

"I knew all the rich guys," he says. "Most of 'em were empty suits."

To this day, George has a knack for going to the tracks in style. As recently as the summer of 1969 George was back at Saratoga, quite comfortable in the home of Harry M. Stevens III, a young Stevens of the family that invented the hot dog, the straw, the paper cup and now caters no fewer than forty-one tracks and stadiums around the country. Sitting on young Harry's porch one evening, George was asked by his host if he wanted to pitch coins at a line for cash.

"Now what would I do with a catering business?" said George.

But let's retreat back to those 1930's again, to the days when Low honestly felt he could make it all the way from his assistant pro jobs into a handsome living on what had become a burgeoning PGA tour.

George started out on the tour determined to make his way as a champion, but, well, it was just too much fun in those days. Card games all through the nights — pitch and bridge, that kind of thing. And there were all of these characters to pal around with — Demaret, Jimmy Thomson, Leo Diegel, Craig Wood. "And that Indian," he says. Which was Ky Laffoon.

"Laffoon is the only man who ever beat me outa something on the putting green," says George. "At the old North and South Open at Pinehurst we got into a game that lasted day and night. I should have known I was in trouble when we putted at night. Laffoon was an Indian and Indians can see at night. I didn't get in that jackpot no more."

Low made an attempt which might generously be described as feeble to win the British Open of 1939. The idea of returning to semi-native soil gripped him, one reason being that he might be able to redeem himself for the last round he had played in Scotland. A long time before, in the British Boys' championship at Edinburgh, George had been beaten 8–7 by a cross-handed Scot, and he was so disgusted about it he heaved his clubs out of a train window. So George and Johnny Bulla sailed on the *Transylvania* in the summer of '39 for England.

The trip abroad took too long for George. Struggling to occupy his time on board ship, he got into a high-stakes game of shuffleboard with a gentleman of nobility, and he lost so much money that he was forced to delay his arrival for the British Open. Instead of going straight to St. Andrews he went with the earl or count or whatever he was to Perthshire. There they would bowl on the green.

"My bankroll looked like an elephant slept on it when I got off the ship," George explains. "Took me three weeks bowling on the green to get it back."

Low finally got to St. Andrews but not in time for a practice round. And he isn't altogether clear on how well he played. "I think I missed the cut — if I teed off at all," he says. "I forget. In those days, me and Clayton Heafner had a bad habit of being withdrew."

Where are the characters on today's tour? That's one thing George would like to know. Where are the fun-lovers, the withdrews? "All you got out there is a bunch of authors and haberdashers," he says.

"All you got to do to write a book is win one tournament. All of a sudden you're telling everybody where the V's ought to point. And them that don't win, they're haberdashers. They sell sweaters and slacks and call themselves pros."

Says George, "There ain't many of 'em knows how to repair a club in a shop. They can bend 'em, but they can't work on 'em until they know what's right. Most of 'em couldn't win consistently if they had Dick Tracy for a partner. I do a little club work for a few of 'em, but there's not too many who'd give the ducks a drink if they owned Lake Mead. They'll pop for a handshake, but those I got plenty of."

One of George's last flings as an active tour player came in 1945, and history confirms that he went out beautifully. Among the more remarkable facts of golf is that George Low helped end the fantastic winning streak of Byron Nelson. It happened in the Memphis Open that summer. Nelson, the Mechanical Man, had won eleven straight tournaments when he got to Memphis to try for the twelfth. Nelson finished third at Memphis behind Amateur Freddie Haas, who shot 270, and none other than George Low, who shot 276.

"Haas win the tournament, but I win the front money," says George. "I was the first pro to beat Nelson. Look it up."

Very shortly after that Low retired to the putting greens forever.

So many legends and half-truths have been written, spoken and whispered about George Low's putting ability, he ought to be a folk song. There are wild tales of George putting with a rake, a shovel, a pool cue and a broom handle and defeating others using a legitimate putter. There are stories of George kicking the ball with his foot and acing five out of nine holes in one round on the putting green. Other stories say that George has given putting "secrets" to Arnold

Palmer, Bing Crosby, Willie Mays, all sorts of celebrities who turn up in his photo albums with their arms around his bulky shoulders. And there are stories that in the old days George took so much money away from tour winners on the putting greens that he should have been given a speeding ticket.

Low only forces a sly grin when the stories are put to him.

"They get started because I live good," he says. "I spend $50,000 a year of somebody else's money, that's all."

Oh, there are a few things George could talk about if he wanted to get himself in some kind of jackpot, as he says, but it isn't worth it. Sure, he can kick the ball with his foot and get it down in two from almost anywhere. For example, at Las Vegas a few years ago he was walking around in a practice session with Bo Wininger when Bo plopped a ball down on the 16th green at the Desert Inn and said, "Three cases of beer to two you can't get it down in two from here." The putt was seventy-five feet long. George called it, put his shoe to the ball and rolled it up within two inches of the cup. And George *can* beat you putting, even if he uses a wedge. "Don't ever try him," Byron Nelson has warned.

"I shall have to admit, in all modesty, that I'm probably the greatest putter who ever lived," says George. "At least I'll try anyone for a nominal fee."

There is a simple reason why George Low is the greatest putter who ever lived. "I've done more of it than anybody else," he says. "Back in Scotland, in Carnoustie, there was a thirty-six-hole putting green right outside our house. I putted for three or four years, eight, ten, twelve hours a day, before I ever started playing golf. I've always been able to do things with my hands anyhow. Build things. I have feel in them. So I putted and putted before I ever played golf, and then I've done nothing but putt since I quit. I can beat anyone on the tour because they have to worry about getting to the green. I'm already there."

George is not keen about giving away his putting secrets — not for free, at least. But he can offer a little advice.

"Everybody has a different problem putting," he says. "The best thing you can have is a quick left wrist. That makes you take the clubhead back on the inside. Most of your weight ought to be on the left foot for good balance. Another important thing is to keep both thumbs squarely on the top of the grip for the right feel."

He goes on, "The feel of the club may be the most important thing of all. When you reach in your pocket for a coin the last thing that touches the coin is your thumb. You use it to roll out the coin. It's the most sensitive finger. That's why you grip the putter with both thumbs on top of the handle."

And on, "After you get the feel of the club the thing to do is be sure you get a good, solid rap on the ball when you hit it. And there's only one way to be sure of doing that. Take the club back on the inside, like opening a door, and then bring it forward. When you open a door you take it back slow. When you close the door, that's the way the putter should meet the ball."

And on, "The worst way for the beginner to putt is to jab at the ball. You'll see some of the pros jab at it, but it's their own method they've worked out, which they think is good for all of the bad greens they putt on. There are a couple of 'em that jab the putt on any kind of green. Billy Casper, for instance, and Bob Rosburg. They're pretty good putters, but there are exceptions to everything. Besides, they jab the same way every time, which is the real key to good putting. Consistency."

And finally, "That's why I'm gonna beat everybody. I'm gonna hit the ball the same way every time, and you're not. And if we putt long enough for the luck to scare off, I got to be the winner."

George Low might be a more mysterious figure than he is if it had not been for Arnold Palmer. When Palmer won his second Masters in 1960, Low's name burst into print as some sort of weird genius of the greens — and all because of a remark Arnold made to the press. That year Palmer sank dramatic putts for birdies on the last two greens to win, not only before the thousands in Augusta, but before millions more watching television. And later on, in an interview, when asked about those heroics, Palmer said, "The only thing I did on those putts was keep thinking what my old friend George Low always says: 'Keep your head down and don't move.'"

A short time after this Low's small but impressive notoriety resulted in an autograph-model putter, the George Low putter, a mallethead type with a marketing slogan that went "the putter with the built-in touch." It was made by a company called the Sportsman's Golf Corporation of Chicago. A few of the pros began using the Low putter, mainly Gary Player. And exactly one year later, back in Augusta again, Player, using the Low putter, won the Masters and George Low got even more publicity.

"But I was lucky," says George. "The putter started selling so well I got fired. It was a relief. With a lot of money in your pocket, it takes away the torment of where you're gonna sleep."

Along about this time another change took place in Low's career. A motel chain, Ramada Inn, hired him as a goodwill ambassador. His job was to follow the tour and guide as many pros as possible into Ramada Inns across the land. They gave him a Cadillac to drive — "the only Cadillac in the press lot" — and let him have free rooms in all of the Ramada Inns he could locate.

"It didn't feel right," he says. "I knew it wouldn't last. Something was missing. The daily challenge that I'd grown used to. The challenge of whether I'd be able to borrow Frank Stranahan's car and lose it to somebody in a coin flip or something. It got so bad for a while I almost bought a pair of shoes on my own."

That wouldn't have been right. George hadn't bought a pair of shoes in thirty years. He'd got them all from Foot Joy. "I been a test pilot for Foot Joy forever. I test their sixty-five-dollar alligator models to see if standing in them for long periods of time in a bar brings them any serious harm. What effect spilling beer has on them."

Rarely is George anything in appearance but the portrait of prosperity. Foot Joy shoes, a handsome plaid jacket that he got from Joe Jemsek, a golf course owner from the Chicago area ("he wears my size") and a Western-tooled, monogrammed leather chair stool, courtesy of Bob Goldwater, Barry's brother.

"No if-come about him," says George. "Bob stands up."

There have been, sad to relate, times when George Low has insisted on paying up himself. Not often, but some. And only in these latter, more prosperous years. One such occasion was in Augusta in 1965 in a place called the Bull Bat Lounge, just off the lobby of the Town House Hotel. George was sitting with a few journalist friends he could trust, drinking beer and getting ready to go search for a cafeteria. He prefers cafeterias to elegant restaurants because they have a lot of vegetables. Anyhow, George was in the middle of an anecdote when an old friend appeared.

"Good to see you, Bubble," the voice said, the voice belonging to a Tampa car salesman named Madman Morris. "Where you been? I been all over. Pensacola. Miami. Everywhere. How come I didn't see you?"

"Madman," said George. "Either shut up or sit down and assume the financial obligation. I got my own lies to tell."

"Sure good to see you, Georgie," said Madman. "I know this guy thirty years. . . ."

"Are you gonna sit down and buy something, Madman, or just stand there looking like a buried lie in a bunker?" George said.

"I been all over, Bubble. Jacksonville. Pensacola. Miami. How come you wasn't anywhere?" Madman said.

"There's a rule in this joint that any guy stands around has to *buy* something," said Low. "Why don't you take your shag bag somewhere else and hit your shanks?"

"Whatta guy," said Madman Morris. "Same old George. I'd see this guy everywhere. Palm Beach. Orlando. Pensacola. Miami . . ."

"I can't get in no jackpot with an unplayable lie like this," said George, excusing himself, sliding out of the booth in the Bull Bat Lounge, paying the check and leaving to go look for vegetables.

There are also occasions when George Low can be persuaded to play a round of golf. Actually play. Naturally, the type of golfing companion George prefers is someone with money and questionable talent, an ego-inspired handicap, perhaps. "Give me a millionaire with a bad backswing and I can have a very pleasant afternoon," George says.

An afternoon like this occurred not so many winters ago at the posh Seminole Golf Club in Palm Beach. George got into a game with the Duke of Windsor and the late Robert R. Young, the railroad magnate. An earl or a duke or a count could always entice George into a game of something. George's putter was good to him this day as it usually is when more than laughs are involved. The other shots he could hit well enough from memory. George came out in good shape, don't worry. Except that when the round was finished Low didn't notice the Duke straining to get in his pocket.

They were all sort of strolling toward the clubhouse — to the veranda, of course — slowly, amid a rather awkward silence. George cleared his throat a couple of times. They stopped and chatted about the nice day, how lovely the course looked this time of year. George shifted his weight from one Foot Joy to another and cleared his throat again.

Finally, Robert Young discreetly took George aside and whispered something to him.

"Oh, by the way, George. I should have mentioned that His Royal Highness never pays money," said Young.

"He don't do *what?*" said Low.

"His Royal Highness never pays. It's custom with him. It's rather a privilege, you see, to play golf in his company."

"Mr. Young," said George Low, the only George Low there ever was or ever will be in golf. "You take care of your railroads and I'll take care of my dukes."

Down South

---

*You'd think I'd never done anything else but hit
that shot. In the Orient for a while I became
known as Mr. Double Eagle, which nongolfers
probably took to mean that I was an Indian chief.*
— GENE SARAZEN,
*reflecting on the shot
that made the Masters*

IT is commonly known among a select group of Masters goers that many of the best shots of the tournament are served in tall paper cups on the upstairs porch of the Augusta National Golf Club. The truly great moments occur out on the course, to be sure, but you have to wait for those, and the porch outside the upper Grill Room is a very pleasant place to wait. There, one can sit where corporate insurgents sit and mill where double eagle makers mill. There too a man can listen to the Masters, not only from the logy, anecdotal mumbling around him, but from the mighty braying of the crowds in the valley below. Off on the fragrant horizon there stands a big, faintly readable leader board reacting to the roars, and near the white porchrail is a contemplative wisteria, and down on the umbrella-dotted veranda there is an ever-present cluster of Conni Venturis and Susan Marrs to holler at. In the whole Renoir of the Masters there is really no better place to await the premonition that Gene Sarazen will hole out a four-wood, or that Billy Joe Patton will slice a spoon into a creek, or that Roberto De Vicenzo will shank his scorecard.

Augusta premonitions come in several different

forms of course. It can be a whoop from up around the
8th green, where, according to one's watch, Arnold
Palmer's gallery ought to be. It can be an ominous
wailing from down near the 10th, where, perhaps Jack
Nicklaus is. It can be a series of red numbers going up
on the leader board for someone who was out of it —
say, Bert Yancey — but who now, suddenly, is back in
it. Or it can sometimes merely be an intelligence
report. A sunburned soul will hike up the stairs to
pant and puff the news that H-Hogan . . . has . . .
b-birdied four holes . . . in a r-row. J-jay and B-bee
. . . and water, please . . . t-tall . . . ice . . . t-twist
. . . aaaaaiiiii, whew.

In all of its years since the beginning in 1934,
the Masters has been a tournament of premonitions
closely followed by explosions. One simply knows that
every afternoon something cinemascopically dramatic
is going to happen, as in no other championship, for
the Augusta course is laid out to make things happen,
to entice the field into grandiose delusions. These
explosions can be of the mild kind that only make the
ice cubes swirl, but they can also be violent enough to
rattle the porch and send everyone scrambling out
onto the course like Hollywood-style Spitfire pilots
darting toward their planes.

Bobby Jones, who started the Masters, must have
had a premonition himself as long ago as 1935, the
year of his second tournament. He had played in the
event (Jones played in the Masters until 1948) and he
was in the clubhouse with most everyone else, toast-

ing Craig Wood as the probable winner, when he decided to wander out on the back nine. He wanted to watch his old friends, Gene Sarazen and Walter Hagen, who comprised the last twosome. Jones reached the 15th green just as they were nearing, Sarazen holding a remote mathematical chance to tie Wood if he could manage three birdies out of the last four holes. Some chance.

Sarazen, as he recalls, was not really thinking about making a double eagle as he stood out there in the fairway of the 15th, waggling a club, his plus-fours fluttering in the spring breeze. All he wanted to do was clear the pond in front of the green, get on in two, and score an easy birdie. Nobody ever thinks about making a double eagle except fourteen-year-old junior champions.

Sarazen lashed at the four-wood from the right side of the fairway, and the ball took off in a high, drawing arc, slightly right of the flag. He might have hit more club, a spoon or brassie, to be certain of clearing the pond, but it would not have done him much good for the shot to wind up in Savannah. The trick was to reach the green and hold it.

"There was a pause and then I heard some yells," Sarazen recalls. "I walked a few yards before I realized it had gone in and wasn't just close for an eagle. Frankly I'm tired of discussing it. You'd think I had never done anything else but hit that shot. In the Orient for a while I became known as Mr. Double Eagle, which nongolfers probably took to mean that I was an Indian chief. To me the most interesting thing about the shot is that both Jones and Hagen saw it."

Sarazen's remarkable shot did not alone win him that Masters of course. He had to par the last three holes to tie, and then defeat Craig Wood the next day in a thirty-six-hole play-off. The fact remains, however, that the double eagle has done more to publicize Augusta than all of the growing of azaleas and pruning of junipers have since. Rudy Vallee had Sarazen re-create the shot the following year for a network radio show, for example, and many a newsreel cameraman has had him trudge back to the scene. And once, in 1955, the tournament committee commemorated the event by staging a double eagle contest on Wednesday instead of a clinic (or the par-three tournament it now holds). Each member in the field took three whacks from where Gene hit the four-wood. Freddie Haas, Jr., was the winner with a shot four feet from the pin.

Few men, including Sarazen, have won the Masters under more desperate conditions than Byron Nelson did — twice. His sub-par barrages on both occasions, in 1937 and 1942, were nearly spectacular enough to make everyone forget all about double eagles. They were, in fact, memorable enough for the green-jacketed sponsors to erect a bridge in honor of his deeds at the 12th hole, a bridge similar to the one they built for Sarazen at the 15th.

The Byron Nelson of '37 was barely twenty-five years old, tall, slender, nervous and usually outfitted in starched dress shirts with the cuffs turned up twice on the order of a pharmacist. But he opened that championship with a 66, the lowest round Jones and his friends had seen in the tournament. Nelson's lead slowly dribbled away to a more experienced Ralph Guldahl, and on the last day, with nine holes to play, Byron trailed by three strokes.

Guldahl was playing one hole ahead of Nelson, who was paired with Wiffy Cox, and when Byron reached his drive down the 10th fairway it was just in time to see Guldahl take a birdie putt out of the cup. "If I don't get a birdie here, I'm four behind with only eight to go," Nelson thought to himself. "I wonder what second money is?"

Without thinking much more about his predicament than that, Nelson hit a good shot into the 10th green and saw it spin up close for a short birdie putt. He made it, and Wiffy Cox said to him, "Kid, I think that's the one we need. It'll show Ralph he can't shake you, and there are plenty of holes left."

Both men got par fours at the long, dangerous 11th, but when Nelson reached the 12th tee, the crowd, he noticed, was scurrying over to him in mad droves, jamming around him. And he thought he heard someone talking about Guldahl taking a double-bogey five on that dandy little water-logged par three.

"My adrenalin really got going," Nelson says. "I suddenly realized I'd been playing negative golf for two days." Nelson, somehow was seized by aggressiveness. He splintered the flag with a six-iron at the 12th and dropped the ten-footer for a birdie two. Wiffy Cox did a little dance.

Now, up ahead on the par five 13th, Guldahl, reeling from Nelson's pursuit, gambled on a second shot to the green, plopped it into Rae's Creek and took a bogey 6. Then Nelson, almost in a dead run, whomped a spoon over the creek and off the left edge of the green, whereupon he took a three-iron and gently chipped in a fifty-foot eagle three.

In just two holes Nelson had gone 2–3 to Guldahl's 5–6, and it was all over.

"I really didn't realize the importance of it at the time," Nelson says. "It was quite a while before I remembered I'd played the first four holes of the back nine four under. In those days, the money was the main thing, the *only* thing I played for. Titles were something to grow old with."

Five years later the Masters saw a different Nelson, this one more sophisticated, confident, popular, established, secure, already, at thirty, the holder of three major championships, those being the Masters, the 1939 U.S. Open and the 1940 PGA. He was Lord Byron, the Mechanical Man, a man obviously reaching his peak ahead of Ben Hogan and Sam Snead, who were among his contemporaries. And a handy thing it was, for only this kind of player could have defeated Hogan, another rising star from Texas, in a classic Masters.

Nelson began that tournament as if he intended to turn Augusta into a Roanoke chicken ranch, shooting

68–67 — 135, tying the thirty-six-hole record. He played ahead to 280 and what seemed like victory, but Hogan, burning inside for his first major title, made up eight strokes over the last two rounds and gained a tie. So it was Nelson vs. Hogan, a couple of old Texas pals, from the same caddy pens in fact, in a play-off. It was a Fort Worth city championship — on the road.

"Still the most vivid thing to me is that many of the players stayed over on Monday to follow us around," Nelson says.

Byron did not begin the play-off like any sort of mechanical man. He double bogeyed the 1st hole, and then bogeyed the 4th, and Hogan stepped onto the 6th tee with a three-stroke lead. But it was from this point on, through the next eleven holes, that Nelson, by his own admission, played the finest golf of his life. All he did was birdie the 6th, eagle the 8th, birdie the 11th, 12th and 13th, and play the next three holes in par. The harsh fact was that Hogan played those same eleven holes in one under par — and lost five shots, not to mention the Masters.

"The round was a little on the cool side," says Byron, who shot 69 to Hogan's 70. "I don't know that Ben and I exchanged many words. It was a big deal for both of us, naturally. The Masters was very much entrenched then as a major championship, more so than in the previous years."

As just about everyone knows who doesn't use rented clubs or tee off in sneakers, Hogan's best years were still ahead of him. He would win the Masters twice (among ten major titles in all), would finish second three more times and would post a record of never finishing worse than tenth in fourteen straight Augusta appearances. For all of this, however, Ben's finest moment came many springtimes after his prime, and it was a very moving moment for the Masters. Where were you on April 8, 1967, the day Hogan almost turned Augusta into a soap opera? If you were in warm, sunny Georgia that Saturday you must have been in Hogan's gallery on much of the last nine holes when he shot a record-equaling 30 and completed the round in 66, the lowest of the week.

Quite possibly Hogan's last nine was the most elegant shotmaking ever in a major tournament. It was certainly an amazing performance for a man only four months shy of his fifty-fifth birthday. Hogan played the nine in six birdies and three pars, without a single error in judgment or technique, without a single fairway miss or a putt of more than twenty feet in length, including the two par fives.

Soft music, please, and build that applause while the graying man in the old-fashioned white, billed cap and the pleated trousers plays it again. Let's see. There was a seven-iron into the 10th for a six-foot birdie, a six-iron into the 11th only one foot from the cup for a birdie, a six-iron onto the 12th for a ten-foot bird, a four-wood onto the 13th in two for a two-putt birdie, a five-iron onto the 14th for a par from eighteen feet, a four-wood onto the 15th for another two-putt birdie, a seven-iron onto the 16th for a par from twenty feet, a seven-iron onto the 17th for par from twenty feet and a five-iron onto the 18th for the last birdie that curled downhill and in from thirteen feet.

Ben had trudged up the last fairway to the building roar of thousands, and when the final putt dropped, the burst of joy from the great crowd must have awakened every tired body in the parking lot. It was followed by endless applause, like a marathon curtain call, and one had the feeling that even on the blasé clubhouse porch there surely couldn't be a dry eye.

For sustained whoops and hollers, and all-record-breaking in Spectator Hop, Step and Jump, no Masters has ever equaled that of 1954, in which a younger Hogan was intimately involved along with Sam Snead and a crazy, chattering North Carolina amateur, Billy Joe Patton. Those were the days when Tournament Chairman Clifford Roberts did not edit the crowds at Augusta. They were larger in the mid and late 1950's, the biggest, trompingest galleries golf has ever known. Mary Queen of Scots doing her naked dance of the rut iron (or whatever she did to get some credit for inventing the game) could not have lured more people into Augusta than the Masters had in 1954 for the Ballad of Billy Joe.

Well, it wasn't so much a ballad as it was a slapstick whodunit. Billy Joe Patton, known only around Morganton, North Carolina, tied for the first round lead, which was unreal in itself, but then he led all alone after thirty-six, and he hung in there five behind

Hogan and two behind Snead, in third place, after Saturday. Bareheaded, bespectacled, grinning, with a faster swing than a kitchen blender, Billy Joe kept the bulk of the throng enslaved with his scrambling tactics and his comments. "I may go for it, and I may not," he would drawl, addressing a shot. "It all depends on what I elect to do on my backswing."

Sundays are always psychotic at the Masters, but this one more closely resembled a South American revolution than most. Hogan and Snead, playing one hole apart, had every reason to think they were going to have their own private little tournament on Sunday, but Billy Joe, two holes ahead of them, got back in it shortly after everyone had teed off. At the 6th hole he hit a seven-iron right into the cup for the loudest hole in one in the history of Morganton, North Carolina, or Augusta, Georgia.

And all anyone could hear from the galleries during the next hour or so as Patton, Hogan and Snead began to shift the lead around, was "Billy Joe gonna do it. He gonna *do* it."

Everybody did it down around Amen Corner, the nickname for a cruel and scenic bend of the 11th, 12th and 13th holes. Snead three-putted himself to a 72 and 289, the highest total that ever looked like it might win. Hogan uncharacteristically hit an approach shot into the water at the eleventh for a double-bogey six and a 75 to tie Snead at 289. But while all this was happening and the hordes were running around like children at recess, Billy Joe threw the Masters so high in the air only the azalea goddesses knew where it would land. At a point when judicious play would have won it for him easily — laying up at 13 and 15 or sure pars in other words — Patton went for the greens on his second shots and landed in the water both times. To the complete horror of his followers he made a seven and a six on those holes for a 71 and missed tying by a stroke. Pars there would have given him 68 and a two-stroke victory.

The 13th hole provided the more important and dramatic incident, for Patton knew he was leading then, that Hogan had just made six at the 11th. He could see too, one presumed, that he had a nasty sidehill lie for his shot to the green with a three-wood. He studied the shot momentarily while the crowd shouted for him to be cautious. Then he looked over at those near him, taking a wood from the bag.

"I didn't get where I am playin' safe," he said, promptly hitting the ball right into the creek bottom bordering the green.

For a moment or two there was still a glimmer of hope for Billy Joe. Walking toward the ditch Patton heard a few frantic calls and saw some members of the gallery pointing down into the high grass below the green. They were telling him the ball had not submerged quite as deep as Conrad Veidt usually took his U-boats, that perhaps it was playable. Soggy and weed-covered but playable.

Patton removed his shoes and socks, rolled up his trousers, grabbed a wedge and climbed down into the ditch. He got set once or twice for a slash at it but finally decided, amid some nervous giggles in the crowd, that it was too risky. He could take fourteen or fifteen slashes at the ball once he got going. So he took a penalty stroke, laid out, pitched up poorly, pitched again and required two putts for his calamitous seven.

The ballad of Billy Joe ended with him sharing a cart with Clifford Roberts the next day to follow Snead's narrow play-off victory over Hogan.

"I wouldn't play it any differently," says Patton. "I was elated to play as well as I did. Going into those last nine holes I knew I had to take a pop at it. What if I'd played safe and lost? That wouldn't have answered anything. I didn't feel I had any lead at all with Hogan behind me. I'm talkin' about the Hogan of *then.* If I'd played it safe I'd always have wondered how good I really was. I'm almost delighted I lost, in fact. I might have turned pro."

The remainder of the 1950's at Augusta were not what you would term unexciting. Certainly the victories achieved by Cary Middlecoff, Jack Burke, Doug Ford, a new fellow named Arnold Palmer and Art Wall, in that order, were not without suspense and splendid play. But the Masters, like pro golf itself, was suffering a disease we might call the In-betweens. It was mourning the gradual but obvious exit of Hogan and Snead and waiting for the real Arnold Palmer.

The love affair between Palmer and Augusta actually began in 1958 when he won the first of his four Masters. He won it with his pants too long, his shirttail out and no one sure at that time whether Latrobe was in Pennsylvania or Poland. Specifically, he won it on the last day with a free lift from an imbedded lie on the 12th hole, an eagle on the 13th and some unfortunate three-putting by Ken Venturi. The affair simmered the next year, Wall's year, when it was Palmer who *lost* the tournament in the last round on the same hole, the 12th, where he had won it with the free lift. With a two-stroke lead he splashed a seven-iron into the creek and about two dozen guys up front, led by Art Wall, regarded the news so jubilantly they birdied every cup in sight, including a few paper ones.

Now, with this buildup, Palmer and the Augusta crowds were ready in 1960 to embrace one another, Swedish film style. He quickly mobilized his now famous Army with a first-round 67 and continued to lead the tournament all the way until the last thirty minutes. The charge of the Winnie brigade was on. At this point, however, Ken Venturi was in the clubhouse caressing a 283, believing he had redeemed himself for collapsing twice before when he had been close. Poor Ken Venturi. He was forced to watch a TV set while Palmer rammed in a thirty-foot birdie on the 71st and then an eight-foot birdie on the 72nd to beat him by a shot.

"I'm sitting there with the press, all pleased and comfortable," Venturi would describe it later, "and when Arnie holes the thirty-footer they leave me like I got the pox."

By 1961, of course, there was only one player in the

Masters — Arnie. The championship was his to win or lose as he saw fit. That Gary Player would have the audacity to share the lead with him at thirty-six and then to open up a four-shot bulge through fifty-four was practically unspeakable. Cries of "Get him, Arnie" echoed through the pines on Monday (Sunday's round was washed out) as Palmer set chase. There was one particularly frustrating moment for Gary as he doggedly tried to hold his lead with Arnold slowly creeping up. Bouncing down the 11th fairway, Gary looked at the big leader board and saw that the scorekeepers had posted a huge impromptu sign on it. It said GO ARNIE.

Player got home with a 74 for 280, but Arnold, working on a 69, had struggled to a one-stroke lead and when he crushed a drive up the center of the last fairway, leaving himself no more than a seven-iron to the green, the Army was ecstatic. The war had been won and they, as much as he, had won it. There were slaps on the back and long, giddy choruses of whoo-ha, Arnie.

The Army had forgotten one thing though. Palmer could go to sleep at times like these, the challenge over, the hard work done. And sleep he did on the seven-iron, which plinked off into a right-hand bunker. Well, that was all right, the Army felt. He would either get it up and down in two or take a bogey, in which case he would simply win it in a play-off the next day with a 63 to Player's 97. And then, right there, before all of those worshipping thousands and before all of the millions watching television, before Winnie and Mark McCormack and everybody, he hit a Joe Zilch out of the bunker. A Sam Sausage.

"He Dick Smithed it," a man quietly said to himself in the stunned gallery. Guy named Dick Smith.

The ball squirted across the green and sped down a far slope into so difficult an angle that no mortal could have chipped back to rescue the bogey. Palmer made six and lost another Masters.

"I guess I was in too big of a hurry to win it," Arnold said later. "Or something. Hell, I don't know what I was up to."

Palmer very nearly suffered a worse humiliation in 1962 when the Masters was all his again in tone, mood and suspense. He grabbed the lead the second afternoon with a blazing 66, tacked a 69 onto that, and although Player and Dow Finsterwald were hovering near enough to the top to cause trouble, most of the porch talk Sunday morning was all about Palmer breaking Ben Hogan's seventy-two-hole record of 274. Why not? All he needed was a piddling 68, which he could surely shoot if he had enough cigarettes with him.

Arnold didn't shoot the 68, but he came close to a 78. In one of the most curious rounds he ever played Palmer frittered away stroke after stroke until he eventually arrived at the 16th hole to find himself two shots behind Finsterwald and Player with par in for a fat 77 and with some of his Army sacrilegiously mixed into Dow's Dragoons.

Then it was like this: Ah, good, says Palmer. Are the TV cameras in focus? Swell. Flick the cigarette. Hitch the pants. And there goes a sixty-foot chip, uphill, downhill and in for a birdie deuce. On to 17. Flick. Hitch. Hitch again. And down goes a six-foot birdie putt. Play-off. Which, of course, he wins, largely with the jolt of a gimme birdie at the 12th hole, good old breezy, bitchy No. 12, Amen Corner, where he had splattered and splashed and won and lost before.

Palmer won the Masters again in 1964, but this one was more or less of a, well, porch-sitter some called it. He led all the way and finished six strokes ahead of the field. And he may win it some more. Harry Vardon, after all, won six British Opens, so there is no law against a man building up his own stockpile of particular major championships. Never again, however, will he dominate the atmosphere of Augusta as thoroughly as he did over those five consecutive years from '58 through '62. Nor does it seem likely that anyone ever can again.

If winning alone could do it Jack Nicklaus would already be there. Think about Jack for a moment. Over the past ten years as an amateur and professional he has not only taken three Masters but nine major championships in all, which is more than anyone other than Walter Hagen (11) and Bobby Jones (13) and Ben Hogan (10). Along the way one of his modest projects at Augusta in 1965 was to fire a 64, equaling a twenty-five-year-old course record, and wind up with a total of 271, seventeen under par, which broke Hogan's record by three strokes. Jack also has wavy blond hair, drives a roadster and is considered well-liked around the frat house. But what he needs for a future birthday is warmth.

Jack's problems are that he has had too much talent and maturity for his age. After all, no one can identify with a beefy rich kid who hits the ball across the state line and goes around beating Arnold Palmer all the time. The warmth is there to those who know him well, but it never transfers to the crowd. They applaud him politely, but mainly for the mechanics.

What Nicklaus *could* do some year to evoke sympathy perhaps is approve a Masters scorecard with a mistake on it and blow a championship. Had it been Jack who did what Roberto De Vicenzo did in 1968, he would have a whole new image, the Rules of Golf would still be under siege and the tournament committee would be hiding out in Pueblo, Colorado.

The 1968 Masters should have been filed away as one of the most dazzling ever played. Just about anyone in town who owned a set of clubs was in the thick of it all four days. Starting the final round, for instance, no fewer than eleven men were all within three strokes of one another, and going into the last nine holes at least six players were seriously in contention. When the day appeared to be over the following results had been produced: twenty-two players had broken par and twenty-one had finished under the par of 288 for the championship, nine more than ever

before. There had been so many red numbers (for
under par) on the leader boards it looked as if the
place had been bombed with Bloody Marys.

Hottest of all were two men who had been, possibly, the least considered as potential Masters winners: Roberto De Vicenzo, a carefree, if elderly, Latin,
and Bob Goalby, a plodding veteran of the PGA tour
whose often brilliant golf was becoming less frequent.
Roberto pitched in a wedge at the 1st hole for an
eagle two and birdied the next two holes, getting off to
the kind of start municipal hustlers enjoy when
they're betting the trailer rent. Ever smiling and looking at times quite astonished, he birdied the 8th as
well and came through the first nine in 31. Goalby
stayed close with a 33.

Roberto kept it up on the back side. He birdied the
12th and then the 15th, but Goalby birdied the 13th
and 14th, playing two holes behind him, and by now
it had come down to just these two. Then as Roberto
stood over a short birdie putt at the 17th, Goalby
addressed a fifteen-footer for an eagle at the 15th. If
both putts dropped they were tied. Both did, as one
was privileged to see on television's split screen, an
utterly delicious moment for the electronic journalists
involved. Roberto now needed par on 18 for 64 and
276, and Goalby needed pars on the last three holes for
65 and the same total.

For the next few moments, both men seemed determined to avoid a play-off. Roberto played a sick three-
iron into the 18th, bunkered it and wound up with a

bogey five and 277. Goalby, meanwhile, having parred 16 three-putted the 17th for a bogey. They were, alas, still in a deadlock — if Goalby could manage a par on the last hole. And he did so with a career two-iron from a hook lie that soared 220 yards, fading perfectly onto the green for an easy two putts.

What no one knew at the time except the Masters officials and De Vicenzo was that even as Goalby played his stirring 18th hole, Roberto had lost a stroke through bookkeeping. Tommy Aaron, his playing companion for the day, had accidentally marked down a 4 instead of a 3 at the 17th hole on his scorecard, a 35 instead of a 34 for the last nine and a 66 instead of a 65 for the round. And Roberto had hastily approved the card. The Rules of Golf state that a player's card stands as he approves it. If it is too many, that's what he gets. If it is too few, he's disqualified.

Most of the Rules of Golf, of course, were written for the days when men played in heavy tweed suits, smoked pipes on their downswings and were galleried mostly by sheepherders. But there was nothing anyone could do about it, least of all De Vicenzo, who would only say, "What a stupid I am," or poor Bob Goalby, who became a Masters champion in the most unlikely of ways since Gene Sarazen's double eagle knocked everyone off the clubhouse porch.

Each year that the Masters reemerges as such a scented and luxuriant success, it strengthens the notion that God must have been a 2-handicapper from Georgia. At least it encourages the legend of how it all seems to get started every spring: either Bobby Jones or Clifford Roberts goes outside the Augusta National clubhouse upon a certain divine morning in April, does a *verónica* with one of those green blazers and, all at once, wonders occur. Grandiloquent pines rise up. Acres of emerald turf appear. Obedient servants begin stirring around. And suddenly great swarms of happy people are encircling Arnold Palmer, who happens to be threshing about in a million or so fresh-blooming dogwoods.

But the Masters does not happen quite like this. It evolved painstakingly, building its traditions and its distinctions. It was caressed, loved, patted and prodded into shape until it finally became the most glorious scene that golf has to offer. Because it grew slowly and mellowed quietly, there is much to the Masters — and Augusta National — that goes unseen by the swarming galleries and even unappreciated by the players, who are the people this particular tournament was made for.

The town of Augusta itself is more than two hundred years old, and for most of those years it squatted in a state of semi-decay on the red clay banks of the Savannah River. It wasn't even important enough for Uncle Billy Sherman to burn down on his march toward Atlanta. And in the early days of the Masters it got to be known as a place where Georgia got even for the Civil War. Hotel accommodations were once as scarce as clean sheets. Jim Murray, the columnist, looked around his hotel room one year and wrote: "I am staying in the house on Tobacco Road that Jeeter Lester moved out of." Dining out, even today, is still the sort of treat that would put Craig Claiborne in the insurance business. Florida killed Augusta as a winter resort, which it was for a time, and nearby Fort Gordon, where the Normandy invasion troops were trained, almost killed it as anything more than the annual meeting place for the Southern Baptist Congregation of Hookers. But despite all of this it is a beautiful town, and it has endured, and for one exciting week every spring it becomes the only place in the whole world to be — to smell and enjoy the visible Masters and to feel that all around you there is another one going on.

Subtle sounds and sudden glimpses help reveal this hidden Masters. It might be the clinking of ice in a cocktail glass as a green-jacketed member moves through the white portals and multicolored umbrellas on the terrace, or a quick look toward a row of cottages along the 10th fairway, with the knowledge that one of them was built for a President. It might be the way the sun drifts through the dark row of magnolias on the avenue leading up to the clubhouse entrance, or Valerie Hogan sitting on the lawn with a handful of cables and letters of congratulation for Ben. It could be a gathering of caddies, lounging in a fenced-off yard, weary from trudging over the course's valleys and too tired to play pool at the table provided for them in the caddie house, or the clacking of typewriters from inside the massive Quonset hut that serves the press. It might be nothing more than the glow of the club at night during a private dinner of the past champions, or something as remarkably simple as a hand-lettered sign on a swinging door leading from the kitchen into a dining area called the Trophy Room where Jones's clubs are displayed on a wall, a sign that advises the waiters: PLEASE TALK JUST A LITTLE LOUDER THAN A WHISPER. Perhaps, most of all, it is a devastating orderliness and a Southern loyalty that almost hurls you back to the veranda at Twelve Oaks where the Tarleton twins are giggling with Scarlett O'Hara.

A behind-the-scenes look at the Masters can well begin with the man who put up the sign to the kitchen help, Bowman Milligan, the club steward. Bowman is a big fellow with a smudge of gray at his temples and a baritonish voice, who has probably heard his name called out more than anyone in the history of Augusta National. But unrattled and dutiful, he maintains the carriage and aplomb of one who has spent a lifetime catering to millionaires. Primarily, Bowman is in charge of hiring and overseeing the Negro employees at the club — the waiters, bartenders, chauffeurs, maids and others. But if during Masters week Claude Harmon cannot get a glass of iced tea fast enough, or if Ben Hogan does not like the look of the lettuce on his sandwich, a holler of "Bowman!" is heard, and somehow Bowman is always nearby. "I work from can't to can't," he says of Masters week. "I try to rise to the occasion. My main job is remembering — trying to remember everything there is to be done."

Bowman, whose father was a groundkeeper on the Harry Payne Whitney estate in Aiken, South Carolina, which is just across the river, came to Augusta National in 1930, before the golf course was built on some nursery land Jones had discovered. He cooked, washed dishes and shined shoes for Roberts and Jones and began to learn the things that have to be remembered for a Masters. At one point Bowman even earned himself some personal prestige by managing Beau Jack, an Augusta National shoeshine boy who fought his way to the world lightweight championship. In the old days, it is said, battle royals were staged in the ballrooms of the Bon Air Hotel for Augusta National people, affairs in which five boxers were in the ring at once, and there Bowman's Beau Jack reportedly won many a fight that does not show on his record.

Today Bowman gets into the spotlight, too, but in a different way. He is official custodian of *the* green coat, that cherished piece of either gabardine or Palm Beach fabric (the player gets his choice) that goes to the Masters champion. Those who have witnessed a prizegiving at the putting green after a Masters may have wondered about the identity of the Negro gentleman in the dark suit, the one who marched, almost to an imaginary drum roll, from the clubhouse out to the course, carrying the green jacket and handing it to the past champion who, in ceremonial turn, slipped it on the new champion. It is Bowman Milligan who carries the coat.

Augusta National did not invent the idea of wearing blazers, even green ones, but it did start the custom of presenting one to its champion, a ceremony that some other tournaments since have copied. However, in the case of the Masters, the champion may leave town, but the green coat rarely does. All the green coats are stored in lockers. There is an unwritten rule that the coats of the past champions and those of members are to be worn only at the club. No one knows exactly what would happen if a man walked into Mike Manuche's wearing his Masters coat and Cliff Roberts were there, but one hates to guess.

The green coat and the winner's check for $20,000 or so are the most publicized of Augusta's rewards to the golfers, but there are many, many others. The champion receives a sterling silver replica mounted on pine of the permanent Masters trophy. The permanent trophy is just that, permanent, principally because no one could lift it. Made in England of nine hundred separate pieces of sterling, it weighs some one hundred twenty-five pounds. The winner also gets a gold medal, a silver cigarette box and, finally, a year later at the dinner for the champions, a gold locket (Cartier) made like a book, with the club symbol — a map of the U.S. with a flagpin where Augusta might be — on the front and a photo of Bobby Jones on the inside of the back cover.

Augusta National gives away almost as many prizes as it serves thin steak sandwiches on toast, a basic part of the club menu that Jimmy Demaret once described as "the back nine of Bowman's cuisine." The pro runner-up gets a medal, the low amateur and runner-up get medals, each day's low scorer gets a Steuben crystal vase, the maker of a hole in one gets a Steuben vase, the maker of an eagle gets a Steuben highball glass, the winner of the Wednesday par-three tournament gets a silver tea service (Reed and Barton, Hampton Court design) or twelve Wedgwood bone china plates decorated with an etching of the clubhouse, the par-three runner-up gets one piece of a tea service or two plates, the third-place finisher gets two plates, and anyone who scores a hole in one in the par-three event gets six plates. There is one other prize for the competitors, which may be tougher to win than the championship, a giant Steuben bowl given for scoring a double eagle. There have been only two — Gene Sarazen's back in 1935 at the 15th hole and Bruce Devlin's in 1967 at the 8th hole.

In addition to all of the above, the Masters gives away to hundreds of officials, volunteer workers, players' wives and members of the press some different kind of remembrance each year. Almost every idea for a gift has been exhausted, but Cliff Roberts always hopes to better an ashtray, a billfold, a card case, a tool kit or whatever. It must be something green — Masters green — and monogrammed. Those are the only requirements.

One of the reasons why the Masters comes off so beautifully, no doubt, is the presence of all of the volunteer workers, who labor for a green billfold under a total of twenty-two committee chairmen. The personnel on these committees rarely changes. For instance, though it takes one hundred forty men to operate the scoreboards and bulletin boards there is rarely a turnover of more than five people. Of the one hundred twenty-five men signed up by the Gallery Guards Committee, there will be only ten or so working next year who were not working last year. The waiting list for such jobs is formidable. The volunteers are rarely Augusta National members — indeed most of them will never even get to play the course — but their loyalty and affection for the Masters seems limitless.

In a quite different way, one Augusta National member made a considerable contribution to the Masters. That was Dwight D. Eisenhower. The late President gave the tournament a lift that would be impossible to overestimate and prestige it could not otherwise have achieved. For example, several cottages seemed to have been sitting over in the woods by the 10th hole for years, but not until 1952 when some anonymous members built one for Eisenhower, which they first named "Mamie's Cabin," did cottage row become a tourist attraction for Masters spectators. It is an attraction seen only from the outside, needless to say.

There are seven cottages in all. Besides Eisenhower's and Jones's, there is Tennessee, built by a group of members from Tennessee; Firestone, which was certainly not built by Goodyear; Peek, built by a late member named Burton Peek and now owned in part by John Hay Whitney; one called Butler, the latest, built by member Thomas Butler and three friends; and one unexcitingly named Duplex, which consists of four compact, identical apartments that were originally used by the club to house guests when clubhouse space was full.

The cabins all appear to be small as one gazes at them from, say, the 10th tee, which is about as close as nonresidents ever get. Inside they are large, however, for they tumble off down a hill in the rear. Butler, the new one, has eight bedrooms on three levels, each with a bath. No one would ever really want to sneak into Butler cottage for a look around. It is, naturally, the Eisenhower cottage that attracts the gallery's attention. It is golf's equivalent of the LBJ Ranch or Bebe Rebozo's yacht.

Eisenhower's cottage is three-storied. On the main floor is Mamie's all-pink bedroom, a dressing room and bath suite, a living room with card tables, a spare suite just like Mamie's, a screened-in porch and a butler's pantry. Over a fireplace hangs a painting by Ike of the 16th hole. Eisenhower's bedroom is on the second floor along with a small office, a large paneled sitting room with more card tables and another bedroom suite. The walls are adorned with photographs of Mamie (dated from 1911 to 1928), pictures of houses the Eisenhowers have lived in at various army posts, five Remington prints and an oil by Ike of his grandson David. Naturally, David is in a golfing stance. One of the most interesting things about the cottages is that ownership did not mean exclusive use, even by Eisenhower before he died. Any of the club's accommodations are available to any member and his wife. This includes the cottages and five suites in the clubhouse. During Masters week another group is also eligible to live at the club: *amateur* participants in the tournament.

The amateur's felicity at Augusta, which certainly harkens back to Bobby Jones, is shown in another way. The week of the tournament three dinners are given for competitors. There is the one for the previous champions, which is held on Tuesday night, and one for the foreign golfers in the field on Wednesday night. But first of all, on Monday night, is a dinner given by the club for the amateurs.

Of these occasions, and, indeed, of all the things from Ike's cottage to Bowman's omniscience, nothing typifies the hidden Masters any better than the dinner for past winners, a tradition started in 1952 by Ben Hogan. No gathering in golf can rival it. On Tuesday night of Masters Week they meet in the Lower Grill Room at Augusta National — Hogan, Snead, Sarazen, Nelson, Palmer, Nicklaus and all the rest, along with Bobby Jones and Clifford Roberts, but nobody else. Absolutely nobody. This is, after all, how the Masters started, a little get-together for Bobby and his friends. A fine wine will be selected — usually a 1945 or '47

Château Lafite-Rothschild. The defending champion, who as host must also pick up the tab, will be responsible for the menu, and like as not out will come the strip steak again, hash browns and those peaches that Cliff Roberts likes. "I think Roberts owns a lot of peach orchards instead of Wall Street," Jack Burke, who won in 1956, once said.

The evening will begin with cocktails and reunions, for some of the oldtimers will just have arrived, and a thirty-minute business meeting of the Masters Club, during which a group photograph is taken, a process that shortens some tempers. Then comes the very carefully seated dinner; Hogan always in the same chair, a few others, for various reasons, always a safe distance apart. Everybody will discuss everybody's health and current activities, the defender will speak briefly and with consummate modesty about how he happened to win last year and no one has ever been able to prevent Sam Snead from telling a few hillbilly stories. Ultimately, the group will enter into a somewhat sacrilegious discussion of how the course and the tournament can still be improved. This bunker will have to go, one will say, that fairway will have to be narrowed, another will point out, this tee is too low, that one is too elevated — all of the talk being somewhat colored by personal experiences with the bunker, or what have you, involved. At some point it will certainly be mentioned, while Gary Player busily looks the other way, that there are too many foreign players in the field. It will be said that there seem to be too many amateurs. Contemplating the size of the dinner check, the defender may even decide that there are too many Masters winners.

Slowly the opinionated discussion will subside, the last bite of Nectar peach will be eaten with the last piece of Brie cheese and the group will move to the Upper Locker Room where the defender gets his money's worth, because everybody watches a movie that shows him winning the Masters last year.

By ten P.M. the bar is closing, the retired champions, with their thoughts of the past, are headed to the homes that they have rented for the week, and the younger champions with some real work ahead of them — Nicklaus, Palmer, Player — are off to reflect on their private tensions, for tee-off time is near. The Augusta National clubhouse is now strangely quiet. Only Bowman and his people are moving through it — talking, of course, just above a whisper.

The Big Window

*Mechanically everything worked fine, including the
jaws of the commentators. Cut your talk in half.
You're not saying anything interesting, anyhow.*
— FRANK CHIRKINIAN,
*at a television production
meeting during the Masters*

E XCEPT, possibly, for a handful of seminomadic qui-
nine hunters somewhere in Sumatra, just about
everybody in the world has come to realize what
American television's basic dedications are. The three
networks are very strong for the elimination of cavities
among kids, dirt among T-shirts, sweating at high
school dances, frowsy wives who can't cook, malnourished pets and freestyle burping. They are also very
strong for the advancement of better mileage, scented
breath, guava-colored jetliners, staying skinny and
tourism to places where everyone looks like Jane
Fonda. This is all terrific for the guys in the industry
who play a lot of paddle tennis and throw around
terms like "thirty-six mill" and "eighty-four thou" as if
these were towns near Old Greenwich. The time salesmen know the viewers will swing in there with whatever comes up in the big window, be it *Secret Squirrel*
or another Bette Davis smoke-a-thon. Anyhow, they
ask, what do the viewers know about love, which is
money? Don't they all have eyes like fusilli with meat
sauce, suffer from chronic neck-aches and want Walter
Cronkite for President? Don't worry about the pro-
gramming, Joe Bob. Anything sells. Let's all just phase

into "21" for the day and do a total face-down in the salad.

Fortunately for at least some of the country's nearly two hundred million dial twisters, the industry is not always so insensitive. There are instances when its thinkers will drive a root canal through the great bicuspid of Madison Avenue and put something live and in color up there in the big window — a political follies, a space shot, or, more often than those, a sports event. When it happens, and when it is done well, TV becomes the electronic pleasure pill that it should be.

One such happy occasion came about in the spring of 1966 in Augusta, at that essential American quilt-spread, the Masters golf tournament. Few annual events, sporting or otherwise, lend themselves to television quite as well as the Masters. For one thing, it is the first major outdoor sports event of the year if you agree that post-season football games really belong to another calendar. And it literally reeks with live action furnished by a pretty well-established cast: Poor Arnie, Big Jack, Black Gary, Darling Doug, Buffalo Billy. It is also accustomed to mixing in some old eagles — gray ones like Hogan and bald ones like Snead — and a variety of Chen Ching-Po's for international flavor, all of this amid the set decoration of dogwood and azaleas. The whole scene is awash with color, Augusta-CBS color, which, of course, is better than the less vivid hues of God, though perhaps not as good as NBC's.

The Masters has continually presented television

with a perfect opportunity to be a newsy, gorgeous, creative show-off, to further enhance the good images left it by, well, Edward R. Murrow's cigarette, Sid Caesar's parodies and Paddy Chayefsky's old dramas. It is, indeed, one of the prestige presentations that CBS has worked hard to keep over the years, like NFL football. Networks have an awful time establishing their identity with the viewer at home, and this kind of show helps. If you ask the average viewer, for example, to tell you the differences among the three networks, he could be hard pressed to explain that NBC is the one with Johnny Carson, Huntley-Brinkley and a lot of funerals, that ABC is the one with the Olympics interspersed by demolition derbies, and that CBS has Cronkite, the war in Vietnam, the NFL and the Masters.

Doing the Masters or any other tournament right is never easy, and not at all what the viewer might imagine — a lone cameraman bounding along a fairway with the equipment on his back and a commentator looking more tanned than usual in the giddy social whirl of the 18th green. To come out with the splendid show CBS did in 1966 required ten years of bungling, worry, argument, mechanical refinement, thought and invention. To be specific, it took months of planning, 150 men, 15 cameras, a bastion of giant trailer trucks, 60,000 feet of underground cable and $600,000.

What this produced was a record four and a half hours of live color coverage that began with Saturday's third round of play and did not end until late Monday evening when Jack Nicklaus won his play-off victory. It is well that this television effort was closely observed, for it has not been equaled since, artistically or journalistically, where electronic golf coverage is concerned.

Backstage at that Masters was a sort of athletic event of its own, a week of flickering madness in the control truck when the show was beaming out to millions, and of bizarre hilarity practically everywhere else, and all of it rotating around a producer-director named Frank Chirkinian, who will slowly emerge as the hero of this story.

The week started, as most weeks do for TV, with a lot of worry — terrible, grave worry. Let's pick up our CBS executives now on the veranda of the Augusta National clubhouse where they are worrying. There they are, all dressed in their dark blue blazers with crests, looking something like a haggard group of AAU officials trying to figure out why amateur athletes take cash under the table. They are concerned about the opening of their show, the fact that it is being written and rewritten, approved and unapproved, and criticized by everyone in town. They are also uneasy about the man who will do the opening on tape.

Their situation takes some clearing up. CBS had agreed to a request by Tournament Chairman Clifford Roberts that each day's telecast would begin with a solemn opening. They had also agreed that the introduction would not only set a prestigious mood, but it would state the fact that there would be a reduced number of commercials in tribute to the importance of the event. Clifford Roberts, of course, is a lifelong friend of Bobby Jones and the man who runs the Masters like Napoleon ran France. Reducing the number of commercials was his idea. No one ever ignored a Clifford Roberts idea, least of all CBS.

When Roberts had first asked the show's sponsors, Travelers Insurance and Arrow Shirts, for fewer commercials, an agency man in New York had said, "What does he think the Masters is, a moon shot?"

The answer was no. Clifford Roberts thought the Masters was infinitely more important than that.

Roberts did manage to get five commercials sliced from the scheduled two days of telecasting — a feat, some said, that was comparable to Bobby Jones winning the Grand Slam. But the tournament chairman also felt that this fact should be announced before and after each show by someone outside the realm of sport. A Walter Cronkite, perhaps. Or a Dwight D. Eisenhower.

For a while, no one involved could think of a satisfactory person. Cronkite and Eisenhower were unavailable. So were George Washington, Abraham Lincoln and Thomas Jefferson. Finally someone in New York decided on a different tack and suggested Ed Sullivan to Clifford Roberts.

"Ed Sullivan!" Roberts reportedly bellowed. "If we

wanted anybody from show business, we could get Randolph Scott."

The man finally suggested by CBS and approved by Roberts was a fellow named Jim Jensen from the WCBS-TV news staff in New York. Roberts had seen him and liked him on the screen in New York. Jensen had a convincing manner and sincere tone and he was handsome in a dignified way. Ah, but the opening. Somehow, in the editing by Roberts and his assassins and by ad agency writers and CBS writers, Jensen wound up identifying himself on the tape as a "news correspondent."

Now that may seem accurate enough to outsiders, but in television there is an important distinction between a correspondent and ordinary Earth people. A correspondent is most properly a man over in Vietnam eyewitnessing assaults on poppy fields, or, at the very least, a familiar face famed for discoursing on vital events. Jensen, whether Masters officials realized it — and CBS was afraid to ask — was a *local* news announcer. This meant that the peak of his journalistic success might involve a description of traffic problems on the Long Island Expressway during a blizzard.

Now, back on the Masters veranda, one could naturally understand the genuine distress among CBS executives. If they asked to edit the word "correspondent" from Jensen's opening by having him retape it, Roberts might get the idea that Jensen wasn't big enough to be doing it, and he might ask to edit five more commercials. On the other hand, with Jensen, through no fault of his own, falsely identifying himself, the phone would be sure to ring at Masters control, and it would be Jack Schneider wanting to know what was going on. Bill MacPhail, the vice-president in charge of sports, would have to take the call, and he didn't really *need* a call like that from Schneider, who is the boss of everyone at CBS except William Paley and Dr. Frank Stanton.

Finally, as they all stood around, Frank Chirkinian said, "Bill, just tell Schneider that Cliff Roberts promoted Jensen."

Chirkinian was not overly worried about the Jensen dilemma. Jensen could introduce himself as Nancy Dickerson and it would be all right with Frank. The producer-director was far more concerned with the camera angles, the audio, and the velvet words that would fill the tense hours of live coverage when the show went on the air.

Bill MacPhail, a gentleman at all times, finally sighed and said, "This is serious and I think worthy of a cocktail."

CBS Sports Director Jack Dolph, who was sort of a self-appointed vice-chairman to MacPhail in charge of Augusta Worry, agreed. So did others. Chirkinian said, "Go ahead. If I wanted a drink, I'd go get Randolph Scott."

Chirkinian, who had long been acknowledged as the best golf director in television, one who had been responsible for all kinds of innovations, proceeded to stroll away, doing one of his favorite things. He sang a parody.

> *You take Lionel, and I'll take Jay.*
> *You take Marty — and I'll take Ed.*
> *Hebert, Hebert.*
> *Furgol, Furgol.*
> *Let's call the Masters off.*

That evening the problem of the program opening and other assorted worries were temporarily put aside, and the elite guard of CBS turned to something of a more pressing nature — its annual, underground Calcutta pool on the tournament. It was held in one of the six sumptuous homes in Augusta that the network rents during Masters Week. It was staged in the house Chirkinian lived in with his close associates and commentators.

The evening began with all of Chirkinian's invited guests mixing several dozen drinks for themselves and tearing into a large ham on the drainboard in the kitchen and then collapsing on the living room carpet, in sofas and chairs and against the wall paneling. Chirkinian and MacPhail decided to take turns auctioneering — selling the players — and Bill Brendle, CBS's publicity director, would do his best to keep the books.

"It might be a little hard for Brendle to write with a drink in each hand," said Chirkinian.

Frank kept up a steady stream of comedy as he sold the top contenders individually.

"What am I bid for Arnold Palmer?" he would say. "I understand he's divorcing Winnie and smoking pot now. What am I bid?"

When Palmer sold for about $500, Chirkinian said, "He's a good buy. I spoke to him today in the hospital. He doesn't think that fall he took off the twelfth tee will bother his swing at all."

As the players were sold, one by one, there would be occasional shouts from the floor.

"Fifteen hundred for Conni Venturi," somebody said.

"That's too much for Ken," said Frank.

"I don't want Ken. I want Conni," the voice said.

Fields were available to the buyers. You could purchase a dozen Dudley Wysongs, say, with a Terry Dill thrown in, for only five dollars. A couple of visitors, being somewhat less than golf-wise, refused to believe that there were any golfers named Cobie LaGrange or Ed Tutwiler in the field.

In the end MacPhail and Jack Dolph were the most active bidders, and later on they had the foggy recollection that they had managed to buy almost everyone, including, they feared, Randolph Scott.

Thursday, the day of the tournament's first round, was important to CBS for two reasons. First, there was to be a complete dress rehearsal, "full fax," they call it, which in television means complete dress rehearsal. Secondly, MacPhail and Dolph had to go to the airport to greet an assortment of brass from New York which included Jack Schneider, John Reynolds, then the president of CBS-TV, and a sales vice-president, Ted O'Connell. The brass had to be taken to the club and impressed by the fact that the veranda was literally teeming with hosts of corporate celebrities.

After the rehearsal Frank Chirkinian held a massive production meeting in a downstairs room of one of the clubhouse cottages to remind everyone that they weren't getting ready to do *Supermarket Sweep* come Saturday. He had not especially liked the rehearsal.

"Mechanically, everything worked fine," he said, "including the jaws of the commentators. Cut your talk in half. You're not saying anything interesting anyhow."

The crew of commentators included Jack Whitaker, CBS's most knowledgeable and presentable talent, at the 18th green, Jack Drees and Byron Nelson at the 17th, Henry Longhurst, the noted British writer, at the 16th, John Derr at the 15th, and Cary Middlecoff down in a clubhouse basement. Middlecoff's job down there was to deliver expertise while staring at hole diagrams, stop-action, or the tournament in progress through a contraption called the TNT Eidophor, a special projection device that provides a screen within the screen and can be clearly explained only by the Swiss scientist who invented it.

When Chirkinian concluded what he called his "harpoon-the-commentators" meeting, he asked if there were any problems or questions anyone cared to bring up.

"No, I don't think so," said Jack Whitaker. "Now

that my morale is destroyed, I'll just leave. If you'll excuse me, I'm taking Dr. Zhivago's calls tonight."

Jack Dolph said he did not want to frighten the crew unnecessarily, but he had received word that the Scotch tape, rubber bands and paper clips had been lost.

"You jest," said Chirkinian.

"I jest not," Dolph said. "You ready? They were shipped to Nevada."

Chirkinian dropped his head and then spoke quietly to the room.

"Gentlemen, for the first time in the history of this network, we're going to do a show *without* Scotch tape, rubber bands and paper clips."

Thursday evening was devoted to that fine old American pastime of tension-relieving. The directors, commentators and brass split in all directions, making the rounds of the private parties that are a feature of Masters Week. A few dropped by a house that had been rented by Bedford Wynne, one of the owners of the Dallas Cowboys and found Wynne cooking steaks in the backyard for a small group of one hundred. Just down the street others went to a similar party being given by the Atlanta Falcons. Most people went to both, doing some fancy hedge-hopping with their drinks.

"I thought this was a golf tournament, not an NFL convention," said Ted O'Connell.

Before the night was over, several of the group wound up at what passed for the late, late show in

Augusta that spring. It was a place called the Key Club. A members-only cocktail lounge — you joined by walking in — it offered a number of treats, namely a combo that could play guitar louder than the siege of Vicksburg, an incredibly lucky blackjack dealer, enough noncoms from nearby Fort Gordon to invade Normandy again, and scads of painted, gum-chewing ladies barely out of their teens.

Someone had insisted on taking Jack Schneider there. It was part of the flavor of the town he ought to see, this being his first trip to the Masters. Having just recently recovered from the unflattering publicity that accompanied Fred Friendly's resignation as head of CBS News, Schneider gazed around the room and said, "Well, here I am. Where's the *Daily News* reporter?"

Friday's dress rehearsal went well, considering the hangovers, and Chirkinian's production meeting afterward reflected this. Frank strolled in good-humoredly, working up a new parody to the Roger Miller tune "Engine, Engine Number Nine." He sang:

> *Clifford, Clifford, Number Nine,*
> *Your old dogwood doin' fine.*

The producer-director made only a few small points. Jay Hebert's name was misspelled on the scoreboard in Middlecoff's basement — the scoreboard that would be superimposed on the live screen.

"Jay Hebert's name is always misspelled," said

Dolph. "We've tried to get him to change it to Herbert."

There had been a little too much talking over the intercom, Frank said. "Let there be one leader." He asked around if Jack Schneider had enjoyed himself and did anyone know when the big boss was heading back to New York? Schneider had left, someone said.

"Kid never did have stamina," said Frank.

Chirkinian went on to say that he hoped there would not be too many green jackets — Masters committeemen — in the control truck tomorrow to tell him all about the mistakes he was making. And finally he announced that the show would begin thirty minutes before air time so they would all have a flying start and be warmed up.

"That's about all," he said. "Good luck tomorrow, and since I'm going back in the dry-cleaning business, let's win this one for me, okay?"

Frank Chirkinian looks almost like Hollywood's conception of a TV director. He is a natty little man, dark-complexioned, with black, wavy hair, horn-rimmed glasses, alligator loafers, jazzy clothes and a 10-handicap. This would be his eighth straight Masters production for CBS. His earlier training had not been in sports. A native of Philadelphia, he had been in the army, done a year at Penn and two years at Philadelphia's Columbia Institute. In Philadelphia he had directed just about everything possible — musicals, news, drama, public affairs, variety and circuses. Along the way to CBS in New York, he had become a golf nut, and this had certainly shown in his work at Augusta as well as on the *CBS Golf Classic*, the best of the canned golf shows.

Chirkinian's job at Augusta was far from enviable. Few creatures, electronic or otherwise, are more imposing than a TV control truck. The one at this Masters was a blinking monster of fourteen screens, large and small, color and not, of live pickup, videotape and stop-action. Frank's job was to watch them all simultaneously while keeping in constant touch with commentators, assistant directors and technicians on his headset, and select which of the different shots to put on the air.

Physically, the network's setup as air time approached for Saturday's one-hour show on the third round was this: Chirkinian was at his table in what television romantically calls the hot truck. He was seated between an assistant director, Roland Vance, and a technical director, Sandy Bell, whose job was to punch a button when Frank said "Take one" or "Take three" or whatever picture he wanted on the huge panel before him. Also in the truck was Lou Scanna, the engineer in charge of the whole rig-up, the man mainly responsible for all of the plugs being in their sockets, the strewn cable and so on, and one of the few men in the world who knew how a person got a picture on his screen at home. MacPhail and Dolph were present, of course, to worry.

Another big truck was situated down near the 16th green, and squeezed in there were Bob Dailey, a fine director in his own right who rates up there with Chirkinian, CBS's Tony Verna and ABC's Malcolm Hemion and Andy Sidaris, as the elite of sports directors. Dailey was acting as Frank's assistant. It was his job to punch up the action from the 15th, 16th and 17th holes as best he saw it, and ride shotgun on the commentators at those locations. The commentators — talent, they are called, perhaps because they earn eighty-four thou a year — were all on their towers in their blazers, and Middlecoff was in his basement, frequently saying to Frank, "I'm here if you need me, Doll."

As show time drew close Chirkinian sat calmly calling up test shots — the scoreboard, Jack Whitaker, various greens, competitors walking along fairways, the gallery.

"Fellows," said Chirkinian in his headset, "let's remember to keep sight reference at all times, and keep silent on the shots. We've got these tees and fairways miked for audio, so I want to hear it when they swing."

He glanced at one of the screens and noted that a cameraman had playfully trained his lens on a shapely, bell-bottomed spectator.

Frank cupped his hands and called out, "Barr-a-cuda!"

Bill MacPhail got nervous and left the truck to step next door to a VIP trailer and get a Coke, and when he returned he asked Frank if he was happy with the opening that Whitaker had been rehearsing earlier in the day.

"The gray eagle will be fine," said Chirkinian. "I'll stick some spurs in him just before we go on, anyhow."

Dolph, trying to think of something useful to do, leaned forward and reminded Chirkinian that he should use as much stop-action stuff as possible because Paley liked it.

"Paley who?" said Frank, without turning around.

Just then Roland Vance, earphones on, stopwatch uplifted, papers spread out before him, announced that it was just seven minutes to go. At about the same time the truck door opened and several CBS friends invited themselves in to stand in the back. They were Dave Marr and his wife, Susan, and Charley Conerly, the ex-Giant quarterback, and his wife, Perian, a pretty plantation owner from Houston named Eloise Rowan, Jerry Danford, then a salesman for WCBS-TV, and Bill Brendle, the publicity man, who began taking drink orders.

"What's the story on the bigger truck we ordered?" Dolph cracked.

With everyone crammed in Chirkinian lit his ninety-seventh cigarette of the day, sat up a little straighter in his chair, adjusted his headset like a bomber pilot engaging some flak and said that great thing that TV people enjoy saying so much.

"One and a half 'til air," he said.

As Roland Vance started to wave his arms and shuffle his papers, Chirkinian began talking to his crew. "Whit, we've got a hell of a tournament. The scores are close. Everybody's in there with a shot at it — Palmer, Nicklaus, all the big guys . . . Hey, you

fellows downstairs! I want that scoreboard up to date
right now. . . . Get the stop-action ready. . . .
We'll get into that pretty quick, Cary. . . . Bobby,
your guys all set? . . ."

Vance practically shouted, "Ten seconds! Stand by."

Chirkinian relaxed and spoke quietly. "Good luck
everyone, and good show."

"Roll Augusta music," cried Vance.

Suddenly on the big color screen surrounded by all
of the smaller screens in the truck, there was Jim
Jensen and what might have been a wisteria behind
him. It was the taped opening.

"Good afternoon," said he. "I'm CBS News correspondent Jim Jensen. Because of the importance of
the program you are about to see, it is being brought
to you with a reduced number of commercials,
and . . ."

Jensen concluded the opening with the line that
was a cue for Jack Whitaker to take it live. "May you
enjoy the show you are about to see," he said.

"We're on!" shrieked Vance.

"Go, Jack," said Chirkinian. "Go, Babe."

Jack Whitaker took over, and in his distinctive,
elegant style began bringing the tournament into
focus. Nicklaus had led the first round. Paul Harney
and Peter Butler had taken over the second day, and
now, today, the big guns were making a move.

Just then, a knock came on the door of the control
truck and Yvonne Connors, a CBS secretary from the
VIP trailer, poked her head in. She said that Bill

MacPhail was wanted on long distance. It was Jack Schneider back in New York.

"Oh, Christ," said MacPhail, getting up.

"Where do you want the body shipped?" said Dolph.

MacPhail, who is a member of the very famous baseball family, returned in a few minutes looking as if he had just heard a rumor that Mickey Mantle's hobby was needlepoint. He smiled weakly and sat down. "Guess what Schneider wanted?" he said.

"I'm sure he didn't want to know why Jensen called himself a correspondent," said Dolph.

MacPhail said, "I just told him it was a conspiracy involving some foreign powers and the CIA would furnish us all with a full report later."

Back on the panel of screens the tournament was beginning to tighten up. The leaders were creeping into view in this corner and that. This is when a director ages. He is likely to have two or three key dramas at hand, and, of course, he can only show one at a time. The trick is knowing the sport and the tendencies of the athletes — exactly how long Nicklaus will take on a putt, when Palmer will stop hitching his trousers and hit a drive, how much study Sanders will give to a chip shot.

Chirkinian seemed to be doing remarkably well in spite of the periodic irritant of Roland Vance shouting something like, "Two minutes past ideal commercial."

To Bob Dailey, the assistant director in the truck down at the 16th Chirkinian said, "Better whip your boys a little, Bobby. They're dragging along, and this is pretty exciting."

Frank went to Whitaker.

"A little more schmaltz, Jack, on the closeness of the race." Frank then dramatized his voice and slowly, mimickingly said, "You could cut the tension here with a hot butterknife."

Dolph and MacPhail let out a whoop.

"It's the wide world of Jim McKay," said Dolph.

Now a crucial moment approached. Jack Nicklaus had come to the 18th tee and Arnold Palmer was back on the 16th, both of them struggling to catch the current leader, Gay Brewer, Jr. The audio picked up a devastating whack as Nicklaus drove into the woods. The camera caught Palmer's shot biting into the 16th green and curling toward the flag.

Palmer striding onto the green made a spectacular image in color, and Bob Dailey had it. Somehow the lighting on Palmer, the emerald turf mingling with the shade of the pines and the pond and the flowers in the background combined to represent, in Chirkinian's mind, everything the Masters was.

"Look at that Picasso!" said Frank. "Good shot, Bobby."

The producer-director's ecstasy was interrupted by Yvonne Connors again rapping on the truck door and peeking in.

"I don't know what to do," she said. "Mr. Roberts just called and said the TV set in his cottage isn't working right and he wants somebody over there to fix it *immediately.*"

"Terrific," said Chirkinian, glued to his screens.

MacPhail looked at Dolph. Dolph looked at Mac-Phail. They both turned and looked at Lou Scanna, the chief engineer, as if to ask if he had a screwdriver. "Yeah, yeah," said Lou, getting up. He edged toward the door, poked his head out and called to a technician. "Hey, uh, somebody go over to Roberts's house and kick the set or something," he said.

Jack Nicklaus at the moment was having worse problems. He was virtually out of sight in the woods at the 18th fairway. Middlecoff's voice then came into the truck. "Frank," he said. "We're gonna *have* to get big Jack in those woods. This is a real important shot."

"Thanks a lot, Doc," said Frank. "I'll see if I can hit a couple of trees with Armenian lightning."

As Nicklaus thrashed around in the woods Palmer was preparing to putt for his birdie at the 16th and Chirkinian stood up.

"Need a little luck here, babies," he said.

Palmer stroked the putt. "Whit, throw it to sixteen," said Frank. The ball rolled toward the hole. "Ready two, and open the fairway on eighteen," he said. "Take two." Nicklaus slashed from the woods, and Palmer's ball neared the cup. "Take remote." Palmer's putt narrowly missed. "Take three." Nicklaus's ball bounded into a bunker. "Take remote." Palmer grimaced. "Gimme a closeup, Bobby." Nicklaus emerged from the woods. "Take one." And Chirkinian sat down.

It had been only thirty seconds of show-biz torture but an excellent moment in good production.

When CBS did its first Masters in 1956 it used only six cameras, all of them trained on the greens, and Bud Palmer was the lone commentator sitting on the 18th and describing the other holes from a monitor. Chirkinian encouraged making it a more sophisticated production his first year, which was 1959.

At that Masters CBS increased the number of cameras to 12, and Frank deployed them so that fairways and tees could be shown, and he upped the number of commentators to three. A year later he began miking the tees and greens. Conduits were put underground to eliminate the cables stretched everywhere for Arnie's Army to trip over. Frank also devised the plus-minus cumulative scoring system that Clifford Roberts himself adopted for the big leader boards (red for under and green for over par). By 1965 Frank had fifteen cameras, helicopter footage, hole diagrams, videotape reruns, stop-action, the TNT Eidophor, more commentators and improved camera positions. And he now had a dedicated, experienced crew.

Everyone thought the Saturday show was beautiful, and with a certain amount of justification, the evening was once again devoted to tension-relieving. There was not so much moving around, however. A couple of downtown bars were visited, but the hard core of tension relievers flopped down in the MacPhail-Dolph-Brendle house, or P. J. Clarke's South as it came to be called, for a fine-old-fashioned dinner of fried chicken and Scotch. It was there that Jack Whitaker and a writer friend who had been loitering around all week completed a parody they had been working on as a tribute to Chirkinian. It would become the underground Masters theme song for the next few years.

To the tune of Steve Allen's *This Could Be the Start of Something Big*, it went:

> *You're walking around the course,*
> *You're on the veran-da.*
> *You're looking for Chen Ching-po,*
> *Or Cobie LaGrange.*
> *You're looking for Downing Gray,*
> *Terry Dill or Rod Funseth, say,*
> *This could be the Masters in the spring.*
>
> *You're standing on seven-teen,*
> *You're up on a tower.*
> *You're looking for Up-de-graff,*
> *Tutwiler or Hunt.*
> *When there in a fair-way dance,*
> *You come upon Lion-el Platts,*
> *This could be the Masters in the spring.*
>
> *With Randy Glover,*
> *You discover,*
> *It's a thrilling day.*
> *And Har-old Henning is the nicest guy.*
> *And Peter Alliss, Michael Bon-al-lack and Dicky Sikes,*
> *With Ramon Sota will be pass-ing by.*
>
> *You're walking around the course,*
> *You're on the veran-da.*
> *You're looking for Chen Ching-po or Cobie LaGrange.*

If you wander all eight-teen holes,
Maybe you will find Neil C. Coles,
This could be the Masters — oh, yes,
This could be dis-astrous — oh, yes,
This could be the Masters in the spring.

On Sunday CBS had the telecast scheduled for an hour and a half but, unlike the old days, it was geared to stay on, hang the expense, until the Masters had a champion. Not too many years ago TV had a habit of bidding farewell to the excitement when its allotted hour was up, and if Sam Snead happened to be bent over a putt for a possible win, that was tough luck.

"We're different now," MacPhail explained Sunday morning. "We're cleared to run over into prime time if we have to. And if there's a play-off on Monday, we'll be here. In fact if there's a sudden death after the play-off Frank thinks we could cover it remote." MacPhail wasn't sure how — perhaps with Whitaker snapping Polaroid shots from a golf cart and Frank preempting Cronkite's news to show the stills. Talk of sudden death made MacPhail sick to his tum tum.

The program opened Sunday with the same dramatic count-down procedures of the day before. A couple of new spectators were in the hot truck, each of them wearing a green jacket. They were crouched down near Chirkinian, presumably to see to it that CBS didn't screw up anything.

"Do they know anything about television production?" someone discreetly asked Jack Dolph.

"Taught Chris Schenkel everything he knows," smiled Jack.

Things went along in an orderly fashion for a while, but then the Masters burst apart with the excitement that it always seems to provide on Sundays. Gay Brewer's lead was far from secure. Tommy Jacobs had moved up to contend. Nicklaus still had a chance. So did Palmer.

Feeling the drama, Chirkinian's voice began to pick up some emotion and strain that it had not previously shown. A delicate ear detected something of a bark. Buzzing Bob Dailey, he said, "Let's drive these commentators a little, Bobby. The players are nervous. There's tension out there. This is the big one."

There was frantic activity everywhere on the closing holes. Nicklaus birdied the 14th, Jacobs birdied the 15th, and when Brewer could only make a par at the 17th, there was the distinct possibility of a three-way tie. Chirkinian leaped up and clapped his hands during all this, and, coming back down, he remembered that he had alerted Whitaker to make a specific point about something or other. But he had now forgotten what.

"Just vamp, Jack," said Frank. "Go."

Whitaker vamped about tension, azaleas, Bobby Jones, Augusta, the veranda, and seemed about to launch into a soliloquy on the old open-cockpit days of aviation when Chirkinian rescued him.

Tighter grew the tournament. Palmer blew a short putt on the 17th, and fell out of it. But Gay Brewer now came up the 18th fairway to a seven-foot putt for a par that might lock up the championship.

"This is it, Doll," said Middlecoff over the intercom.

Chirkinian said to Whitaker, his anchor man, "This is it, Jack. This is the most important putt of Gay Brewer's life."

And Whitaker said to Videoland, "This is the most important putt of Gay Brewer's life."

If it was, that was too bad, for Brewer missed the putt. He was thus in a tie with Tommy Jacobs, and Nicklaus, too, could tie if he could manage pars on the last two holes. Jack played deliberately, just missing a short birdie at the 17th and driving safely off the 18th tee.

"I want to really hear that sound," said Frank, getting poised for his big finish. "When Jack comes up the fairway near the green, I want to hear the crowd. I want some emotion. This is a hell of a finish . . . This guy may birdie the hole, and I want a reaction . . . *I* may have a reaction . . . Who's got Nicklaus in the pool, anyhow? . . ."

Nicklaus had a tremendously long birdie putt on the 18th for a win, and it seemed that a play-off was assured, but Chirkinian wanted a buildup.

"Jack," he said. "There's Brewer and Jacobs, watching from the edge of the green. They have no other recourse but to watch, right? . . . Wait! Don't repeat that crap."

Frank, giggling at himself, wheeled in his chair

toward MacPhail and Dolph. "My resignation will be on your desk tomorrow morning," he said.

Nicklaus rapped a fine putt that came down from the back of the green and curled slowly toward the cup, dying away just at the lip, amid Chirkinian's chaotic shouts of, "Take one, take five, take three," and the agonizing groan of the gallery on the audio.

Whitaker rapidly did a résumé and a wrap-up and the show signed off, and Dolph spoke for everyone in the truck when he said, "I don't suppose we'd do anything like have about nine thousand cocktails?"

Compared to the roaring finish of the previous day, Monday's play-off was tame. The network managed to make the most of it though. Nicklaus was pretty much in command by the time they came on the air. Jacobs was hanging in with a chance, but Gay Brewer had played like Chirkinian. The show had some fill in it — a lot of taped replays of Sunday action, and some Middlecoff lectures on big Jack's swing. But it worked all right.

At one point, Chirkinian got annoyed at a couple of camera shots. One had been an intimate closeup of a spectator's hand. "What's *this*? Frank said in the headset. "I want Jacobs and you gimme a *hand*?" Another time, a green-jacketed official had marched out in the center of the 17th fairway, right in front of a camera, and obscured Nicklaus from view. "That's it, that's it," said Chirkinian. "You and me, Mr. Green Coat, we'll swing along down to Wall Street together."

There was only a dim chance that Jacobs could

make up enough strokes on Nicklaus to force a sudden-death play-off, but Lou Scanna had put in motion the sudden-death preparations, just in case, when Nicklaus and Jacobs had been tied through nine holes. Now he had a question.

"Frank, is sudden-death canceled?" he asked.

Chirkinian roared with laughter, and the hot truck gently swayed.

"Lou, you're beautiful," he said.

"Well *is* it?" said Scanna. "My guy's on the headset and he says it's not only getting dark out there, they've taken out the pins everywhere and they're watering the greens."

The truck exploded with laughter again.

"That's the bottom line," said Dolph. "That's the merciful ending we've been waiting for."

Had Nicklaus not maintained his lead and won the 1966 Masters, it would surely have been the most fascinating sudden-death in golf history. It would have been played Tuesday morning, and CBS could have done it as a two-minute commercial on a *Leave It to Beaver* rerun.

Several weeks later, after all concerned had recovered from the battleground that was Augusta, Frank Chirkinian was in Toots Shor's one evening and happy as an Armenian dry cleaner who had discovered the white knight. He had accepted an Emmy award for CBS sports. It had not been won for the Masters — which was a shame — but for the·CBS *Golf Classic*.

And the awards committee had also presented an Emmy to NBC and ABC sports. A three-way tie, like the Masters had been. Still it was an Emmy.

"Who'll ever know?" said Frank. "Anyhow it doesn't look bad on the hood of the car."

Wide Open

I'm gonna be a Spaniard instead of a Mexkin as soon as I get some more money.
        — LEE TREVINO,
        *on the eve of winning the U.S. Open
        championship*

SUPER MEX is what he called himself. Super Mexkin. A laughing tub of enchiladas in bright red socks with a caddy-hustler's game from Dallas. That was Lee Trevino. Then came the cross-handed sergeant, Orville Moody, who had a name like a bowler or a dragstrip mechanic and who didn't even have a hometown to be poor from. Just Sergeant Moody from fourteen years of Fort Hoods and Koreas. And, suddenly, there they were, implausibly and inconceivably, out there among the striped ties and gold pins, the blue coats and armbands, enhancing the tradition of the Nobody in that incorrigible old shrub-judging and weed-stomping contest known as the United States Open Golf championship. Gentlemen, play away. Mexkin, play away. Sergeant, hit it.

Here was the Open, as it is so simply known, almost seventy years old as it neared the end of the 1960's, crammed with all the class and propriety, the crustiness and aplomb that men like Bob Jones and Ben Hogan, like Harry Vardon and Gene Sarazen, like Jack Nicklaus and Arnold Palmer, had given it. Here was the Open, exaggerated into the greatest tournament in the world, played from year to year on only

the most aristocratic and brutal courses, offering a
title which guaranteed a wealth and fame that no
other golfing event could match. But there came these
two Nobodies, this Mexkin at Oak Hill in Rochester in
1968 and then this sergeant at Champions in Houston
in 1969, serving as a reminder that the Open is for *all*
the people and that somebody must have been right a
long time ago when he said that nobody wins the
Open, it wins you.

Before the Mexkin and the sergeant most enthusi-
asts of the game thought they knew what the Open
was supposed to be. Some club named Oak-something
got doctored up to look like a Scottish moor, a group
of men who looked like delegates to a world money
conference moved onto the veranda, a flag went up
and Ben Hogan won for the two dozenth time while
Sam Snead lost again. Before Hogan it was always
Jones. And after Hogan it was a blend of Boroses,
Caspers, Middlecoffs, Nicklauses and Palmers. Some-
bodies.

Oh, of course, there would be these metaphysical
years now and then when players with names like Lee
Mackey, Bob Gajda, Bobby Brue, Rives McBee, Les
Kennedy and Al Brosch would seize the first round
lead or shoot a course record the second day. But they
would follow up those rounds with characteristic 91's
and return to their club jobs back in Willoughby,
Ohio. A couple of them *had* won, as Sam Parks, Jr.,
did in 1935 at Oakmont and as Jack Fleck did in 1955
at Olympic, but those occasions were so rare that they

were written off as the natural catastrophes that occur to any lasting institution. A catastrophe every twenty years is not so bad. Even a little quaint.

Thus, one got used to an Open and knew exactly what to expect of it. Every year in mid-June didn't we read stories something like the following:

OPEN FIELD MAY REVOLT

OYSTER BISQUE, N.Y. — A glittering field on the eve of the National Open golf championship agreed today that there is so much exotic plantlife bordering the narrow fairways of historic old Baltus Oak Country Club that only a malnourished hippie could walk down the middle of them without snagging his britches.

During today's final warm-up round two foursomes actually got lost in the foliage of the back nine holes and wound up at a Southampton lawn party.

Gardner Dickinson, chairman of the PGA tournament players committee, said he was withdrawing from the championship because he had never learned how to hit golf shots out of waist-high asparagus.

The irate Dickinson said, "If this kind of thing doesn't stop we might not have a spot on the tour for the USGA next year. The sponsors may have the tents, but the players have the dog acts."

UNKNOWN LEADS OPEN

OYSTER BISQUE, N.Y. — Jesse Ray Rives, an unheralded driving range pro from Hoot, Utah, grabbed the opening round lead in the National Open here today with a sizzling even-par 70 on historic old Baltus Oak, the course where Bobby Jones first wore knickers.

Rives, who wore coveralls and a straw hat with a band on it which said "Root for Hoot," birdied the first nine holes and blew out a full row of lights on the IBM scoreboard, and although he bogeyed the entire back side for a 44, his score held up against an array of glamorous challengers.

Incredibly, Rives took only six putts for the round, tying a record set by Bob Rosburg. He tied another Open record held by Don January when he holed out eight sand wedges.

Rives, 25, said he would feel better about his chances if he weren't so lonely so far away from home. "I wisht my uncle Clyde and my pet bobcat was here," he said.

OPEN JOLTED BY SECOND MYSTERY MAN

OYSTER BISQUE, N.Y. — R. J. (Bo) Mackey, an obscure pro at a putt-putt course in Clump, Calif., seized the halfway lead in the National Open here tonight when he added a 65 to his first-round 81 for a 36-hole total of 146, only 6 over par on historic old Baltus Oak, the course where Walter Hagen had his first hangover.

Having teed off at 5:14 A.M., Mackey was one of the day's early finishers at 4 o'clock in the afternoon as the field of 150 moved along briskly despite the 101-degree heat. Sweating out his lead in Baltus Oak's non-air-conditioned clubhouse, Mackey had some anxious moments until shortly before midnight when defending champion Jack Nicklaus came in.

Nicklaus had threatened to overtake Mackey until the 17th hole. Jack finished with a horrendous 13 and then a 15 on the last green when his children persisted in clinging to his back when he swung the club. He failed not only to catch Mackey but to make the 36-hole cut.

"I'm tired of golf," Nicklaus said. "All I really want to do anymore is go to family reunions and take my kids to Astroworld."

First-round leader Jesse Ray Rives also failed to make the cut, largely because a lurking animal — believed by some to be a bobcat — swallowed his ball on the 10th fairway.

Mackey, who wore khakis and a tool dresser's helmet, confessed that he had received a lot of help in molding his game. He said he owed a lot to the crew on the B. W. Roberts No. 2 oil rig in Clump. They had encouraged him to leave town, he said. He also specifically singled out two men who had pieced together his compact swing: Ralph Tibitt, his ex-warden, and Roy Sangry, his parole officer.

UNKNOWN LOG JAM IN OPEN

OYSTER BISQUE, N.Y. — Billy Tom Riddle, an assistant pro from Harper Valley, Tenn., playing in his first professional golf tournament, tied for the 54-hole lead in the National Open here today with four amateurs, all from the powerful University of Houston. Their score was 223, only 13 over par on historic old Baltus Oak, the course where Harry Vardon tripped on a dining room carpet.

Best known of the Houston collegians was Rex Zark, who has been the Western, Trans-Miss, Southern, North-South, Broadmoor, British and Idaho State amateur champion every year since the age of 9. The other talented members of the Texas team are Kermit Blank from Albany, N.Y., Babe Stimmett from Seattle, Wash., and Joel Wuthergrind from Worcester, Mass.

None of the leaders could rest easily, it appeared, for only 16 strokes off the pace, poised to make one of his patented stretch runs, was Arnold Palmer.

The championship was struck with an indelicate misfortune during Saturday's third round when R. J. (Bo) Mackey, the putt-putt pro, was disqualified on the first 9 holes of his round. A USGA spokesman said Mackey had been warned repeatedly since Thursday to refrain from making obscene gestures and comments to women in his gallery but that he had refused to heed the warning. "We had no other course of action to take," said T. Phillip Carter duPont Lawrence, a USGA vice-president. "This, after all, is the Open championship. Not Orlando."

HOGAN WINS UNPRECEDENTED NINTH OPEN

OYSTER BISQUE, N.Y. — With the coveted National Open championship all but sewed up, Arnold Palmer caught his backswing in a flowering banyan today on historic old Baltus Oak, the course where Tommy Armour once bought lunch, and Ben Hogan, looking tanned and fit despite his 67 years, breezed past him to win an unprecedented ninth Open.

Palmer caught his swing in the tree at Baltus Oak's 17th hole and had to be rescued by a demolition team from the Corps of Engineers. Palmer was unable to complete the round and the tournament, and thus he will have to endure sectional qualifying again next year.

"It's pretty disheartening to know you can finish 10–10 and win, and then not even be able to play," said Palmer.

Hogan shot a flaming 67 in the final round for a 72-hole total of 301, only 21 over par. Hogan's round was the lowest since architect Robert Trent Jones had revamped Baltus Oak, placing a number of bunkers in the center of some tees and forcing carries of 280 yards or more over water.

There was a moment of pure drama at the final green after Hogan finished, flashing his familiar outgoing, quick-smiling expression. Hogan went over to Jones and shook his hand until the architect knelt down, uttering a bit of a whimper.

"I brought the monster to its knees," said Hogan.

Sam Snead, who mailed in his scores, again finished second.

None of the third-round leaders managed to finish. Billy Tom Riddle, tormented by the sight of his first gallery, picked up at the 3rd hole after striking his ball 21 times in a bunker. The entire University of Houston team, including Rex Zark, quit after 9 and mysteriously departed for West Lafayette, Ind., the site of next week's NCAA championships.

Palmer was one of several blowups as the Open pressure mounted late in the day.

Billy Casper needed only to play even bogey over the last 9 holes to tie Hogan, but he suffered a sneezing fit because of pesticides which had been sprayed on the fairways and shot an incoming 46. A man of great inner peace, however, Casper smiled and said, "Boy, it looks like the Lord got up on the wrong side of the bed today."

Miller Barber, who kept swallowing diet pills throughout the round, could have parred the 72nd hole for victory, but he hit a 5-iron an amazing 240 yards over the clubhouse and the massive marble statue on the veranda of T. Phillip Carter-Hughes Bentley McCarver duPont Lawrence, Sr. "Well, you get pretty revved up out there," said Barber.

Finally, Julius Boros, chewing on a weed and sipping a can of beer, nonchalantly tried to backhand 3 successive putts on the final green, missed them all, and lost by the same margin as Casper, 2 strokes.

As Hogan accepted the unprecedented ninth Open trophy in a moving ceremony at the putting green and in turn presented the USGA with his full set of clubs and his wife Valerie for the Golf House museum, some 30 players were still out on the course, completing the last 9 holes in the dark. Word circulated momentarily that one of them, Frank Clack, a driving range operator from Davenport Iowa, could tie Hogan with 2 birdies over the last 4 holes. Officials, however, dismissed the news as wild, malicious rumor.

In its only other action of the day the USGA announced that next year's Open had been awarded to the Upper

Course at historic old Baltus Oak, the club where Jug Mc-
Spaden first fore sun glasses.

As strange as this imaginary Open may seem, it is
no more strange than many which have been played
since a nineteen-year-old named Horace Rawlins won
the first one in 1895 at Newport on October 4 with
rounds of 91–82–173. Just about every established
star has played as carelessly in the Open as he has
played splendidly, and Open blowups have been more
numerous in golf than doddering foursomes.

The statement may seem foolhardy, but both Bob
Jones and Ben Hogan, the grandest players the Open
ever produced, managed to lose as many Open championships as they won, and officially they captured
four apiece. Hogan unofficially can count five, for in
1942 a Hale America National Open was played at the
Ridgemoor Club in Chicago for the benefit of several
service organizations, and Hogan won it. The championship is listed in the USGA record book, and Hogan received the same kind of gold medal for winning
it that he was presented for winning in 1948 at Riviera, in 1950 at Merion, in 1951 at Oakland Hills and
in 1953 at Oakmont, but no one credits Hogan for
having taken a fifth Open.

Except Hogan.

A number of us journalists who loiter around the
sport like to recall with relish an afternoon when Ben
was sitting in a locker room at Cherry Hills in Denver,
having failed in a bid for the 1960 Open championship,

the tournament Arnold Palmer won with a crushing 65 over the last eighteen.

Someone said to Hogan, "Ben, do you think you'll *ever* get that fifth Open?"

"Sixth," said Hogan. And the conversation ended.

It does not appear likely that any golfer will ever post a better continuous record in the Open than Hogan. With his game styled to narrow, target-type courses — Open courses — he had a stretch of playing in sixteen straight Opens from 1940 through 1960, never finishing out of the first ten. The record reads: fifth at Canterbury in 1940, third at Colonial in 1941, first at Ridgemoor in 1942, fourth at Canterbury in 1946, sixth at St. Louis in 1947, first at Riviera in 1948, first at Merion in 1950, first at Oakland Hills in 1951, third at Northwood in 1952, first at Oakmont in 1953, sixth at Baltusrol in 1954, second at Olympic in 1955, second at Oak Hill in 1956, tenth at Southern Hills in 1958, eighth at Winged Foot in 1959 and ninth at Cherry Hill in 1960.

Hogan worshippers also like to point out that Ben missed five Opens during his prime — three because they were canceled during World War II, the 1949 Open because of his automobile accident, and the 1957 Open because of a shoulder injury.

Even in losing Hogan dominated the atmosphere of a U.S. Open. Always the big favorite, he tended to create as big a stir with his near-misses as with his victories, so much so that the winner, whoever he might be, was looked upon as a man "touched," or someone who had lapsed into what came to be known as an "Open coma."

Among Hogan's more famous losses were these: a three-putt on the 72nd at Canterbury in 1946 to miss tying with Byron Nelson, Vic Ghezzi and Lloyd Mangrum; a four-wood that crazily bounced out of bounds as he led the field in the third round at Northwood in 1952; the miracle of Jack Fleck's birdie-par-par-birdie finish to tie him at Olympic in 1955 and Fleck's subsequent 100-to-1 shot victory in the play-off; a thirty-inch par putt on the 71st at Oak Hill which curled out of the cup in 1956 and cinched the title for Cary Middlecoff; and a wedge shot that failed to clear a pond by an inch on the 71st at Cherry Hills in 1960 when he was tied with Palmer.

All of this made the Open Hogan's tournament, which in turn gave the championship a class and importance it might not otherwise have attained. Two decades earlier, Bob Jones had done the same thing.

Jones played in only eleven Opens, but his record was fantastic. He was eighth at Inverness in 1920, fifth at Columbia in 1921, second at Skokie in 1922, first at Inwood in 1923, second at Oakland Hills in 1924, second at Worcester in 1925 (losing a play-off to Willie MacFarlane), first at Scioto in 1926, eleventh at Oakmont in 1927, second at Olympia Fields in 1928 (losing a play-off to Johnny Farrell), first at Winged Foot in 1929, and of course first at Interlachen in 1930 when he scored the Grand Slam.

One of the least remembered things about Jones's

Slam is how close he came to failing in the Open
at Interlachen in Minneapolis while playing some of
the best golf of his career. For one thing, he half-
topped a spoon shot at the ninth hole of the second
round and it went directly into a lake. But then it
skipped across, rather miraculously, and got Jones a
birdie instead of a six. For another, he had to birdie
three of the last five holes on the final eighteen, including a forty-footer on the 72nd, to edge out Mac-
donald Smith by two golden strokes.

In the pre-Jones era of the Open, there are three
years well worth mentioning, all because of the brilliant Englishman Harry Vardon and what he meant to
the growth of the game.

There is first the year 1900, Vardon's first to tour the
U.S. in a series of exhibitions. He concluded his trip
by playing in our Open at the Chicago Golf Club, a
chore he did not particularly warm to. Our Open at
this time, of course, was of no more importance to
Vardon than, say, the Singapore Open is to Jack
Nicklaus today. But Vardon played and naturally Vardon won. The way he won, however, demonstrated
the utter disdain that he held for the title. He casually
whiffed a putt on the final green, shrugged, and still
walked off with the championship. Vardon next returned in 1913 with his friend Ted Ray, a large man
who was considered the world's second-greatest
player. The U.S. Open had gained considerably in
stature by then, but not so much that Vardon and Ray
weren't supposed to smother the field at The Country

Club in Brookline, Massachusetts. And smother it they did with the lone exception of a twenty-year-old, wide-eyed, homegrown amateur named Francis Ouimet.

To the astonishment of everyone, including himself, Ouimet finished the tournament birdie-par to tie Vardon and Ray. He then walked home, slept a comfortable thirteen hours, got up, walked back and shot 72 to Vardon's 77 and Ray's 78 in the play-off. The legend is that Ouimet's feat made golf front-page news in America, but the truth is that his conquest hardly got onto the sports pages of any newspapers outside of Boston and New York. It would be inaccurate to say, however, that the deed did not eventually help popularize the game along the Eastern seaboard.

Vardon's last appearance in our Open was in many ways one of the great accomplishments of his career, which included the taking of no fewer than six British Opens — the *real* Open of his day. This was in 1920 at Inverness in Toledo, Ohio. Vardon was fifty years old, but he thoroughly dominated the tournament. In fact he led by five strokes with only seven holes to go. Unfortunately a vicious gale came up, and Vardon played those holes in even fives, allowing the larger and stronger Ted Ray to overtake him and win by a stroke. It was a shame that Vardon could not have crowned his career with that victory in his fiftieth year, for he was, by all evidence, the best swinger until Jones. He was so perfect in the swing, in fact, that Walter Hagen once admitted, "In times when my own swing would leave me, I could bring it back by remembering Vardon and trying to imitate him."

The period between Bob Jones and Ben Hogan — the Thirties — can safely be regarded as the goofiest era of the Open, a decade into which champions like Lee Trevino and Orville Moody would have fit perfectly.

No sooner had Jones retired than the Open responded to his absence in 1931 by producing the longest golf play-off in history. Billie Burke and George Von Elm had to play seventy-two grinding extra holes at Inverness before Burke won by a single stroke.

In 1932 Gene Sarazen found himself seven strokes behind with twenty-eight holes left to play at Fresh Meadow in Flushing, New York, so he promptly swept over those holes in 100 strokes, which included a final round 66 — nine under par in all — and which of course produced victory.

A year later a lightly regarded professional named Olin Dutra, who also happened to be suffering a severe stomach ailment, put on an equally impressive stretch drive. He was eight behind with thirty-six to go, and all of the leading players of the time were ahead of him at Merion, including Sarazen.

One by one Dutra passed them all to defeat Sarazen by a stroke, thanks in large part to a triple bogey seven Sarazen made at Merion's 11th hole, which thereafter earned fame for its Baffling Brook.

If Sarazen could suffer a blowup, so could lesser men, the Open having by now become the one championship in golf that a winner could truly cash in on where endorsements were concerned. Perhaps Jimmy Thomson, first of the long hitters with the steel shaft, had dollar bills in his eye when he three-putted away his one and only chance at a major title in 1935 at Oakmont. Thomson even managed to four-putt one green in the last round to allow the absolute nobody Sam Parks, Jr., to win.

In 1938 at Cherry Hills a dashingly handsome and personable player, Dick Metz, was gradually running off from the field through fifty-four holes. At this point he was told that an Open victory would get him a glamorous movie contract. Metz promptly shot 79, and the quiet, brooding Ralph Guldahl took his second Open in a row.

The Thirties concluded with Sam Snead's first and most often discussed Open tragedy. Snead came to the 72nd hole at Spring Mill in Philadelphia, with par five to win and a mere bogey six to tie. Nothing to it. Except Snead came apart in a fairway bunker, took a disastrous eight, and Byron Nelson went on to win. Snead never fully recovered from that experience in the Open, and thus he never won America's biggest championship, although he won nearly one hundred other titles.

"If I'd won that one I might have won ten others," Snead frequently said.

The post-Hogan phase of Open history belongs pretty much to Arnold Palmer — right up to the Mexkin and the sergeant.

Palmer won his only Open championship in 1960 at Cherry Hills in a typically Palmer way, with a rousing 65 in the last round.

Throughout the 1960's, however, the Open would never be his again, although it would several times *almost* be his. He had to three-putt twelve greens at Oakmont to fall into a tie with Jack Nicklaus and lose the play-off in 1962. He had to blow to a wild 77 in the third round at Brookline in 1963 to fall into a tie with Julius Boros and Jacky Cupit and lose the play-off to Boros. He had to blow a seven-stroke lead on the last six holes to drop into a tie with Billy Casper in 1966 at Olympic and lose that play-off.

The fact that it seems impossible for Arnold Palmer to win another Open somehow is partly the reason why the victories of Lee Trevino and Orville Moody seem all the more mysterious.

Golfing America had a legitimate question: how could a Mexkin and a sergeant win a tournament that the country's darling couldn't?

The answer of course is as elusive as the perfect round of eighteen birdies, and the thing that makes the game itself so irritatingly unfathomable at times.

There was Lee Trevino at Oak Hill, cracking jokes to his gallery and the press, acting as if just being *close* to the leader, Bert Yancey, was good enough for a Mexican from Dallas, an impoverished lad who had never won a tournament and who in fact had been on the professional tour only a little more than a year.

For three days it was Yancey's championship, clear and simple. He was golf's best putter, everyone agreed, and everyone knew how much Yancey *wanted* the Open, and his slow, smooth swing was considered to be among the more picturesque of the game's bright new stars. He would be a splendid Open champion. And he was beginning to get used to the idea himself. After the third round interview with the press, he quietly asked a friend, "How did I sound?"

Meanwhile, Trevino against the backdrop of Oak Hill's yawning clubhouse and verandas — a place which seemed to combine all of the elements of Wuthering Heights and Jay Gatsby's mansion at West Egg — was an oddity, golf's credibility gap. Well, it had been fun to have him up there challenging, saying things like, "I'm gonna be a Spaniard instead of a Mexkin soon as I get some more money."

But he couldn't win.

Oh really? All the Mexkin did on Sunday was go out on Oak Hill paired head-to-head with Yancey the way a hustler likes it and turn that pretty swing into a wreckage of broken rhythm and disturbed concentration. Yancey began missing putts and Trevino began making them.

Lee would ask his followers, who already had assumed the name of Lee's Fleas, "What am I doin' out here? I don't know if I'm gonna hook it or slice it."

The crowd would whoop and holler, "Whip the gringo."

Trevino buried Yancey over the first nine holes that day and he then stood up to a late rush by Jack Nicklaus, who was playing behind them. At his rear, the crowd would explode for a Nicklaus birdie, but Trevino would respond with a wisecrack and a slashing recovery shot out of Oak Hill's weeds.

"I was tryin' to get so far ahead I could choke and still win," he said later. "But I had to keep playin'."

And suddenly all Trevino had done was not only blast Bert Yancey into a trauma and win the U.S. Open, he had shot a fourth consecutive subpar round, a 69 — which had never been done before by Hogan or anybody, four subpar rounds in the Open — and his total of 275 merely tied the seventy-two-hole record set the previous year by Nicklaus.

Now here came all of that instant lore. Yeah, Trevino had come out of a hustler's game in Dallas, and sure he could play you with a Dr. Pepper bottle, using it fungo style and putting with it like a pool cue. Try him. For money, try him. He said his name was Super Mex and that some of the pros knew him before this, even if the public didn't. He sent a few of them home from El Paso in a Greyhound bus when they came out there to try him. What's that? Oh, the Band-Aid always on his forearm? Oh, that covered up the name of an ex-girlfriend that he once had tattooed on. "I get rid of 'em when they turn twenty-one," he said. The red socks and the red shirt he wore? "That's my payday outfit," he said. Finally, Trevino didn't know whether he had proved that Mexicans can play golf, but he thought he had proved that one of them can. And that was Super Mex, the unlikeliest Open champion ever — until a year later.

Here now came Orville Moody to compound the felony at Champions in Houston. Like Trevino, the sergeant had never won a professional tournament, aside from a few Korean Opens, and also like Trevino he had only been on the PGA tour for slightly more than a year. Nor did his cross-handed putting method particularly recommend him since no man had ever putted cross-handed and won more than a kick in the ass with a cold boot, as the saying goes.

As Oak Hill had been Bert Yancey's tournament for three days, Champions had belonged almost exclusively to a tour veteran, Miller Barber. Barber was not an exciting player, with the loop in his backswing, the dark glasses he wore and his quiet, keep-to-himself nature. But he was solid, he had been a winner on the tour, and to see him up there in front at Champions was no real surprise.

Champions was playing long and tough and the humidity was at times unbearable, but Miller Barber had destroyed par for three days. He was four under, sitting on 276 in other words, and if he didn't come back to the field on Sunday, the championship was over.

Orville Moody, who was thirty-five and had spent

fourteen years in the army, was the nearest man to Barber, and they were paired together on the final day, just as Trevino had been paired with Yancey.

"A guy like me can't think about going out and winning the National Open," Moody said that morning. "I'll just play along as best I can and see what happens."

He said he had liked the army, that the army had been good to him. He had made staff sergeant E6. He had gone in the first time for six years because of a girlfriend that done him wrong. "A kid don't know what he's doin' sometimes," he said. Then he reupped for three more years because he didn't know exactly what he would do if he got out.

By then, he said, he had become a pretty good golfer and he thought he'd like to try the tour. So in 1962 he got out of the army again, rounded up a likely sponsor for a try at the tour, qualified for the National Open, went to the Open and missed the cut. "My sponsor come down a little on the money he promised when I blew the cut," Orville said. "So I went back in the army." Total time out: two weeks. Amount of time back in: five years.

Moody had played the tour most of 1968, but he had won only $13,000. He seemed to have a good, sound game, however. His swing was compact and smooth-looking. He had fair distance. He stood up to the ball well. But there was that business of the putting stroke.

"Anything over six inches long, my grip comes loose if I putt normal," he said. "I'm just a lousy putter, so I got to go cross-handed."

Moody arose on the morning of the last round and drove with his wife and his two children about an hour out to Champions from a Holiday Inn across town. Obscure motels are where Nobodies stay. He reflected briefly in the locker room about the fact that he was playing pretty good. "I'm hittin' my irons exactly where I'm aimin' 'em," he said. "I guess I ought to start shootin' for the pins."

So he went out with Miller Barber and just played steady golf. He played 72 golf, two over. He played 281 golf, one over at Champions. But it was more than good enough. No one broke par on Sunday. The wind came up and the flags were tucked behind bunkers and ponds, and Moody's 72 was quite a score for a guy in contention. Miller Barber, meanwhile, got too conservative, too cautious. Bogey after bogey assaulted him, and after nine holes Moody had the lead.

"Miller kept tryin' to cozy it," said Orville. "He knew a seventy-three or four was all he needed, but he knew he was in the National Open too. It isn't easy out there."

It seemed easy enough for Moody. When he got to the last hole he needed a par four to beat two other contenders who had slipped up on Barber, Bob Rosburg and Al Geiberger.

All he said to his caddy was, "I got to get me a four here somehow." He nailed a driver down the middle, then he split the green with a five-iron, just twenty feet from the flag. Two more putts would do it, except that the first putt stopped about fourteen inches short. Moody looked at it and turned his cap sideways, the way a man does when he's made a dumb mistake and knows it. But he walked up to the short one, took no time, and dropped it.

Maybe the Open daze made that par for him and maybe not. Maybe the Open coma won it for Lee Trevino. Back-to-back Nobodies is asking a lot for us to believe. But perhaps there is something more to it. It is just possible that the right player can come up to the right course at the right time. The fairways bend to his shots and the greens suit his stroke. Somehow he also gets to thinking that he *can* win and, more important, that he *deserves* to win. In the case of Trevino and Moody, it may also be that a little bit of disrespect for the institution and the establishment doesn't hurt anything.

Trevino did it with an obvious brashness and defiance. Moody did it with a cold sort of you-can-bet-me-if-you-think-you-can-play attitude. They were both hustlers and a hustler likes a big game, and there is no game bigger than the Open. Looking back, they even made it look easy, and one had to be reminded of that old story about the Turnesa family. They had learned the game as caddies where their father was a greenskeeper, and when it once looked as if Joe Turnesa might win the 1926 National Open some members of the club, having heard the news on the radio, rushed out on the course where the father was clipping grass. "Mr. Turnesa," one of them cried. "Joe's winning the National Open."

"Why shouldn't he?" said the old man, without looking up. "All he's ever done is play golf."

Maybe it's as simple as that, after all, for a Jones or a Hogan, or a Mexkin or a sergeant.

Winner and Loser

---

*Claude Harmon not only taught me most of what
I know about the golf swing, he took me out of
Argyle socks.*

— DAVE MARR,
holding court on 52nd Street

O N one of those dazzling nights in Manhattan that a visitor from Minerva, Ohio, might classify as being heavy on the celebs, Dave Marr, a young man from the robot life of the professional golf tour, stepped into one of his favorite 52nd Street restaurants and began moving through the glitter like, let us say, Sandy Primetime.

It was a tired room, filled with those ever-present clusters of familiar midtown drinkers: Giant fans, Jet fans, Met fans, high handicappers from Winged Foot, broadcasting immortals, ex-athletes, magazine folk, network worriers, directors, producers, panelists — all sorts of people who sometimes pass for celebrities when there isn't a real heavyweight on the street. But suddenly the room seemed to be refreshed by Marr's arrival.

Tanned and beaming, resplendent in his double-breasted blue blazer, trim and handsome, all Guccied and Dunhilled, Marr shot his hand out in varying directions as he greeted individuals and groups at the bar up front, working casually toward a table in the rear. All around, there were happy blurps of worship: "Hi, Dave," "Hey, pro," "Put it in the vise, champ."

And all around, there were friendly, happy needles: "Missed the cut, right?" "Got arrested for impersonating a golfer, right?"

Marr grinned and pushed along, accepting a vodka and tonic from somebody, lighting a cigarette, shaking hands. Laughter trailed after him, for he, too, was dropping lines.

"Hey," he said to Mike Manuche, the proprietor. "Did you read where Arnold's been talking about the governorship of Pennsylvania? Man, I think that hip injury must be movin' up to his *head*."

By the time he reached his table, he had enough pals with him to play a good game of half-court, and the table quickly expanded like a bar at 5:42 P.M. All sorts of people had been in lately and asking about him, Marr was told. Alex Webster, the Giant coach. Frank Gifford. Bing Crosby. Bob Newhart. Tucker Frederickson. Don Meredith. Paul Hornung.

"A great thing about my line of work," Marr said to a friend. "I'm O-and-eighty but nobody's singing 'Good-bye, Davey.'"

And so Dave Marr was at home, doing his thing, holding another seance in sport, being his charming, likable, entertaining self, getting on the outside of his share of cocktails, being, for whatever it may be worth, the pro of 52nd Street. Later on, when he would move to other bistros in the big city, *his* city now — to Toots Shor's, no doubt, perhaps to "21" the Unicorn, Mister Laffs — a hearty band would follow and others would be collected. The end would finally come in the early morning. It would be signaled mercifully by the placing in front of him of that salvation of Western man: the bacon cheeseburger. Dinner at last. It would come in the back room at P. J. Clarke's after all of the golf tour's problems had been threshed out, after the future success of the New York Giants had been assured, after the city had been saved, the wars ended, the new books discussed, the world's oxygen preserved, the pollution problem solved. Surviving another evening on the town, the final triumph, would be shared with Marr by such stay-awakes as Danny Lavezzo, the owner of Clarke's, by maybe Jack Whitaker, the broadcaster, perhaps by an old ex-Giant or two, and surely Jimmy Martin, just an old friend from Yonkers.

The point is, Dave Marr would have done it again. His thing, whatever it is. This thing of just being alive and being around, laughing a lot, knowing everybody, being known, reveling in the fact that although he is just little Dave Marr from Larchmont out of Houston by way of Claude Harmon and golf shop flunky — just another of those steady, faceless guys on the PGA tour — he can move through the big town like the emcee of a talk show, like Arnold Palmer *should*, considering his fame.

And done what? On such nights as these, had Dave Marr only proved that he can drink and go back to the Hartford Open and hit five-irons? Proved he can stay up later than Joe Namath? Proved he knows more people than Paul Hornung? Proved he is the checkgrabbing champion of the fashionable East Side? Well, let's see. Maybe part of this. Maybe all of it. But then again maybe none of it. Maybe David Francis Marr was only having a good time with friends, genuine friends, who constitute much of his real wealth. He is *not* just another pro exempt from qualifying, and he knows it, and an inner circle knows it and, after all, what other pro wears Guccis and always leaves you laughing?

Dave Marr would go back to the grind of the tour to finish twenty-third of course, to miss the cut perhaps, to *not* win another tournament, to become one of those hundred or so players out there who hit very good shots but who are not Arnold Palmer or Jack Nicklaus or Gary Player or Julius Boros or Billy Casper, or even, in terms of crowd recognition, Doug Sanders or Lee Trevino. But he would go back and make the stylish living that provides nicely for his pretty wife and his three children. He will play well enough to keep the house in Larchmont and the summer house on Long Island, to pay for first-class air travel, for the best hotel rooms in the best hotels, to be able to "whip out" for the restaurant checks, the theater, the nightclubs, the moving around town, the clothes, the schools and all that. In this sense Dave Marr is a bigger winner than he ever thought he might be.

But he knows the way it is. Attention to oneself in pro golf is not easily gained except by winning — repetitious winning. And even then it can be difficult as evidenced by the public's slow warm-up to Jack Nicklaus. Nobody wins more than Nicklaus but the public says ho-hum, he should lose some weight, overlooking the fact that Jack is pleasant, at times witty and thoroughly likable. It has been said that Palmer did it not just by winning but by fighting a course in his furiously dramatic way. Tony Lema drank champagne and did it. Chi Chi Rodriguez danced on the greens and did it. Doug Sanders wore wild clothes and did it. Billy Casper ate buffalo meat and did it. But on the intolerant surface Dave Marr occupies the role of so many others. He hasn't done it outside of New York and Houston and when he comes down the fairway with Mason Rudolph or Frank Beard or Charley Coody, the crowd wonders who is who.

And so it goes for most of the so-called stars of the game. Aren't they robots in a curious way who plod along pondering their destinies as someday club pros? Their personalities tend to be the same: uncommunicative. Their look is the same: blue shirt, white cap, gray slacks. Their wives are the same: simple but nice, with outdated hairdos. Their politics are the same: unphilosophically conservative. Their food is the same: steak, baked potato, salad with Roquefort. And their complaints are the same: Palmer's gallery is a pain in the ass, Nicklaus plays too slow, Trevino talks too much, Sanders is dizzy, the pins are brutal, the travel is expensive, the caddies are lazy, and where the hell is the courtesy car the tournament chairman promised?

The weeks grind into months and the months grind into years. A major championship breaks up the routine with its abnormal excitement and pressure — "Boy, the press is really here" — but there are only four of those, the Masters, the U.S. Open, the British Open and the PGA, and then it's back to the real tour, back to the Buick Opens. It is back to the blurry dreariness of Holiday Inns and Imperial South Motels. Take the kids out by the pool. Give the wife some money to go shopping. Is there anything good on television? What was the name of that Polynesian restaurant? Frank Beard wants to get up a bridge game. Ken Still wants to go to a ball park. Man, did you see that chick following Raymond Floyd today? Christ, it's hot in Chicago. The lady scorer is a sun-scarred Wasp and the friendly, ingratiating chairman made a million dollars selling hydraulic jacks so how come his blazer doesn't fit? Why in the hell can't a contestant get a table in the dining room? Who let all those kids inside the ropes when we came off the 18th? Boy, Jack Tuthill better get on the ball. The greens are grainy and the rough is a zoo. The TV crew will cost you two shots at least. How about getting paired two straight weeks with Jerry Barber? The fairways are too high, the greens are too damp, and Jesus, Dave Hill never shuts up. If Nicklaus is anywhere near his game he'll win by six. If he isn't, then it must be Casper's turn again. It isn't Dave Marr's. It never is.

But it beats working, they say. It's the golden goose, they say. Just make the cut every week and you'll break Byron Nelson's money record of 1945. What does the touring pro do that's hard? He plays golf six days a week and not exactly on public courses with a pull-cart. He hangs around country clubs with rich guys and takes down $40,000 if he can't play at all. Where's the grief? California in the winter, Florida in the spring, the big cities in the summer. Couple of trips to Europe or the Far East. Some TV stuff. Some appearances and exhibitions. Snappy clothes for cost or zip, a big bag, four dozen pairs of shoes, three dozen new balls every week from the companies, courtesy cars, limousines and drivers, air travel, celebrities, room service, lolling around on verandas, parties, outdoors, fresh air, vodka and blondes, playing a game, for God's sake, and calling it work. Let the brooding dummies overhaul diesel trucks for a living and see how they like it.

One of the engaging things about Dave Marr is that he understands the paradox of the tour better than his contemporaries. It *is* good when you reach a certain plateau, he will say. Everybody likes attention, being made to feel important. The money is there. Status is there. But it is also a terrible grind, almost an addiction, that bleeds the brain, puts a strain on the family, and keeps the ego bouncing like a basketball.

"Your ego is everything," Marr has admitted. "And if you don't get that pumped up regularly, you can't last."

The pro is an athlete above all else, Marr explained, a special kind of athlete who has to control his emotions. Most of his strain is mental, but much is physical about his sport. Play six straight rounds of golf *walking* and you will see that the pro's legs have to be in decent shape. Stand close to a pro hitting an iron shot and look at the deep, slashing divot he takes and you will see that good golf requires some strength. Few things in sport move any faster than a clubhead going through a ball when a touring pro makes a pass at a shot. Whether the player has an easy swing, like Marr, or a gritty one, like Palmer, there is real speed involved at contact — one of the things which separates the pro from everybody else at the country club.

"There's no doubt that the mental part of the game is the toughest," Marr said. "Trying to keep the dog from comin' up in you when you're in shape to win. But when guys tell me there's nothing physical about playing the tour, well, man. I start thinking about all the travel, aside from the practice. Follow me around for two or three weeks and I'll guarantee you, you'll be a tired mother."

Restoring the ego is the constant concern, according to Marr. Small things can do it — a kind word from a respected player, a series of good rounds. The driver can come back from the dead, or the short irons. The putter can get hot. But the best source for the non-winner is a new venue each week. You're starting all over with renewed faith. There is new hope, new anticipation. You have a whole new set of friends. Different admirers are fawning over you, oblivious to the fact that you missed the cut last week. There's

Gardner Dickinson, who wears a cap like Hogan. There's Gay Brewer, the guy with the pug nose. There's Art Wall; he makes holes in one. There's Bob Rosburg, who uses a baseball grip. And isn't that Dave Marr? Didn't he win something once? The PGA, or something?

"You can play real good in a tournament and even if you don't win it, it'll carry you a week or two," says Marr. "A win, of course, can carry you for weeks or months. And a major championship can carry you a whole year, or longer, depending on what you make out of it. There's a very depressing feeling when the year's over and you no longer hold the title. It's back to what have you done lately? But if you've put the title to work it'll stay with you for a long time."

Dave Marr is the perfect example of the young man who has, of necessity, put *everything* to work in order to carve out a nifty existence that he had no right ever to expect. He has nothing spectacular about his game other than a picturesque swing. He has no length, and his putting is absurdly bad. Inside the ropes he has no special charm. He is just another guy in a Jantzen shirt and Foot Joy shoes, slight of build, expressionless, blond, good-looking and usually one or two over on the scoreboard. Ronnie Runnerup, his good pal Frank Gifford calls him, to which Marr says, "who'll ever forget old number fifteen?"

How, then, could this man have become the tour's best-liked, most personable, articulate socializer — golf's major link with television, Hollywood, Broadway, the George Plimpton party and maître d's throughout the broad plain of America? Why is it always Dave Marr with Paul Hornung in the Palm Bay Club? At Tucker Frederickson's party after a Giant game? With Arnold Palmer and Don Meredith at John Murchison's cookout in Dallas? With Dick Shawn at the Pine Inn in Carmel? With the lead columnist or broadcaster in every town? With all of those vice-presidents at Ruby's Dunes in Palm Springs? With Bing Crosby at Manuche's in New York? With Bob Newhart at Shor's? With Alex Webster and Charley Conerly and Gifford at Clarke's? Why him?

"Because I live in New York," smiles Marr.

That, of course, is part of it. Put Marr back in Houston where he came from and none of his accomplishments — the PGA championship in 1965, mainly — would have mattered nearly so much. He would not really still be "Claude's boy," meaning Claude Harmon, the man who gave Marr most of everything; his opportunity to work at Winged Foot and Seminole, to learn the game, his sophistication, his introductions to the big town and his friendships with real millionaires in Palm Beach, Palm Springs, Westchester County and Long Island, and not just the pretenders.

"Claude Harmon not only taught me most of what I know about the golf swing, he did something almost as important," says Marr. "Man, he took me out of Argyle socks."

Claude Harmon, noted for his teaching, has had a lot of protégés, as everyone knows, players who shuttled in and out of Winged Foot, leaving for the tour with infinitely more knowledge about the game, but Marr is surely Harmon's favorite for at least three reasons. First, Dave did more with less, and Claude watched him rise from sweeping out the shop to bon vivant along 52nd Street. Second, he was immensely popular, both around New York and Palm Beach (when Claude would transport his staff to Seminole in the winter). And third, Dave *stayed* in New York, buying the home in Larchmont, even after making it on the tour.

Marr could have lived anywhere, of course, after proving that he could survive on the tour with a victory now and then in Seattle or somewhere and steady checks. He could have gone to Florida as many did, or to California or to Dallas, a convenient place to "get out of" when you have to roam about the country, or he could have gone home to Houston where he had turned pro at nineteen, foregoing a college scholarship. There were close ties in Houston, not just his mother, who had worked in a Howard Johnson's as a waitress after his father died, or two younger brothers and a sister, but several cousins named Burke who were involved in golf, Jackie Burke being one.

"That was hardly what I'd been working for, to get back to where I started," says Marr. "Houston, I love it, but Houston is where I couldn't beat anybody even as an amateur and where the wolf was at the door. It's Jackie and Jimmy's town. Man, I had to go East and pick on those Italian assistants before I could find anybody I could beat."

New York is where he had to be and where he had to stay.

"All of my old friends on the tour — Mason Rudolph and Johnny Pott and Tommy Jacobs, we came out together, sort of — think I'm crazy living in the East. They think, hey, man, where do you go fishin'? What do you do for black-eyed peas and ribs? I just tell 'em, hell, if I live in Clarksville, Tennessee, how am I gonna see the Giants play on Sunday?"

Marr talks with a twinkle and a grin, explodes with boyish laughter at a funny line, his or someone else's, and sets himself apart from most of the pros by not taking his game too seriously in conversation. Football occupies much of his talk, and good food, good books, the theater, politics, current events. His golf talk is dotted with expressions that he either picked up from Burke or Demaret or spewed out himself.

"Always fade the ball. You can't talk to a hook," he says. To someone who strikes a low shot or tops one, "I didn't think you had enough runway for a minute." Or, "I'll take anything in the air that doesn't sting." To a spectator or a marshal or a scorer standing in his way: "Sir, would you mark yourself, please, while I try to get this one up?" After starting a round with a mini-hangover: "If I try to leave the hotel tonight, put out a contract on me." To Arnold Palmer about his wardrobe: "You think Latrobe Dry Goods would make up some of those slacks for me?" On Tommy Aaron blowing Roberto De Vicenzo's scorecard at the

Masters: "What player on the tour would you *least* want to figure your income tax?" On Orville Moody winning the U.S. Open after Lee Trevino: "What does it matter who Orville is? At least he brought the title back to America."

Marr further authored two spontaneous comments in the course of tournament play that have practically become legend; at least they seem to get repeated endlessly in locker rooms and 19th holes and in New York saloons.

Once, it seems, Dave was paired with Jerry Barber in a tournament in Florida, and Barber is never an easy pairing. He can be very slow and meticulous as well as contrary. Marr, who manages to overcome his own temper tantrums rapidly because of his wit, nevertheless can get "hot," as he likes to put it, and lash back at anybody. So on a particular hole Barber, after hooking atrociously, quickly looked over at Marr and said, "Your foot moved."

And just as quickly and coldly Dave said, "When I *walk*. I put the first one here and then the next one there, and pretty soon, I'm moving."

And then there was the day in Augusta, during the last round of the 1964 Masters when Marr came to the final hole paired with Palmer, who was winning the championship by six strokes.

Marr himself was playing superbly and was, in fact, about to finish in a tie with Nicklaus for second, all of it on the glory of national television, a condition that Dave insists created more fame for him than all four of his tour victories spliced together.

At any rate, there stood Palmer and Marr on the last tee, chatting. They were waiting for the big crowd to clear so they could drive up toward the 18th green. Marr and Palmer were already good friends, and Arnold was delighted to see Dave doing so well.

Just before teeing up Arnold glanced over at Dave and said, "Anything I can do to help you here?"

"Yeah," grinned Marr. "Make a twelve."

A year later Marr helped himself to a small part of the glory that Palmer and a few others had been wallowing in by winning a major championship. With sheer tenacity overcoming his lack of distance, and while enjoying a week of unbridled confidence, Marr fought off Nicklaus and Casper and won the PGA on the big course at Laurel Valley in Pennsylvania. It was sort of the American Dream come true, and in his moment of triumph, for all of his cynical wit, Marr could not fight back a tear. All he could think of were the hours, days, weeks and years of sweeping out golf shops, selling cashmeres, giving lessons to the inept, slowing down his swing, struggling to get rid of the dog in him and rejoicing over $400 checks. Now here was a major championship, something few golfers achieve, and something *most* players on the tour will never achieve.

"All I could think of was that the title was for everybody who had helped me — Claude, Robie Williams, Jackie, all the men at Winged Foot who first put me on the tour," says Marr. "The $25,000 was for me, and the prestige was what I would spread around New York and see what it could bring."

It brought a good deal more than it would have anyplace else, to be sure. Dave Marr has been reaping rewards ever since, appearing on TV, in ads, playing exhibitions, being a "name" he had no right to be. One little thing he originated then is still paying off. In New York, he decided that a corporation or two would like to have twenty of its important clients enjoy a round of golf, a clinic and lunch with a top pro — him. Dave arranges the game and the club. He plays three holes with each group, thereby putting himself into the company of everyone in the course of a full round, and he tell his jokes, and drinks are enjoyed, and all of the friends of Union Carbide or Allied Chemical go home happy. He, of course, is paid a fee, and he plays as many of these in a year as he can promote. And this adds up to enough money to pay his bill at Manuche's.

In golf it is acceptable to put down the PGA championship as sort of the low rent member of the Big Four. The Masters and U.S. Open have more prestige and enjoy much broader coverage, and the British Open has the PGA up on the front tees where tradition is concerned. But there is hardly a better title to win for the journeyman pro, mainly because once you are a PGA champion you never have to qualify for another tour event. Never.

The PGA is also, quite possibly, the hardest of the four to win because it annually has the toughest field. A great many good players don't get invited to the Masters, and a good many don't qualify for the Open, and an awful lot of Americans do not make the effort to play in the British Open. But *everybody* is in the PGA, and this, after all, is a championship glorified by such winners as Walter Hagen, Gene Sarazen, Ben Hogan, Byron Nelson, Sam Snead, Gary Player and Jack Nicklaus and made all the more intriguing by a list of some nonwinners. Arnold Palmer hasn't won it, nor has Billy Casper or Gene Littler, and Jimmy Demaret, Cary Middlecoff and Lloyd Mangrum never won it, for some instances.

"Say it again," grinned Marr. "This is my ego lesson for the day."

Another thing the PGA championship did for Marr was put him on the Ryder Cup team, which is sort of the Oscar awards of pro golf every two years. He went to England and helped lead the Americans to another victory over the British at Birkdale, one of the toughest courses there is. On the wall of his den in Larchmont is a sketch made by a British artist showing every shot played by Marr and Palmer when they teamed up in one of the Scotch foursome matches, a round in which Dave and Arnold shot eight under fours.

"Anyone who says they don't think the Ryder Cup is thrilling can bust me," he said. "I didn't know how I'd feel until I got there on the first tee and listened to "The Star-Spangled Banner" and then "God Save the Queen." Man, I wanted to throw a block on one of those U.K.'s."

A man does not stay a major champion, of course,

except perhaps in his own home, surrounded by his trophies, and Dave Marr knows it. Since 1965, he has had to be content with such modest successes as teaming up with Tommy Jacobs to win the CBS Golf Classic, and tying with Frank Beard for the thirty-six-hole Music City Open in Nashville, a gigantic feat for which he received a five-hundred-dollar guitar.

But despite the fact that too many years have sped by since he last won a tournament he remains devoted to the tour. It is partly because the money is so good, partly because he believes he can still play championship golf, partly the fun, and partly his interest in the game. Some club jobs have tempted him, but he is still in his mid-thirties, too young to quit.

The family would be happier if he quit. Every family of every pro would be. At first, the wives think the tour is glamorous, but eventually it becomes a bore, an inconvenience for the children. And without the family for any length of time, the pro finds himself faced with temptations that are not altogether good for him. Too many parties, too much drink, too many available ladies, all of this preying on his loneliness, his ego lag, and his bad putting streak.

Marr said, "We all have to face the problem of the future. How good are you? Can you stay out there with the big hitters? In my case, I can play my best but I might not win if I don't hole everything because Nicklaus can slop it around and out-birdie me. Do I take a club job? I'm still young. I think I can still play good enough to win. You come close a few times and you *know* it. You go through a tournament playing super, but you don't win. So you look back and see one missed putt of about three feet on each nine holes. That's eight strokes you lost by, but you played good."

Dave Marr suffers the dilemma of all of the non-greats. But he is mostly what the tour is made up of. A man with style, temperament, knowledge, and all the shots, but one who rarely wins. But it is not so true that as Marr goes, so will go the rest. He has a more complete background than most, coming up as an assistant, coming out of a golf family, being exposed to Claude Harmon, Jack Burke, Jimmy Demaret, taking a deep interest in the well-being of the game and worrying about its public relations. Somewhere, there is a special place for him, perhaps as another of the great, personable teachers that Claude Harmon is, backdropped by New York, thrust into all of the glamor he seems to find there.

And then again he just might start to win. Wouldn't it be nice to play consistently, he thinks, the way he did in the 1969 Open at Champions in Houston? Shoot 286, close to the top, and pick up the good check every week. Be patient, playing fairways and greens, and let the putts fall where they will. Get your $70,000 a year in prize money and do another forty thousand on top of that in extras.

"That's fine," said Marr. "But as Claude has always said, you can't turn it on and off. Only Hogan could do that. You've got to be totally committed to the tour, out there working all the time."

What truly keeps someone like Marr out there, whether he knows it or not, can best be told by reciting an incident that happened in Houston in the summer of 1969. It happened during the U.S. Open, in which he played superbly, enjoying one of those pleasurable spurts of his, surrounded by all sorts of old friends and relatives.

Completing the first round, he came to the 18th hole needing to hit a four-wood to the green to get his par 4. Standing behind the green was an old friend of his, chatting with a rather well-known spectator—Ben Hogan, wearing, as Dave later said, his Marty Fleckman cap.

Marr hit a tremendous shot, cutting a high four-wood out of the rough and onto the green, a shot which bounded up to within three feet of the flag for a birdie. The crowd had exploded appreciatively, and, afterwards, Marr asked his old friend what Hogan had done.

"What'd the Hawk say when I cut one in there for three on eighteen?" Marr grinned.

His friend grinned back.

"He said it was too much club."

Dave Marr, the pro of 52nd Street, broke up.

"I guess that's what it's all about," he said. "That's where it all is."

The Glory Game

Clutch, Mother Zilch.
— MORON TOM,
standing on the
18th tee at Goat Hills

GOAT HILLS is gone now. It was swallowed up a few years ago by the bulldozers of progress, and in the end it was nice to learn that something could take a divot out of those hard fairways. But all of the regular players had left long before. We had matured at last. Maybe it will be all right to talk about it now, about the place and the people and the times we had. It could even be therapeutic. At least it will help explain why I do not play golf so much anymore. I mean, I keep getting invited to Winged Dip and Burning Foot and all of those fancy clubs we sophisticated New Yorkers are supposed to frequent, places where, I hear, they have real flag sticks instead of broom handles. It sounds fine, but I usually beg off. I am, frankly, still overgolfed from all those years at Goat Hills in Texas. You would be too if . . . well, let me tell you some of it. Not all, but some. I will try to be truthful and not too sentimental. But where shall I begin? With Cecil? Perhaps so. He was sort of a symbol in those days, and. . . .

We called him Cecil the Parachute because he fell down a lot. He would attack the golf ball with a whin-

ing, leaping shove — more of a calisthenic than a
swing, really — and occasionally, in his spectacular
struggles for extra distance, he would soar right off the
end of elevated tees.

He was a slim, bony, red-faced little man who wore
crepe-soled shoes and heavily starched shirts that
crackled when he marked his ball, always inching it
forward as much as possible. When he was earth-
bound, Cecil drove a delivery truck for a cookie factory, Grandma's Cookies, I think, and he always
parked it — hid it, rather — behind a tall hedge near
the clubhouse. When the truck was there, out of sight
of passing cars, one of which might have Grandma in
it, you could be pretty sure that not only was Cecil
out on the course but so, most likely, were Tiny, Easy,
Magoo and Foot the Free, Ernie, Matty, Rush and
Grease Repellent, Little Joe, Weldon the Oath, Jerry,
John the Band-Aid and Moron Tom. And me. I was
called Dump, basically because of what so many partners thought I did to them.

There would be an excellent chance that all of us
would be in one hollering, protesting, club-slinging
fifteensome, betting $800 million. Anyhow, when
Cecil the Parachute had the truck hidden, you knew
for sure that the game was on.

The game was not exactly the kind of golf that
Gene Sarazen or any of his stodgy friends ever would
have approved of. But it was, nevertheless, the kind
we played for about fifteen years, through a lot of the
1940's and most of the 1950's, at a windy, dusty,

indifferently mowed, stone-hard, broomstick-flagged, practically treeless, residentially surrounded public course named Worth Hills in Fort Worth, Texas. Goat Hills we called it, not too originally.

It was a gambling game that went on in some fashion or another, involving from two to twenty players, almost every day of every year. If someone missed a day, it could only have resulted from the fact that he got married or found a pinball machine he could beat. In any case, he would be back tomorrow. The game thus survived — overwhelmed, outlasted — not just my own shaftbending, divot-stomping presence, but heat, rain, snow, wars, tornadoes, jobs, studies, illnesses, divorces, births, deaths and considerations of infinity. If there were certain days when some of us thought the game might help pay part of our tuition through Texas Christian University, a jumble of cream brick buildings across the street from the course, there were other days when it seemed we had plunged into a lifetime of indebtedness. Either way, you were emotionally if not financially trapped, incessantly drawn back to the Hills, like Durrell to Alexandria.

Nearly all of the days at the Hills began the same way. We would be slouched in wicker chairs on the small front porch of the clubhouse, smoking, drinking coffee, complaining about worldly things, such as the Seventh Street Theater not changing its movie in weeks. Say it was August. We would be looking across the putting green and into the heat. In Texas in

August you can see the heat. It looks like germs. In
fact, say it was the day of the Great Cart Wreck.

A few of us were collapsed on the porch. Matty,
who had a crew cut and wore glasses, was resting
against a rock pillar, playing tunes with his fingernails
on his upper front teeth. He could do that. Learned it
in study hall. For money he could play most any tune
and it would be recognizable. I had heard him play
"Sixty-Minute Man" and "Rocket 88," both of which
were popular at this time and place on the jukebox at
Jack's out on the Mansfield Highway. Jack's is where
we went at night "to hustle the pretties," as Moron
Tom would phrase it, or watch truck drivers fight to
see who bought the beer.

I was reading. Something light, I believe, like *The
Brothers Karamazov*. Any kind of book brought out in
the presence of Tiny, a railroad conductor, or Weldon
the Oath, a postman, or Grease Repellent, who
worked at a Texaco station, would prompt a whoop.

"Hey, Dump," one of them would say. "What you
gonna do with all them book things clangin' around in
your head?"

Be a writer, I would mumble, and grow up to marry
Marlene Dietrich.

"That's good," another would say. "All I know is,
you ain't gonna be no golfer."

Foot the Free, which was short for Big Foot the
Freeloader, would be present, practice-putting at a
small, chipped-out crevice in the concrete of the
porch, a spot that marked the finish of the greatest

single hole I ever saw played — but more about that later. Little Joe would be out on the putting green, trying to perfect a stroke behind his back that he felt might help him rob somebody. Magoo would be talking about how unlucky he was and how there couldn't be any God after the way he played the back nine yesterday.

Presently, on the day of the Great Cart Wreck, John the Band-Aid showed up, striding grimly from the parking lot, clubs over his shoulder, anxious to go play. He had whipped a Turf King pinball machine somewhere over on University Drive, and he had some money.

"You, you, you and you and you and you, too," said John. "All of you two, two, two. Automatic one downs and get-evens on nine and eighteen. Whipsaw everybody seventy or better for five." John had lost the day before.

We began tying our shoes.

Magoo said. "I don't guess anybody's gonna let me play since I didn't drop but a young fifty yesterday."

"You're here, aren't you?" said John, removing three clubs from his bag, which he dropped in the gravel, and swinging them violently in a limbering up exercise. "Me and Joe got all teams for five match and five medal. Dollar cats and double on birdies."

Little Joe, who played without a shirt and had a blond ducktail haircut, said, "Sure wish I'd get to pick my own partner someday. You gonna play good, John, or scrape it as usual?"

"Ain't no keep-off signs on me," said John. "You want some of your young partner?"

"I try five," said Little Joe in a high-pitched voice.

"Five and a R-ra C." It was caddy talk, meaning Royal Crown Cola, the champagne of Negro caddies.

Little Joe and I took an electric cart, one of those two-seaters with three wheels, and John and Magoo took one. The rest walked, carrying their own clubs. We were an eightsome, but if others showed up later they could join in, and there would be plenty of action for them. It was not unusual for two or three players to catch up to us, or drive their cars around the course until they found us, park, hop out and get into the game right then. It was Matty one afternoon, I remember, who drove his red Olds right up near the 3rd green, leaped out with his golf shoes and glove already on, and said, "Do I have a duck in the car?" He had driven straight to the game from the University of Oklahoma where he was enrolled, a distance of about two hundred miles. And he had a live duck in the car in case anyone wanted to bet he couldn't hit a duck hook.

With only eight players this day the game was fairly simple to bookkeep. It worked like this. You played each of the other seven individually on the front nine, the back and the eighteen. And you and your partner played all other two-man combinations, or nine other twosomes, the same way. Any man or team who got one down automatically pressed, which meant starting a new bet right there. And everything was doubled, tripled, quadrupled — whatever it took — to get you even on the 9th and 18th holes if you were losing. It was certainly nice to birdie the 9th and 18th holes sometimes.

Naturally, there would always be a long, long pause on the ninth tee while everybody figured out how they stood, like this particular day. John the Band-Aid, who earned his nickname from bleeding a lot, had shot even-par 35, but he was down to everyone.

"All right, Magoo," said John. "With you I'm out, out, out, even, even, one down and one down. I press your young ass for ten. Let's see, Foot. You got me out, out, out and one down with your friggin' birdie on seven. I'll push you eight." And so it went.

John the Band-Aid, who wore a straw hat and kept a handkerchief tied around his neck to protect him against sunburn, rarely observed honors on the tee. In fact, the game sort of worked in reverse etiquette. The losers would jump up and hit first.

The 9th tee at the Hills was on a semi-bluff, above a rather desperate dropoff into a cluster of undernourished hackberry trees, a creek, rocks and weeds. It was a par-four hole, going back toward the clubhouse and slightly uphill. The drive had to carry the big ravine, and if you hit it straight enough and far enough you could get a level lie, about a seven-iron from the green.

John the Band-Aid was teed up first, after all of the figuring out about scores, and as he addressed the ball, spreading his feet, he said, "I'm gonna hit this young mother right into Stadium Drive."

"Outhit you for five," said Magoo.

"You're on," said John, tightening his lips, gripping the driver. "Anybody else?"

"Hit it, Daddy," said Little Joe, his partner.

John the Band-Aid then curved a wondrous slice into the right rough, and coming off of his follow through he slung the club in the general direction of Eagle Mountain Lake, which was thirty miles behind us. He just missed hitting Little Joe, who nimbly ducked out of the way.

"Man, man," said Joe. "They ought to put you in a box and take you to the World's Fair."

John folded his arms and stared off in another direction for a moment, burning inside. Then, suddenly, he dashed over to his bag, jerked out his two-iron and slung it against the water fountain, snapping the shaft in half.

"That ass hole friggin' club cost me a shot back on the fourth," he explained.

I was fairly outraged, too, as I remember. Not at John. I had broken more clubs than he had ever owned. It was because I was one under and no money ahead. Maybe that's why I pointed the electric cart straight down the hill and let it run, putting Little Joe and myself instantly out of control, and headed for oblivion.

Over the rocks and ditches we were speeding, breaking the sound barrier for carts, and when the front wheel struck a large stone, sending us spiraling into the air, all I recall was hearing Little Joe's voice.

"Son of a young . . ." is all I heard him say.

We both went over the front end, head first, the bag and clubs spewing out behind and over us. I suppose I was out for ten seconds, and when I came to the cart was heaped on my left leg, battery acid was eating away at my shirt, and gnarled clubs were everywhere. Little Joe was sitting down in the rocks examining his skinned elbows and giggling. The others were standing around, looking at us, considering whether to lift the cart off my leg — or leave me there to lose all bets.

Magoo glanced down at Little Joe's white canvas bag, already being eaten into by the battery acid.

"Two dollars says Joe don't have a bag before we get to eighteen," he said.

My ankle was so swollen I had to remove my golf shoe and play the remainder of the round in one shoe and one sock. Little Joe's bag lasted until the 14th green where, when he went to pick it up after putting out, nothing was left but the two metal rings, top and bottom, joined together by a wooden stick and shoulder strap. And most of his left trouser leg was going fast.

"Two says Joe is stark naked by the seventeenth," said Magoo.

We finished the round, somehow. I do remember that both Little Joe and I managed birdies on the last hole because Magoo and John the Band-Aid talked for weeks about the time they got beat by a cripple and a guy who was on fire.

In or out of a runaway cart, our game frequently

took on odd dimensions. Utterly bored, we often
played Goat Hills backwards, or to every other hole,
or to every third hole, or entirely out of bounds except
for the greens, which meant you had to stay in the
roads and lawns, with only one club, or with only two
or three clubs, or even at night, which could be
stimulating because of all the occupied cars parked on
the more remote fairways.

One of the more interesting games we invented was
the Thousand-yard Dash. This was a one-hole marathon, starting at the farthest point on the course from
the clubhouse — beside the 12th green — and ending
at the chipped-out place in the concrete on the porch.

I have forgotten who invented it. Most likely it was
either Foot the Free, Matty or myself, for we had once
played from the old Majestic Theater to the Tarrant
County courthouse in downtown Fort Worth without
getting arrested. We had been driving around town,
scraping fenders and breaking off radio aerials, when
we stopped the car near the Majestic. Matty hopped
out, opened the trunk of my car, got out a club and a
ball and smashed a drive straight down Throckmorton
Street, wonderfully straight, over automobiles and
people. It rolled forever. Foot and I did the same. We
played on with putters to the courthouse lawn, frequently falling down and flopping over like laughing
fish. But, anyhow, there were about twelve of us who
each put five dollars in the pot one day for the Thousand-yard Dash.

And off we went, flailing away, cutting across fairways, intruding on other foursomes, cursing and carefully counting the strokes of those who had chosen the same route as us. Some went to the left of the stone outhouse that perched atop the highest point of the course, and some played to the right of it. I followed Foot the Free because he could never afford to lose. He carried the same five-dollar bill for about eight years, I think. So we hooked a driver, hooked another driver, hooked a third driver, then hooked a spoon — you had to hook the ball at Goat Hills to get the roll — and that got us within pitching distance of the clubhouse porch. The others were out of it by now, lost in creeks or the flower beds of apartment houses which bordered the No. 1 fairway.

My approach shot carried the porch, hit hard against the clapboard wall of the clubhouse, chased Wells Howard, the pro, back inside the front door, brought a scream from his wife Lola, glanced off one of the rock pillars supporting the shingled overhang on the porch, and finally came to rest — puttable if I moved a chair — about twenty feet from the crevice.

Foot played a bounce shot, lofting a high wedge, letting it plop in front of the porch on the gravel. It hopped up beautifully over the curb and skidded against the wall, ricocheted off a chair leg and slammed to a halt only ten feet or so from the hole. Hell of a shot.

We quickly got a broom and began sweeping dirt particles off the porch to improve our putting lines, and we took off our shoes because cleats are very bad for putting on concrete. The other players gathered around and started making side bets. We put Wells and Lola at ease by convincing them that this would look good in our biographies one day after we had all gone out and won the young National Open and got ourselves famous.

A couple of rent-club players strolled out of the golf shop, and Foot asked them kindly not to step in his line. "Smart-ass punks," one of them said.

My putt offered one distinct danger, that of tapping it too hard and having it roll past the crevice and into a row of pull carts lined up at the far end of the porch, which is precisely what happened. I tried to argue that the carts were an unnatural hazard and that I deserved a free lift, but Wells Howard, no doubt believing the game to be my idea, ruled I had to play it. On in five, I eighteen-putted for a 23. Against anyone else I might still have had a chance, but Foot was one of the greatest putters in history on any kind of surface. He calmly tapped his ten-footer and it dribbled slowly, slowly over the concrete, wavering, wobbling — and in.

Foot's six was about the best hole I ever saw played, and I have seen several Odessa Pro-Am's. The only thing I ever even heard about that came close to equaling it happened in Austin, Texas, a year or so later. A friend of mine named Bud Shrake, a Hills man on and off, a novelist and *Sports Illustrated* writer and the author of this book's Foreword, made a 517 against another friend, Jerre Todd, from the Lake

Austin Inn to a brown leather loafer in the closet of Todd's apartment near the University of Texas campus.

I am sure that the longest hole we ever played was from the 1st tee at Goat Hills to the 3rd green at Colonial Country Club, roughly fifteen blocks away, regardless of whether one played down Stadium Drive, past the TCU football field, left on Park Hill and over the houses, or down Alton Road and Simondale, past the homes where wealthy roofing company owners and Rotarians lived.

The first time we played it, Tiny wore his bright red, elastic-waisted slacks — he was six foot three and weighed close to three hundred pounds — and Rush's dad, a retired oilman, caddied for him in a big black Lincoln, and Cecil the Parachute got bit by a cocker spaniel.

Playing through neighborhoods requires an unusual shot. The trick, we learned, was to stay in the streets as much as possible to get distance, so a good club to own was a blade putter. You can swat the ball low with a blade putter, guide it pretty well and get lots of extra roll on the pavement. We all kept one around.

I happened to have sliced a putter shot into a bed of iris on Alton Road and was searching for it when I noticed Cecil down the driveway, contemplating a difficult shot. It would have to rise quickly to clear a backyard cyclone fence, and then duck sharply to get under an oak, and then hook more severely to get around a tile roof and then slice back to land in the street. As he studied the shot a dog was barking at his ankles.

Cecil leaped at the ball in his customary manner and drove the shot straight into the Cyclone fence, about eight feet in front of him, and his follow-through carried him forward onto his elbows and stomach, like a man being dragged behind a team of horses. He slid head first into the fence, and the spaniel quickly chased after him as if it were retrieving a sock.

Cecil scrambled up and came tiptoeing back toward me down the driveway, saying, "Hurried the shot. That sucker was a-growlin' at me, and just when I started to swing I seen a lady cussin' me through the kitchen window."

We picked up — "I.P.'d," as one said at the time, meaning the ball was "in pocket" — and began looking for all of the other competitors in backyards along the way toward Colonial. Tiny had quit at a fishpond. Grease Repellent had struck a sundial and lost his ball. Easy Reid had met a fellow and stopped to sell him some insurance. John the Band-Aid had broken his blade putter by throwing it against a chimney. The only two still in contention were Foot and Magoo, whom we found hitting seven-irons out of Bermuda grass lawns over the rose-covered fence and onto Colonial's 1st fairway. They had to play out fast because some Colonial members had sent a caddy back to the clubhouse to get the club manager, Vergal Bourland, who would call in the 82nd Airborne. Foot and Magoo each wound up with a nineteen and hustled back over the fence before Vergal could get their names.

Quite an argument followed, I recall, about the play-off. Magoo suggested playing back to Goat Hills, to the soft drink box in the lunchroom. Foot wanted to play to Herb Massey's restaurant on Eighth Avenue, only three miles away, because he felt like a chicken-fried steak with cream gravy and playing the shuffle bowl machine. Herb's is where we spent almost as much time as we did at Goat Hills, playing gin, betting football games, drinking beer, talking about girls and God, about the thirteen roads leading out of town and wagering on the pinball and shuffle bowl machines. It was where I once saw Matty come in one day with his pants and shirt on backwards and his glasses on the back of his head, and shoot 280 on the shuffle bowl — backwards. Foot and Magoo finally wound up splitting the money from Colonial, and we all went back to the Hills and got in a putting game that lasted until midnight.

To at least partly understand why anyone would hang around a municipal golf course for one-third of his life playing games such as these, you have to understand something about the town and the state and what golf means there.

First of all, Fort Worth is basically a quiet place. It is an old country town with a flexible society (anyone with money can join), a river, the Trinity, a fragrant stockyard on the North Side where no one ever went except to eat Mexican food at Joe Garcia's, a General Dynamics plant, a couple of newspapers, a lot of beer taverns, a downtown area sparkling with loan companies, a few elegant neighborhoods and a university, TCU, which was and is primarily noted for turning out Sam Baugh, Davey O'Brien, Jim Swink and Bob Lilly. It is a town where little has happened, outside of a few big college football games, since Vernon Castle, the dancer, was killed during World War I when his training plane crashed in a suburb. Nor has anyone cared to make something happen except, occasionally, on the golf courses.

Fort Worth is where Ben Hogan and Byron Nelson grew up, and this is one of the first facts a kid learns. There you are one day, out in the front yard brandishing a yardstick like a sword, playing Errol Flynn in *The Sea Hawk*, when, suddenly, your parents decide you have a natural swing. They then tell you about Hogan and Nelson, about Jimmy Demaret, who came from Houston, and about Lloyd Mangrum, Ralph Guldahl and Harry Cooper, who came from Dallas, and they shove you onto the nearest course and tell you not to come home until you're ready for the Ethiopian Four-ball. So you stay twenty years trying to cure a shank and learning to love a duck hook.

Essentially because of the climate — there are few weeks in any year when a man would not play golf in Texas — the sport for about thirty or forty years has been second in importance only to football. This is true throughout the state: in the north-central area of Fort Worth and Dallas, through the heavy pines of East Texas, in the hills and woods around Austin, along the arid, palmed coasts of Houston and Corpus Christi and all across the peach-colored plains of West Texas and the Panhandle, where the fairways wind around mesquite and oil pumps and players can be seen wearing glistening tool dresser's helmets and coveralls, or Stetsons and khakis.

Golf has always received luxurious attention in the newspapers. As soon as you were old enough to read you could see headlines about people like Gus Moreland and Harry Todd playing in some fascinating thing called the Ranger Invitation. Just about every town with a service station clock used to have some kind of invitation tournament for amateurs. All kinds of places — Abilene, Lubbock, Tyler, Longview, Eastland, Waxahachie, Dublin, Midland. They would begin in mid-March and continue through mid-September, there being from ten to twenty each week, scattered all over, and it was possible, and I presume still is, for a good high school or collegiate golfer to play competitively for twenty or so weeks every year, winning, if he was talented enough, more sets of clubs, TV sets, silver trays and wristwatches than he could ever sell to get money to gamble with.

It was this vast amateur circuit that gave us Hogan and Nelson and Demaret, and then Jackie Burke, Jr., Tommy Bolt, Billy Maxwell, Don January, Wes Ellis, Earl Stewart, Shelley Mayfield, Don Cherry, Dave

Marr, Bobby Nichols, Miller Barber, Charley Coody, Ernie Vossler, Don Massengale, Homero Blancas, Rex Baxter, Jacky Cupit, Dudley Wysong, Joe Conrad and dozens of others who made it and dozens who didn't. I can relate with a certain amount of pride that Goat Hills produced its share of touring pros, not the least of which were Vossler, Coody, Massengale, Jack Montgomery and Jerry Edwards. Coody, Massengale and Montgomery came along after our goofy games were over, but Vossler and Edwards came right out of them. Ernie was a relentless competitor who could never understand why anyone other than he ever sank a putt. Sometimes, when a player like Weldon the Oath would hole one, Ernie would stalk straight to the clubhouse and brood. Vossler was never as proficient as, say, myself at breaking club shafts. In one streak I broke my eight-iron every day at the 17th tee for a week because I couldn't make a ball hold that dinky, par-three green. But Ernie had his moments. He bladed a six-iron one afternoon at the 6th hole, I remember, and almost killed us all. He hurled the club straight into the brick fairway, and the shaft snapped. Both parts of the club bounced into the air. One jagged end sprang back and hit Ernie in the palm, causing five stitches. The other glanced toward Weldon and myself, sending us sprawling, as if threatened by repetitious lightning bolts as the steel shaft sparkled in the sun and danced around us.

Later that same day Weldon the Oath had one of his talking fits — talking to the ball. He took oaths on the golf course. Outrageous vows and oaths. Wearing his postman's cap and playing without golf shoes, he had rushed to the game so quickly, I can still hear him giving the ball a wonderful lecture on the 14th tee. The 14th was the easiest hole on the course, a down-hill, with-the-wind par four you could drive. If you didn't birdie this hole you broke at least three clubs. But here was Weldon on the tee, fearful of his usual slice.

"This is your last chance," he said to the ball, addressing his drive. "You lousy little crud. If you slice on me one more time I'm gonna bite you right in half and chew your rubber guts up. Now you go straight! You hear me? Do you *hear me* tellin' you this? There's no by God reason why you got to slice on me ever' time, damn it. Grreeeoood daaaammmm, you, aaaiiii!"

And Weldon hit a world-record slice.

It crossed at least two fairways to the right, a marvelous half-moon of a shot. The ball had scarcely left the clubhead before Weldon was spinning around in circles, pawing at the air with his driver, slugging at imaginary evils, whining and cursing. He ran over and started beating the driver head against a wooden tee marker. He hauled off and beat the ground with it, over and over. He stomped on the face of the club and wished he were wearing cleats to scar it forever. Then he suddenly stopped and got morose.

"Let me hit one more, just for practice," he said, calmly. "I got to figure out what I'm doing wrong."

Weldon hit another glorious slice and simply bent the shaft of the club over his knee and broke it.

"Gaaaaaa, rrreeeee, aaaddd," he exploded again. "I'm bam-dad finished. This is my last day on any gaaad rrraaapp golf course son of a badddeerd bat rop ditch bastard crapping pee." He was so mad he couldn't make his words come out right. "You picks have guyed me damn stick. This rotten stinking miserable low-life friggin' spick nigger whore game."

Weldon the Oath hiked to the clubhouse, but he was, of course, back the next day.

After I holed out a thirty-foot putt to halve a gimme birdie one afternoon on the 14th, Vossler left for good. He moved on to more glamorous things, to the big money games at Ridglea, to become city champion, state amateur champion and ultimately onto the PGA tour. He won a couple of tournaments out there, made good money and finally settled down to a fine club job at Quail Creek in Oklahoma City. I have always considered Ernie our honor graduate.

For a while, all of us thought Jerry Edwards would make it, giving Goat Hills another star in pro golf. Jerry would go around shooting things like 29's and 30's on the back nine at the Hills, driving the ball four miles, or roughly the distance to old Paschal High School (now Tech), a Gibraltar of education that turned out most of us with diplomas in Library Pass Forging, Double Lunch Period Registration, Boiler Room Smoking, Basketball, Abortion Arranging, Tire Screeching and Secret Marriage. Jerry got in the money pretty often on the tour but never managed a win and eventually gave it up. His greatest publicity came when he was rumored to have gone AWOL from the army in 1962 to play in the U.S. Open. "A true Hills man," Magoo said.

Although Vossler and Edwards were the only two who succeeded, unless you want to count Coody, Massengale and Montgomery who came later, all of us at one time, I believe, envisioned a pro career. Easy Reid, for example, bought a huge black bag and an umbrella and some alligator shoes and turned pro, but the closest he came to the big time was missing the cut at the Odessa Pro-Am with me as a heavy partner. Grease Repellent turned pro one day after he shot 62 at the Hills, eight under par, breaking the course record that five of us had shared at 65. But Grease didn't go on the tour, and he didn't take a club job. He only refused to play in any more amateur tournaments, which he didn't enter anyhow.

Sadly, my own dreams were constantly spoiled by collisions with reality. The first time it happened was when I went to the State Junior tournament in San Antonio convinced I would win only to get beat three and two by a cross-handed Mexican wearing tennis shoes. I returned, thirsting for revenge, the following year and lost to a barefoot fourteen-year-old who had only five clubs.

But if those experiences were not enough to convince me, the Waxahachie Invitation should have. The Waxahachie Invitation was not exactly the Masters of Texas, but it had a lot of entries every year

that we thought were awfully dazzling; players like
Don Cherry, Earl Stewart, Don January, Billy Maxwell and Joe Conrad, to name a few. It was a real
privilege to get beat 6–5 by any of them, we felt. I
remember an unusually strong field one year at Waxahachie because it took a 70 to qualify for thirty of the
thirty-two places in the championship flight. Un-
luckily, I shot 71 along with eleven others, so there
had to be a sudden death play-off — swatfest, it was
called — for the last two spots. A swatfest meant a
gallery. Bad deal.

One by one we teed off on the 1st hole, a par three,
and nine players bogeyed and were eliminated. I
envied them all. One player got a birdie and was in.
Two of us made pars and had to go another hole for
the remaining berth, or the honor of being buried by a
Cherry, a January or a Maxwell the next day.

The other fellow was a tall, twangy Texan named
Shelby, and I did not realize until a few years later
that it was the same Carroll Shelby who raced automobiles. This might have been the traumatic experience that made him change sports. The small crowd
hung around to watch us play another hole, the 2nd, a
par-five that bent around a deep cavern and was
bordered on one side by a wire fence that separated
the course from a cotton field. I recall teeing up my
ball and overhearing a couple of spectators behind me.

"Who you want?" one said.

"Aw, neither, axe-you-ly. They both chili dippers,"
said the other.

Whatever Shelby did, I did better. He hooked, I

hooked. He hit one over the fence, I hit one over the fence. He got lost in the cavern, I got lost in the cavern. He landed in a bunker, I landed in a bunker. At one point a man in the gallery said, "Well, I been to two county fairs and the Dublin Rodeo, but I ain't seen nothin' like this." I finally won the hole with a ten to Shelby's eleven most likely on a bookkeeping error.

One did not have to venture out of town — out on the *tour,* so to speak — to enrich the game back at Goat Hills. You could go across town to any of a dozen other courses that Fort Worth had. You could certainly sneak onto any of the country clubs and play from No. 2 through No. 17 frequently replacing all of the flagsticks in the bunkers instead of the cups for reasons which seemed hilarious then.

Our game, I think, was substantially influenced by those at the other courses. At one time we believed that the really good players in town were mostly at another public course, Meadowbrook. They did things like win the city championship all the time, which is something, incidentally, that neither Ben Hogan, Byron Nelson nor I could ever do. In our respective eras we each finished second in our best effort. So if anyone ever asks what Hogan, Nelson and Jenkins have in common, you now know.

And then there was Ridglea. Ridglea had players who might not have been as skilled as those at other courses, but they could sure outbet you. Legendary guys with names like Spec, Snapper and Simpo played at Ridglea, and while they weren't all that great from tee to green, they could talk you out of your savings account just by moaning. Occasionally you would get deluded by a 67 at wide-open Goat Hills and take your swing over to narrow Ridglea. You always came back busted, but at least you had been to the shrine where Titanic Thompson used to hang around.

Titanic Thompson was the adopted name of one Alvin C. Thomas of Rogers, Arkansas. During the 1920's and 1930's Titanic earned fame as the greatest golf hustler who ever lived. Right-handed or left-handed, Ti would bring you in crisp. Everyone had heard about the time at Ridglea long ago that Thompson beat Byron Nelson head-to-head, taking $1000 off Byron's backers.

At Ridglea you could sit around and listen to all of the good stories about Thompson, some of them maybe even true. People would tell how he got his name: from a guy called Snow Clark in a pool game in Joplin ("The way you're sinking everybody they ought to call you Titanic"), how he could throw a key into a keyhole, shoot a sparrow off a telephone wire, throw a watermelon over a hotel, bet it would rain in thirty minutes — and win, outrun a jackrabbit, bet he could hit a green with his driver from four hundred yards (he would walk to the green and tap it with the club, you lose), how he could sail fifty-two cards into a hat and beat anybody playing golf if the price was right. And all the other tales. You would like to have known Titanic Thompson more than any other man.

Since that was impossible the next best thing was

just being at Ridglea sometimes, back in those days before they turned it into a country club for Jaycees. The fact that Thompson had spent some time there left Ridglea with a tradition to uphold, it seemed, and a lot of fellows worked hard to uphold it.

On one of the lazy afternoons I best remember, Raymond Gafford, the pro, and a hell of a fine player, climbed up on a wooden table in the old golf shop with a four-iron, put a ball down on the table, addressed it and aimed it out the open door toward the 1st green, a par five.

"I believe I can make a five from here," said Raymond.

"Five where?" asked Spec, a subtle, moon-faced man who rarely begged off from any action. "From there to your pocket?"

"Oh, I think I could make five from here on the first hole," said Raymond, waggling the club.

"Well, I'll tell you one thing," said Spec, taking out a roll of bills. "I ain't had nothin' this good lately."

"Can I get all that off you?" asked Raymond.

Spec grinned. "I'll guarantee you this man has *got* to make me total rich some day, and there ain't nothin' I can do about it."

"All I know is, I can make five," Gafford went on, waggling the club, looking out the door.

"Well, I don't know a whole lot about it," said Spec, "but I know a man can't make five on number one at Ridglea off no tabletop."

"Just get it on," said Raymond.

"On?" said Spec. "On's here in my hand."

A few others got in, do or don't, and Raymond calmly struck a nice four-iron right off the tabletop, out the front door and a good ways down the fairway. It was obvious that he would have only a three-wood and another iron to reach the green and make his five.

"Piss on the fire and call in the dogs," said Spec. "The hunt's over."

And it was. Raymond made an easy five.

After this, we hit a lot of shots off the shingle roof at Goat Hills, and did a great deal of chipping off the hoods of our cars and, in fact, designed a very interesting hole that would start on top of the card table in the locker room, dogleg through the restaurant noted for its cold, greasy meatloaf, cut through the golf shop, bend around the putting green and conclude on the 1st green. Par was twenty-three.

It was, alas, in the last few years of Goat Hills, shortly before the city sold those sacred 106 acres to TCU so the school could build several more cream-brick buildings, that the games grew too big, too outrageously expensive for working men or students. Some guys got to where they couldn't pay what they lost and others didn't want to collect it. Nor was it any fun to play for scraps of paper. And then, of course, many of us were developing other interests — snooker, eight-ball, bridge, divorce. That sort of thing.

Looking back, our game might have dwindled out purely because of Moron Tom.

He had come to us as a likable, muscular West

Texan on a football scholarship at TCU, but he had quit football when he discovered he had to work out every day during the fall. Moron Tom hit a long ball in one direction or another, and he loved to bet. Anything. He would bet he could drive over anything, or under anything, shoot anything, not shoot anything or hold his breath longer than you could. He could drink a can of beer in four seconds — for money — by inhaling it. And when he was doing nothing else he kept you puzzled or aching from the fast code that he spoke. Moron Tom almost never spoke English. It was a wild kind of gibberish that you either had to learn and speak in or never know exactly what you were doing or how much you were losing.

Everything was usually "quadruple unreal" to Moron Tom, whether it was a good drive or a bad one, a lay-down gin hand or garbage, a good-looking girl or a dog. Things would also move Moron Tom to poetry. "Hit it fine, Por-ke-pine," he would say. Or, struggling over a difficult shot, "Lemme toil, Olive Oil."

There was a very special day in the history of Goat Hills — the day of the last truly big gambling game — that began with Moron Tom speaking his own language on the clubhouse porch.

"I'll take toops and threeps from Youngfut, Youngjun, Youngmut and Youngruss," he said.

Translated, that meant Moron Tom wanted two up and three up from young Foot, young John, young Matty and young Rush. He wanted other bets too.

"Ten and ten with Grease's men," he said. "Two and two with Dump-Magoo."

Everyone sort of drifted out to the first tee, making wagers, choosing partners, taking practice swings.

Moron Tom, who had a habit of aiming thirty yards to the right of every target and bringing a giant hook around and into the fairways or greens, stood up to his tee shot on No. 1 and aimed straight at the row of apartment houses on the right.

Before anyone had a chance to giggle or ask if Moron Tom could hook the ball that much he said, "Think I can't, Cary Grant?" And he smashed a big one that slowly came around and found the fairway.

"Cod Ee-rack Fockle-dim," he said. That was his pronunciation of Doc Cary Middlecoff spelled backwards and a compliment to the way he had hit the shot.

Somehow Magoo and I had wound up as partners against all other combinations, and this was bad. Magoo was a strong player, but he, well, he was unlucky. Once in the Glen Garden Invitation in Fort Worth — that is the course where Hogan and Nelson caddied in their youth — he hit a splendid shot to a difficult green but lost the ball. After looking for about twenty minutes he found it in a man's mouth, being cleaned. Things like that happened to Magoo. It was also hard for him to play well when Moron Tom was in the game because he found himself continually laughing.

But this day Magoo and I were in good form. We teamed together awfully well, taking turns making birdies, and we had everybody screaming and bleeding half to death.

"Cod Eerack God damn Fockle-dim," Foot would say as Magoo drove repeatedly down the middle, just playing superbly.

Moron Tom's losses were mounting, but he remained good-natured as always. "Wod Daw-ret-sniff," he would say, hitting a shot. That was Dow Finsterwald spelled backwards, and it represented a cry of doom.

By the time we came off the 17th green, Magoo and I had birdied something like six holes in succession, and we began calculating that if we could only par the 18th, which was an easy par four, a birdie hole really, we would win so much money that we couldn't get it all home in a Grandma's Cookie truck.

"Ain't this somethin'?" said Foot on the 18th tee. "I ought to go somewhere and stand in line to give up."

"Ever day's a holiday and ever meal's a banquet," said Magoo. "Do I hear a young press?"

"Your ass is pressed on your backswing, your downswing and your follow-through," said John the Band-Aid.

Magoo smiled.

"My window's open," I said.

"Dump City," mused Foot. "I'm bein' took to Dump City by two clutch artists."

Easy Reid said, "Man, man. I don't want the cheese, I just want out of the trap."

Said John the Band-Aid, "I'm out, out, out, out, out, out, out and out. Press for fourteen million."

We finally figured up that we would win about $600

total with a par on the 18th, counting all of the get-even presses, and it was finally time to tee off.

The 18th at Goat Hills was slightly uphill. You teed off from a windy knoll with the south wind always helping and drove across a tiny creek and a couple of sycamore trees. A big drive would leave you only twenty or thirty yards short of the green, and many of us had, at times, driven right to the frog hair around the putting surface. Even a poor tee shot left you only one hundred yards from the green with a good chance at a birdie. It was almost impossible to make worse than four unless the green hadn't been mowed and you three-putted.

The only conceivable trouble was far, far to the right, across the 10th fairway, where Stadium Drive was out of bounds, but in all my years I never saw anyone slice that badly, or that far — only Magoo when Moron Tom spoke to him for that money.

At the height of Magoo's backswing, when he was coming out of his shoes to try and drive the green, Moron Tom quietly said, "Tissim, Oogam." Which was "Miss it, Magoo," spelled backwards.

Needles were commonplace in our game of course. Coughing, sneezing, dropping a full bag of clubs on a putt, yelling, burping, all such as that. It was something you expected when you were winning, and no one ever complained. Normally you just ignored it. But Magoo came apart with laughter at Moron Tom's remark and hit the drive like a two-ton Cecil the Parachute, almost falling down.

Everyone collapsed with laughter at the funny-looking drive, even Magoo and me, his partner, who had yet to tee off and who now would have the full weight of the $600 on his shoulders.

"Mighty fine, Por-ke-pine," said Moron Tom. "Oogam dewalb the Nepo," which was, "Magoo blowed the Open."

Magoo simply looked at his club after a spell and then at me and grinned, "If you don't make a four, I'm gonna stamp this Tommy Armour right on your young forehead."

Now, just on the other side of the creek down below us at the 18th, set upright into the embankment, there was a storm drain, roughly three feet in circumference. We used to pitch at it with old balls from the ladies' tee, but it was a remarkable thing if anyone ever hit it. From up on the men's tee, 100 yards or so back, it was an incredibly small target. In fact it never even entered my mind as I got set to drive the ball 300 yards to the green or know the reason why. I would get a birdie to make up for Magoo's misfortune, and that would be quadruple unreal.

But at the top of my swing Moron Tom whispered something else.

"Clutch, Mother Zilch," he said.

I didn't fall completely down coming through the shot, but almost. The clubhead hit about two inches behind the ball, and the shot snaphooked into the ground just in front of the ladies' tee, took a big hop to the right off of some rocks and — I swear to you — went straight into the storm drain.

It remains the only hole in one I ever made, and it is, of course, the shot which semi-retired me from golf forever.

The Dogged Victim

Fancy seeing you here.
— Arnold Palmer,
winning the U.S. Open

H E first came to golf as a muscular young man who could not keep his shirttail in, who smoked a lot, perspired a lot and who hit the ball with all of the finesse of a dock worker lifting a crate of auto parts. Arnold Palmer did not play golf, we thought. He nailed up beams, reupholstered sofas, repaired air-conditioning units. Sure, he made birdies by the streaks in his eccentric way — driving through forests, lacing hooks around sharp corners, spewing wild slices over prodigious hills, and then, all hunched up and pigeon-toed, staring putts into the cups. But he made just as many bogeys in his stubborn way. Anyhow, a guy whose slacks are too long and turned up at the cuffs, who matches green shirts with orange sweaters, a guy who sweats so much, is *not* going to rush past the Gene Littlers, Ken Venturis and Dow Finsterwalds, the stylists, to fill the hero gap created by the further graying and balding of Ben Hogan and Sam Snead. This is what most of us believed around 1960, even after Palmer had won his second Masters, even after he had begun to drown everyone in money winnings. *This* was a suave new godlet of the fairways, a guy out of Latrobe Dry Goods?

We were, of course, as wrong about him as the break on a downhill six-footer, as wrong as his method seemed to us to be wrong: hit it hard, go find it, hit it hard again. We knew we were wrong one day when the bogeys suddenly went away. No one understood why or how, except that Palmer willed them to. And now he had become a winner like none we had ever known. He was a *nice* guy, of all things. He was honestly and naturally gracious, untemperamental, talkative, helpful and advising, unselfish of his time, marvelously good-humored; he had a special feeling for golf's history and he was honored by its traditions; and with all of this he remained the gut fighter we insisted he be, a man so willing to accept the agonies of pressure and the burdens of fame that for a few years we absolutely forgot that anyone else played the game he was dominating and changing.

He actually started *being* Arnold Palmer in that summer of 1960, a stupidly short time ago it seems. He became the Arnie of whoo-ha, go-get-'em Arnie on a searingly hot afternoon in Denver when, during the last round of the U.S. Open, he exploded from seven strokes and fourteen players behind to win. Two months earlier he had finished birdie-birdie on national television to win the Masters and now he had created another miracle — again on national television.

Much has been written into the lore of golf of how it was that day, of the epic 65 he shot in the final round at Cherry Hills, of the day that really made him, but not by anyone who had lunched with him, kidded him, and then happily marched inside the gallery ropes with him, scurrying after Cokes, furnishing cigarettes, and hoping to put him at ease.

During lunch in a quiet corner of the Cherry Hills locker room before that round, Arnold was cheerful and joking as he ate a hamburger, drank iced tea, and made small talk with a couple of other players, Bob Rosburg and Ken Venturi, a writer named Bob Drum, and myself. He talked of no one else who might win. All he seemed concerned about was Cherry Hills's 1st hole, a comparatively short, downhill, downwind, par four. It bugged him. He thought he could drive the green, but in three previous rounds he had not done it.

"It really makes me hot," he said. "A man ought to drive that green."

"Why not?" I said. "It's only three hundred and forty-six yards through a ditch and a lot of high grass."

"If I drive that green I might shoot a hell of a score," he said. "I might even shoot a sixty-five if I get started good. What'll that bring?"

"About seventh place. You're too far back."

"Well, that would be two-eighty," Arnold said. "Doesn't two-eighty always win the Open?"

"Yeah," I said. "When Hogan shoots it."

Arnold laughed and walked out to the first tee.

For a while I loitered around the big clubhouse waiting for the leaders to go out, as a good journalist should. In the process of milling around, however, I overheard a couple of fans talking about an amazing thing they had just seen. Palmer, they said, had driven the first green. Just killed a low one that hung up there straight toward the mountains and then burned its way through the USGA trash and onto the putting surface. Got a two-putt birdie.

I smiled to myself and walked out onto the veranda and began edging my way through the spectators toward the 1st tee where the leader, Mike Souchak, would be going off presently. But about that time a pretty good roar came up from down on the front nine, and seconds later, a man sprinted by panting the news that Palmer was three under through three.

"Drove the first, chipped in on two and hit it stiff on three," he said, pulling away and darting off to join Arnie's Army. Like the spectator and a few thousand others who got the same notion at the same time, I tried to break all records for the Cherry Hills Clubhouse-to-Fourth Fairway Dash. We got there just in time to see Arnold hole his fourth straight birdie.

Wringing wet and perishing from thirst, I staggered toward the fifth tee, stopping to grab a Coke at a concession stand. I ducked under the ropes as an armband permitted and stood there puffing but excited.

Arnold came in briskly, squinted down the fairway and walked over. He took the Coke out of my hand, the cigarettes out of my shirt pocket and broke into a smile.

"Fancy seeing you here," he said. "Who's winning the Open?"

Palmer birdied two more holes through the 7th to

go an incredible six under, working on an incorrigible twenty-nine out. But he bogeyed the 8th and had to settle for a 30. Even so, the challengers were falling all around him like wounded soldiers, and their crowds were bolting toward him, and the title would be his. Everything would be his now.

Later on, somewhere on the back nine holes, I remember sizing up a leader board with him and saying, "You've got it. They're all taking gas."

"Aw, maybe," he said, quietly. "But damn it, I wanted that twenty-nine."

There have been other major victories, as we know, and scores of lesser ones, and precisely because of him the professional tour has tripled, quadrupled in prize money. He has become, they say, something immeasurable in champions, something more than life-size, even though he has turned into his forties, the hip hurts, and a lot of other big ones have slipped away.

This is true, I think. He *is* the most immeasurable of all golf champions. But this is not entirely true because of all that he has won, or because of that mysterious fury with which he has managed to rally himself. It is partly because of the nobility he has brought to losing. And more than anything, it is true because of the pure, unmixed joy he has brought to trying.

He has been, after all, the doggedest victim of us all.

Afterword

by Dave Marr

Any kid who grew up in Texas in the 1940s and 1950s instantly recognizes the public golf course that Dan Jenkins created in The Glory Game chapter of this book—the particular flavor of the setting, and the cast of characters who fought it out there in some of the strangest golf competitions imaginable. Dan's Goat Hills, of course, is Worth Hills in Fort Worth. For someone like myself whose home town is Houston, Worth Hills is interchangeable with Memorial Park with its sprinkling of sand tees and almost grassless greens and its cast of characters: the guy who played oboe in the Houston symphony orchestra; the garbage man; the Edsel dealer; the beer salesman; the bookies; the oil man; the insurance salesman; and the college kids who could find a few minutes away from their studies. From time to time, Jack Burke or Tommy Bolt or Jimmy Demaret would show up at your home town public course, and you'd find yourself lured into Demaret's specialty: I-can-beat-you-standing-on-one-leg. In those days, people like Jimmy had to live by their wits. For lack of a better word, they had to hustle. Jimmy would keep laughing at the guy who was trying to set up a game with him, until the guy gave him too much. Curtains.

Looking back at more recent times, even Ben Hogan had his game—the game that he would propose that his foursome play during the practice rounds before a tournament. Don't get the wrong idea—Hogan was a darn good putter—but in this game he was proposing, the only strokes that counted were those you took from the tee to the green on that round. He felt that you'd miss a green now and then, and he didn't expect to.

You know, looking back, it was a great time to grow up in Texas. Golf and the movies—that's about all we had in those pre-television days. Now the kids can see a Terry Bradshaw or a Larry Bird or a Tom Watson strut his stuff on the tube. They get to see the best athletes at a pretty early age, and whoosh—they're off learning the correct technique at an indecently young age. In my time, we all needed a helping hand. Like Blackie Sherrod, the sports writer and editor. He was one. He gave Dan Jenkins and a lot of other young men the foothold they needed in journalism. When I say that, I think of Claude Harmon and the role he played as the head professional at Winged Foot, up in Westchester. In those days they were just starting to recruit golfers for college teams at places like North Texas State, so fellows like Claude were responsible for your learning the vocabulary of golf. Not just how

*to explode the ball from a fried-egg lie in a bunker,
or how to play the other shots a good player needed
to know. What I mean is that he arranged for you to
receive an invaluable all-around education by ex-
posing you to club members who, without your
knowing it, would show you, by their example, this
or that slice of life and how to appreciate it. They
opened wide new vistas for you. When I think of
what we learned from the people we met at Winged
Foot and other places—my goodness, did we ever
have help!*

*You travel when you're on the tour, and you get
to meet writers of all kinds. Many of them try to
write humor, but I can think of only three who are
true humorists—Dan Jenkins, of course; Jim Murray of the Los Angeles* Times-Mirror, *whose humor
is of an entirely different sort; and Charlie Price of*
Golf Digest, *who has been turning out hilarious
stuff for decades. There's one thing we all know
about people with the gift of humor: they are deep
and serious people, and their ability to see the funny side of situations is a kind of insulin they need
to function right. Dan, as no one needs to be told, is
a fine writer, because he knows what he writes
about thoroughly and also senses the subtle extra
dimensions. He knows how to ask questions that
really stimulate you. He's absolutely trustworthy.
He doesn't take notes, but he quotes you perfectly.
He's not afraid to express his thoughts on any subject. If he is critical, say, of Notre Dame football, he*

expects that a lot of *Notre Dame* alumni will write in and tell him where to get off. He is never deterred. There is a lot of steel as well as humor in Dan Jenkins. He does not do assassinations. What he is is an expert observer. He is like a skillful cartoonist or an outstanding mimic, like Rich Little. He knows the power of making it clear who he is writing about by exaggerating certain personal traits. I know a lot of people to whom golf is important, but I can't think of anyone who loves golf more than Dan does or is more devoted to it. He may well be the doggedest victim of us all. He covers this up in his writing and in his easy manner, but I think it is evident to all of his friends.

There are many reasons why I like to be in Dan Jenkins' company. He's that rarity—a man of wit who is a superb listener. When he is with an old friend, things are never dull. He likes to toss out a bone—some statement he knows will stir up your wrath—and then he sits back comfortably and listens to your rebuttal. There is never any basic difference in his behavior. He is the same person whether he is at P. J. Clarke's or at Elaine's, the clubhouse at the Augusta National or the lush fairways of Brackenridge Park on the outskirts of San Antonio. I love to see him and to pull up a chair with Drum and Sonny and Roone and Frank and Bud and Rather and Blackie and the other old familiar faces.